Building Software
A Practitioner's Guide

Titles in the
Auerbach Series on Applied Software Engineering
Phillip A. Laplante, Pennsylvania State University, Series Editor

Building Software: A Practioner's Guide
Nikhilesh Krishnamurthy and Amitabh Saran
0-8493-7303-4

Global Software Development Handbook
Raghvinder Sangwan, Matthew Bass, Neel Mullick, Daniel J. Paulish,
and Juergen Kazmeier
0-8493-9384-1

Antipatterns: Identification, Refactoring, and Management
Phillip A. Laplante and Colin J. Neill
0-8493-2994-9

Software Engineering Quality Practices
Ronald Kirk Kandt
0-8493-4633-9

Building Software
A Practitioner's Guide

Nikhilesh Krishnamurthy
Amitabh Saran

CRC Press
Taylor & Francis Group
Boca Raton London New York

CRC Press is an imprint of the
Taylor & Francis Group, an **informa** business

CRC Press
Taylor & Francis Group
6000 Broken Sound Parkway NW, Suite 300
Boca Raton, FL 33487-2742

First issued in paperback 2019

© 2008 by Taylor & Francis Group, LLC
CRC Press is an imprint of Taylor & Francis Group, an Informa business

No claim to original U.S. Government works

ISBN-13: 978-0-8493-7303-9 (hbk)
ISBN-13: 978-0-367-40353-9 (pbk)

Library of Congress Cataloging-in-Publication Data

Krishnamurthy, Nikhilesh.
   Building software : a practitioner's guide / authors, Nikhilesh Krishnamurthy and Amitabh Saran.
      p. cm. -- (Auerbach series on applied software engineering)
   Includes bibliographical references and index.
   ISBN 978-0-8493-7303-9 (alk. paper)
   1. Computer software--Development. 2. Computer software--Quality control. I. Saran, Amitabh. II. Title.

   QA76.76.D47K734 2007
   005.3--dc22   2007010186

Visit the Taylor & Francis Web site at
http://www.taylorandfrancis.com

and the CRC Press Web site at
http://www.crcpress.com

Dedication

To my parents

– A.S.

To my parents and Dr. HKS

– N.K.

Contents

Preface

This book began with a discussion we had in Portland, Oregon, a few years ago. We were talking about the problems related to software development and how they had not changed radically over the years. We were still finding issues of quality and delivery schedules, of confusion about requirements, and problems with communication that existed years ago. Only the technologies were different, and the people we were dealing with were perhaps younger. It seemed as if there were deeper structural issues that people were not recognizing, understanding, or acknowledging. Were we, in the software industry, oversimplifying things and thereby causing problems, or overcomplicating them with the same consequence?

We started looking into some of these issues, trying to organize our knowledge in some fashion. We thought one logical place to start looking at was systems science. Although it has "systems" in its name, it appears to have been ignored by most of the people practicing software systems development. Perhaps it was just a case of practitioners ignoring theory, or using theory without realizing that such a theory existed. It is a vast field and we decided to look at a few thinkers who offered some important insights that a system designer or architect could use, indirectly, if not directly.

We also realized that many in the software field are not reading enough, or certainly not reading widely enough. When we encounter a problem in software development, our first tendency is to look for an ingenious way of solving it. We forget that most problems possibly have good, proven solutions in non-software domains. Land records have been kept for centuries in "databases," the military has been dealing with the problem of secure communications for ages, etc. There is a lot that can be learned from a cross-domain study using a systems approach. In this book we look at certain examples.

There are many practical insights that we include based on experience — ours and others. A practitioner needs to know some simple techniques that are almost always bound to work. One also needs to know many of the softer skills required to deliver successfully. Considering that thousands of newcomers enter this industry every year, and the experienced persons hardly have any time to mentor them, learning can be difficult and slow. We hope some of the insights in this book will help younger designers and developers bring out better systems.

Our findings led to the creation of a framework for *thinking* about the systems to be developed. We call it SEE — Solutions, Engineering, and Execution. The term "framework" refers to a way of approaching the problem. It is *not* a new process or methodology for software development. We illustrate how all aspects of building software can be approached through the SEE framework.

The one aspect that we do not cover in detail is *how* to build systems. We do not present "components" or "patterns" to plug and play with. Neither do we offer a "20-step plan" to ensure systems success. The objective of this book is to trigger thinking, not offer readymade solutions. We have selected issues that come up time and again in software development. For example, most of us still have trouble distinguishing between requirements and desires, or between customization and personalization and configuration. We discuss larger lessons that can be learned from a situation or problem. Enterprise applications such as SAP® or Oracle® should be viewed as new cultures being introduced in the organization: parts of the receiving organization can employ tactics of resistance similar to those used by living organisms resisting external attacks.

The book is aimed at software designers, architects, senior developers, and managers who have experience in designing software systems and managing software projects in product companies, consulting organizations, or information technology (IT) departments. Those working in the nontechnical departments of computer companies, and having to deal with project managers and technical personnel, will also find the contents insightful and interesting. Those interested in general systems and management aspects of software development will find the coverage helpful. The context of the "you" or "one" that we use should be apparent from the content — we sometimes address the architect, the designer, the manager, or the developer.

The contents of the book have been organized to enable random access. The chapters do not have strong dependencies on prior chapters. Each of the topics is related to the building of good systems, although there are many other topics — some basic and others advanced — that are covered better and in more detail in other software engineering books. A book can cover only so much, and choices must be made. Finally, it helps to keep in mind the caution given in the military: *the map is not the territory.*

Acknowledgments

We wish to thank many of our friends and mentors who encouraged us and gave us timely suggestions. The list includes, in no particular order, Alok Arora, Rashmi Prakash, Sanjay Mathur, Raj Rajen, Dina Bitton, Ramesh Balasubramaniam, Terence Smith, Chennagiri Jagadish, Kelly Luce, Divy Agrawal, Jean Jaiswal, Pranay Palni, and Jaak Tepandi.

We are exceedingly thankful to Amit's father, Sri Ram Saran, for unselfishly giving his time for reviewing and proofreading the entire manuscript at short notice. His edits and comments were indeed invaluable to us.

No book is complete without drawings. We wanted ours to be illuminative, yet with a lighter note. Our special thanks to Leena Jacob for the artwork and creative metaphors she painstakingly prepared.

Our thanks to Phillip Laplante for his encouragement during the early days of the book. We thank our editor John Wyzalek for his guidance throughout the writing process. Catherine Giacari and Andrea Demby, in the Taylor and Francis publishing team, have been especially kind and flexible with us, and we thank them for it.

It is not easy to do justice to a book while working full-time. On this note, we wish to thank our families for their patience and constant encouragement. It helped a lot when the task appeared daunting. Amit wishes to thank Terje for the morning coffee refills and for managing affairs while he was busy with the book over the past couple years. Nik would like to thank Uma, Amrita, and Ashwini for their support and encouragement, and Terje for the care she took in supporting this effort.

Introduction

In the software world, one often wonders what goes into making a system good. How does one build it? How does one have fun while building it? How does one ensure that it works reliably? This is a book that touches on some of the creative and managerial aspects of building systems.

Software as a profession has attracted millions of people around the world. Most of them learn on the job. A lot of good software has been delivered by individuals and their teams who did not have any formal or theoretical backgrounds in computer or systems science; just as many good managers never went to any management school. It is equally true that such learning on the job becomes more useful to the individual and to the organization when it is combined with a conceptual framework, together with an organizing influence to support it. Such organization enables one's learning to become cumulative, less fragmented, and easily transferable.

In this book, we present such an organizing method. We recommend that the reader approach all software design, development, and management through this simple framework consisting of Solution–Engineering–Execution (SEE) (Figure 0.1): find a good solution to the problem at hand, engineer the solution well, and address all aspects of delivery associated with the solution being built and delivered. SEE reinforces this.

Solution (in SEE) refers to the *thinking* of the solution from a holistic systems perspective. We use "system" to describe a set of entities that act on each other, and for which a logical model can be constructed, encompassing the entities and their allowed actions. One knows that any problem may have multiple familiar solutions, in which case one needs to think through them before selecting a solution. If the solution is not obvious, then one must work on determining a good (and right) solution.

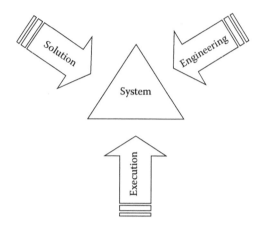

Figure 0.1   The SEE framework.

The systems approach teaches us to look at things beyond the sandbox in which they (appear to) operate and consider the ecosystem around them. This requires that the problem is properly understood and defined. To give an example, if a company wants to increase its technical support service hours, the solutions could be to run the call center in three shifts, or to open a self-service portal, or run the call center during office hours and provide e-mail support later, etc. There may be other solutions, such as outsourcing the technical support or providing extended service to a subset of customers. We would like to encourage system designers to draw more from other, non-software domains. For example, continuous coverage (a.k.a. high availability) is a problem that has been addressed in hospitals, and by security companies that provide security for important installations.

One should not start looking at Engineering aspects only after finalizing the Solution aspect; in the SEE framework, the problem must be approached simultaneously from all three angles. Engineering covers activities such as architecture, design, technology selection, delivery development method-ology to be used, and testing approach. That is, the extended definition of Engineering would be everything that is required to *build* the deliverable. One must understand and plan for all aspects related to building the solution — coding is only one aspect of Engineering. For example, a lack of good usability can cause more problems in software delivery than perhaps some technical limitation of a programming language.

Execution encompasses all aspects of *delivery*. It goes beyond the building of the deliverable to cover its release, implementation, marketing, enhancements, and even its support, staffing, and financial returns. Remember that a solution that does not specify how it is to be built, and managed, is an incomplete solution.

Most of us are familiar with life-cycle models, such as the *waterfall model* for software development. It would therefore be natural to assume that we are referring here to a (yet another) three-step process. We, in fact, are not. One can use any model that works. However, at every step or phase, one will need to approach the situation from all three aspects within SEE. For example, in the Requirements phase, think about the different ways to get good requirements, what would constitute a good set of requirements, and how to identify the business entities and people who could give a complete picture. Simultaneously, ensure that one has thought of the engineering aspects of the requirements (not the engineering aspects of the application one is preparing requirements for), such as how the requirements document will be structured and constructed (document or presentation, topics to be covered), and what techniques must be used to gather the data (interviews, questionnaires, etc.). The Execution aspect would cover how you would manage the process of creating, verifying, delivering, disseminating, and filing the requirements.

Using this SEE framework in the book, we discuss topics that can help the reader understand, and improve, many of the processes and techniques employed in thinking about and creating a software system. The topics discussed in this book often come from three areas: (1) systems thinking, (2) software engineering, and (3) project management. These three areas have been interacting and interplaying in software development for years. Our hope is that we will be able to help the reader approach familiar issues in a fresh and interesting light. To give an example, we are all familiar with how damaging "simple" software bugs can be — one missing character in the code can cause enormous harm to the system, and to the data. In this book we draw attention to the nonlinear nature of such behavior, which is one reason why software development becomes complex. Would it not be good if there were a more linear relationship — for example, a mistake of one character had only a small effect, while an entire module misbehaving would cause major damage? Some readers may not have looked at the familiar problem of software bugs from this angle. Once readers view aspects familiar to them using these different concepts, their minds will get jogged and may, with luck, lead to a different and better solution.

Software professionals need to reach out to domains beyond software, to learn about problems and solutions in other systems. The problems and situations that software designers and architects encounter might have been encountered in other fields. And it is quite likely that they may have already been solved in these areas — far away from the field of software.

For example, libraries and government offices have been cataloguing and retrieving information about books and land ownership for centuries. The military has many command and control procedures proven over time. The trading systems in different societies offer a lot that can be learned. Still, many designers do not pay sufficient attention to non-software systems, and thereby miss valuable opportunities to improve their thinking skills and design strengths. Good system design has not only to draw on a large body of topics and experience, but it must, in fact, be a synthesis in thinking across multiple domains. It must complement the analytical thinking that exists in abundance among software practitioners.

Workers in the software industry often complain of a lack of time. Either because of this or for other reasons, they are not eclectic readers. There are ideas in philosophy, logic, art and literature, systems science, practically every other field of knowledge that a good software professional can make use of. We discuss a few — Occam's razor, Ashby's work on variety, McLuhan's concepts in innovation, Forrester's work on system dynamics, Churchman's views on better thinking — which would definitely help a system designer, or a project manager, do his or her work better. Many of the topics are discussed in an introductory manner, as access to detailed information is available on the Internet.

Tiger Woods said, "It wasn't by accident that I learned to play golf from the green back to the tee." For similar reasons, we begin this book with a discussion of *failure*, something that one wants to avoid. We look at the definition of failure in software, and the reasons why software fails, and what we can do to minimize its chances. The remainder of the book deals with how better systems can be built, by introducing good practices and also avoiding bad ones.

Software development is done in the context of business strategies that drive IT investment and project work. Ignoring, or being ignorant of, business strategy could lead to software that gets built with great effort and yet must be shelved. Strategy plays a role within IT itself: the kind of strategic choices that must be made relate to enterprise technology, outsourcing, build-versus-buy decisions, and such.

The requirements that one builds to are meant to solve problems. One needs to distinguish between "true" requirements, which would solve the problem being addressed, and the "requirement specifications" that two parties have agreed to deliver and accept as part of a commercial agreement. Stakeholders are key to the requirements: a stakeholder is anybody who is impacted by the application when it is being built and when it is rolled out. There are often more stakeholders than generally assumed. Requirements also straddle both technical and business areas; and to maintain this distinction between them as seriously as some people do is to do a disservice to the way problems get solved and solutions get delivered.

Architecture and design are essential to good software. They are foundational aspects of software development. Architecture differs from design — one is global while the other is more local. If an application is complex, it should be built using a proper architecture.

Life cycles and processes are other two important concepts that should be understood. A life cycle is a coarse-grained process model. It allows one to get a good picture of the entire process but does not get lost in details. Processes, on the other hand, allow for the performance of highly repeatable tasks. Good processes help while bad processes hinder. Managers need to know how to design and implement good processes. We discuss processes that act as a feedback system between the specifications and the deliverables, and are invaluable in keeping the deliverables in control.

Not all software development is from the ground up as in the old days. The trend is toward using off-the-shelf products wherever a functional match exists. Off-the-shelf products may require extensive customization before use. However, customization facilities vary widely by product, leading to the failure of many (expensive) customization projects. We look into issues related to the selection of off-the-shelf software and its subsequent implementation in an organization. Closely related to this is the fact that most of the work done by IT departments is either migration or maintenance work. Migration projects get triggered because the existing application has reached its natural limits or else there is a business situation driving the move. We discuss how migration efforts can get ruined due to technology, the ecosystem, or data-related issues.

When one looks back at failed projects, one realizes how important good communication is for successful software development. Software development is basically a process of communication between customers, developers, and machines. We focus our attention on this important topic mainly because miscommunication can lead to significant rework and delays, and consequently rising costs.

Data and information are what software professionals deal with, day in and day out. Early ways of distinguishing data from information were simple: information was a report and data resided in a database or file. Trying to distinguish between data and information with such loose definitions can be difficult, because data, when organized in a certain way, can convey information. We discuss the multiple sources of information, both formal and informal, and how critical it is to adequately categorize, store, and manage it.

Reports have high visibility within an organization. Complex systems are judged, sometimes unfairly, on the quality of reports generated. The report portfolio can be linked to Maslow's well-known hierarchy of needs because reporting should map to management needs at various levels. We look at various aspects of good report design, viz., the need to be goal oriented and to take a problem-solving approach. One must change one's point of view — to look at its purpose and intended audience. We also discuss methodologies for clear status reporting and concise documentation in software projects.

Due to the increasing vulnerabilities in the environments in which software operates, it is time to pay more attention to the security aspects of deliverables, raising it, perhaps, to the same level of importance as functionality and performance. We conclude this book with a discussion of how a good security system covers business, technical, human, and process factors related to the systems being implemented.

The Use of Terms

Familiar and frequently used terms can remain elusive. Terms that refer to similar or closely linked ideas are often not probed further, under the assumption that the distinction is clear. However, this lack of distinction is the cause of much muddy thinking, ineffective communication, and often results in wasted and overlapping efforts.

Since 1852, the English language has had *Roget's Thesaurus*, a reference book of synonyms and equivalent words. Writers use this reference to select words with the right weight and shade of meaning, thereby improving their writing considerably. Scientific terms and expressions in professional usage appear to be far more well-defined and precise than normal English words: a glossary of terms is considered sufficient. Appendix A discusses terms that systems professionals often use — and confuse. The idea is not to arrive at a particular definition, but to explore ideas underlying multiple definitions or interpretations.

Good reading and, more importantly, better systems!

About the Authors

Nikhilesh Krishnamurthy has been managing software projects and consulting practices for over 25 years, working on MRP II, CRM, and other systems. He began his career with computer-aided design programs and then went on to the design and development of a comprehensive MRP II system. After many years of product development, he moved to the consulting field and managed consulting practices delivering custom applications. He is currently working with a large services company in the San Francisco Bay area, managing some of their business intelligence and information applications. He has a master's degree in industrial and systems engineering from the University of Illinois.

Amitabh Saran is an "ideas" person. He has spent most of his 18 years of professional experience designing and creating successful software products for institutions such as TCS, Philips, NASA, HP, and TriVium. He has been exposed to diverse kinds of systems — from compilers to networking, from utility billing to banking and finance, and from Web 2.0 to VoIP. Amitabh's technical work has been published in conferences, journals, and books. He holds a Ph.D. in computer science from the University of California, Santa Barbara, with specialization in distributed systems.

The awareness of the ambiguity of one's highest
achievements (as well as one's deepest failures)
is a definite symptom of maturity.

—**Paul Tillich (1886–1965)**

Chapter 1

Failure

Fail better.

—Samuel Beckett,
"Worstward Ho," 1983

Civilizations perish, organisms die, planes crash, buildings crumble, bridges collapse, peaceful nuclear reactors explode, and cars stall. That is, systems fail. The reasons for failure and the impacts of the failure vary; but when systems fail, they bring forth images of incompetence. Should we expect perfection from systems we develop when we ourselves are not perfect?

All man-made systems are based on theories, laws, and hypotheses. Even core physical and biological laws contain implicit assumptions that reflect a current, often limited, understanding of the complex adaptive ecosystems in which these systems operate. Surely this affects the systems we develop.

Most people recognize the inevitability of some sort of failure although their reaction to it is based on the timing of the failure with respect to the life expectancy of the system. A 200-year-old monument that crumbles will not cause as much consternation as the collapse of a two-year-old bridge.

In software, failure has become an accepted phenomenon. Terms such as "the blue-screen-of-death" have evolved in common computer parlance. It is a sad reflection on the maturity of our industry that system failure studies, causes and investigations, even when they occur, are rarely shared and discussed within the profession. There exist copious amounts of readily available literature analyzing failures in other industries such as transportation, construction, and medicine. This lack of availability of information about actual failures prevents the introduction of improvements as engineers continue to learn the hard way by churning out fail-prone software. Before arguing that a software system is more complex than most mechanical or structural systems that we build, and that some leeway should be given, there is a need to look at the various aspects of failure in software.

A Formal Definition of Failure

Although the etymology of "failure" is not entirely clear, it likely derives from the Latin *fallere*, meaning "to deceive." Webster's dictionary defines failure as "omission of occurrence or performance; or a state of inability to perform a normal function." It is important to note that it is not necessary that the entire system be non-operational for it to be considered a failure. Conversely, a single "critical" component failing to perform may result in the failure of the entire system. For example, one would not consider a car headlamp malfunction a failure of the car; however, one would consider a non-working fuel injection system as a failure. Why the distinction? Because the primary job of a car is conveyance. If it cannot do that, it has failed in its job. The distinction is not always so clear. In some cases, for example, while driving at night, a broken headlamp might be considered a failure. So how do we define software failures? Is a bug a failure? When does a bug become a failure? In software, failure is used to imply that:

- *The software has become inoperable.* This can happen because of a *critical* bug that causes the application to terminate abnormally. This type of failure should never happen in an end-customer scenario. Most organizations have mandatory guidelines about QA (quality assurance) — that no software should ship to a customer until all *critical* and *serious* bugs have been fixed (see Chapter 12 on quality). All things being equal, such a failure usually signifies that there is a problem outside the software boundary — the hardware, external software interacting with your software, or some viruses.

- *The software is operable but is not delivering to its desired specifications.* This may be due to a genuine oversight on the part of the development team, or a misunderstanding in the user requirements. Sometimes these requirements may be undocumented, such as user response times, screen navigations, or the number of mouse-clicks needed to fulfill a task. By our definition, a critical requirement *must* be skipped in development for the software to be considered a failure. Such a cause of failure points to a basic mismatch of the perceived criticality of needs between the customer and the project team.

■ *The software was built to specifications but has become unreliable to a point that its use is being impacted.* Such failures are typical when software is first released, or a new build hits the QA team (or the customer). There could be many small bugs that hinder the user from performing his or her task. Often, developers and the QA team tend to overlook inconsistencies in the GUI (graphical user interface) or in the presentation of data on screens. Instances of these inconsistencies include, but are not limited to the placement of "save" and "cancel" buttons, format of error messages, representation of entities across screens (e.g., "first name" followed by "last name" in one screen, and "last name, first name" in another). These cannot be considered bugs; rather, they are issues with a nuisance value in the minds of users, "putting them off" to a point that they no longer consider the software viable.

Failure Patterns

Failure as a field has been studied extensively ever since machines and mechanical devices were created. In the early days, most things were fixed when they were broken. It was evident that things would fail at some point in their lifetime, and there had to be people standing by who could repair them. In the 1930s, more studies were conducted, and many eminent scientists (including Waloddi Weibull) proposed probabilistic distribution curves for failure rates. The most commonly accepted is the "bathtub curve," so called because its shape resembles a Victorian bathtub (Figure 1.1).

The first section of the curve is called the "infant mortality." It covers the period just after the delivery of a new product and includes early bugs and defects. It is characterized by an increasing and then a declining failure rate. The second section, the flatbed of the bathtub, covers the usual failures that happen randomly in any product or its constituents. Its rate is almost constant. The third section is called "wear-out," in which the failure rate increases as the product reaches the end of its useful life. In physical terms, parts of a mechanistic system start to fail with wear and tear.

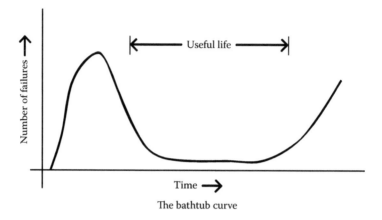

The bathtub curve

Figure 1.1   The bathtub curve.

Until the 1970s, the bathtub curve remained the basis of scheduled maintenance for physical machines and production plants, where parts of such systems were regularly replaced regardless of their wear and tear. All this changed in 1978 due to the work of Nowlan and Heap. They worked with many years of data obtained from the airline industry and disproved the concept of a *defined useful life in systems*. Their studies revealed (Figure 1.2) that greater than 70 to 90 percent of all failures were random, leaving only a very small percentage of age-related failures. These failure patterns made it clear that scheduled maintenance could have the reverse effect on the life of a system. Any intrusion (part replacement) could potentially cause more damage because the system would reset to its infant mortality failure rate (which is higher) from its random failure rate. Nowlan and Heap created the concept of Reliability Centered Maintenance, a concept later extended to other systems by Moubray in 1997. His idea is that as more bugs and problems accumulate in a system, its reliability starts deteriorating. As experienced managers and engineers, we need to know when to schedule component replacements and perform system maintenance; and Chapter 12 (on quality) further discusses this.

The Dependability of a Software System

Dependability is a combination of reliability — the probability that a system operates through a given operation specification — and availability — the probability that the system will be available at any required instant. Most software adopts the findings of Nowlan and Heap with respect to failures. During the initial stages of the system, when it is being used

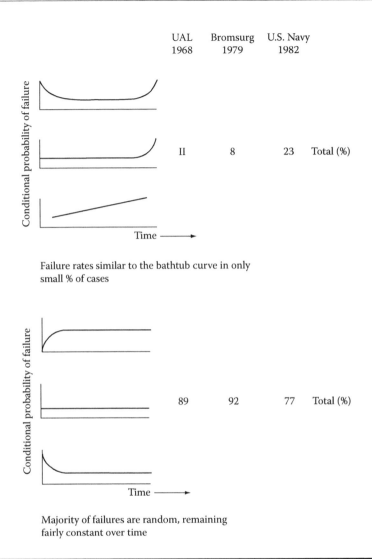

Figure 1.2 Nowlan and Heap's findings.

fresh in production, the failure rates are high. "Burn-in" is a concept used in the electrical and mechanical industries, wherein machines run for short periods of time after assembly so that the obvious defects can be captured before being shipped to a customer. In the software industry, alpha and beta programs are the burn-in. In fact, most customers are wary of accepting the first commercial release (v 1.0) of a software product. The longer a system is used, the higher the probability that more problems have been unearthed and removed.

For most of its useful life, the usage of any software in the production environment is very repetitive in nature. Further, because there is no physical wear and tear, the rate at which problems occur does remain the same. The reality, however, is that during the course of its usage, there is a likelihood that the software system (and the ecosystem around it) has been tinkered with, through customizations, higher data volumes, newer interfaces to external systems, etc. Each time such changes occur, there is the chance that new points of failure will be introduced. As keen practitioners, one should be wary of such evolving systems. Make a call regarding the migration of the production environment (see Chapter 11 on migration). This call will be based on more abstract conditions than simply the rate at which bugs are showing up or their probability — it will depend on one's experience in handling such systems.

Known but Not Followed: Preventing Failure

Software systems fail for many reasons, from the following of insufficient R&D processes during development to external entities introducing bugs through a hardware or software interface. Volumes have been written about the importance of and the critical need for:

- A strict QA policy for all software development, customization, and implementation
- Peer and buddy reviews of specifications, software code, and QA test plans to uncover any missed understanding and resource-specific flaw patterns
- Adhering to documentation standards and following the documentation absolutely
- Detailed end-user training about the system, usage, maintenance, and administration
- Feedback from user group members who will interface with the system and use it on a day-to-day basis
- Proper availability of hardware and software infrastructure for the application based on the criticality of its need
- Frequent reviews, checks, and balances in place to gather early warning indicators about any untoward system behavior

There is little need to reiterate the importance of this list. The question one wants to tackle is: if these things are so clearly recognized, why do we continue to see increasing incidence of failure in software systems? Or do these policies come with inherent limitations because of which they cannot be followed in most software life cycles?

Engineering Failures: Oversimplification

Dörner, in his book entitled *The Logic of Failure*, attributes systems failure to the flawed human thinking process. Humans are inherently slow in processing various kinds of information. For example, while one can walk and climb stairs with ease (while scientists still struggle to remove the clumsiness in the walking styles of smart, artificial intelligence-based robots), one is not as swift in computing primitive mathematical operations such as the multiplication of two large real numbers. It is this apparent slowness that forces one to reduce analytical work by selecting one central or a few core objects. We then simplify, or often oversimplify, complex interrelationships among them in a system. This simplification gives one a sense that things are in one's control and that one is sufficiently competent to handle them (Figure 1.3). On one hand, this illusion is critical for humans to maintain their professional self-esteem. On the other hand, it forces one to make choices that may not be right for the overall system. And because one is unable to think too far ahead, and unwilling to comprehend very complex temporal behaviors of the system one is proposing to create at the onset, one inevitably leaves pitfalls in the system that can cause its failure.

It is a good idea to regularly document the assumptions made at various stages of design and development, and to have them reviewed by domain experts or actual users. A building's structural engineer not only needs specifications about the layout of the proposed building, but also of the

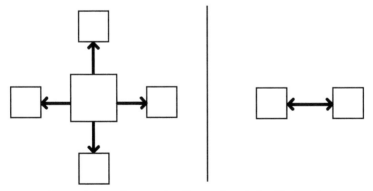

Human beings often oversimplify complex relationships by selecting one central object or a few core objects because it reduces analytical work

Figure 1.3　Simplifying relationships.

land orientation, soil composition, water table, wind (or snow) or environmental conditions, etc. So while the building code for earthquakes may not require anything exceptional if the land is far from a fault line, the presence of an active railway track nearby may result in similar conditions and thus must be considered *a priori*. Mission-critical software has been known to fail because of trivial assumptions such as measurement units (e.g., meter-kg-second instead of foot-pound-second). Developers may have found it difficult to create a system with definable units, or perhaps they were unaware of measurement systems used in different parts of the world. Assumptions that are wrong are a bane of the software world.

Execution Failures: Overruns under Pressure

Often, software does not even reach a stage where it is put in front of users; the project fails before the software is released. The causes of such failures are usually time, resource, or scope overruns. Many times, project managers and architects are not 100-percent aware of the domain's complexity or the new technologies that would be used for the proposed system. Such failures are common in porting projects (see Chapter 11 on migration) where managers tend to estimate project costs on the basis of the origin and destination technologies without looking into the details of the features used. The complexity involved in porting a system from Microsoft SQL Server DB to Oracle DB can vary immensely if triggers, stored procedures, and DB-dependent system calls have been used extensively.

Functional Failures

Unclear user requirements and undocumented "understandings" between the client and the sales team of the vendor are causes of project cost overruns. In their enthusiasm to close a deal, meet and beat their sales quota, or because sales people do not have an adequate understanding of what it will take to deliver the software, project costs may be severely under-quoted. It is advisable to have a technical person involved with the sales process, before the final estimates are shared with the client. All expectations should be documented as formal features in the requirement specifications. Sometimes the client innocently adds requirements, often immediately before signing the deal. These can cause several problems. Nontechnical verbiage such as "one of my sales staff works from another city and will need a copy of the database on his computer" or "we have some data in our existing small computer we used, which you can move to your new system" can completely alter delivery times.

Failing to follow a pre-decided formal change management process is another cause for delay. A potential problem occurs in the development of a system when a programmer needs to implement an obscure or vague specification. Consultants and experts in the domain may not be accessible in time to get advice or clarification. If clarification is not sought or received, any guesswork on the part of the programmer can lead to unwanted results, and even cause system failure. For example, the programmer may have specifications that fields, which are not explicitly filled by the user on a screen, should default to certain values when the user hits the "save" button. When a change is introduced, adding a new field to the screen, the programmer may not get a clear specification about its default value and decides to select the one "that makes sense." This could lead to problems in the data being displayed elsewhere in the application.

Ecosystem Failures: Uncoordinated Efforts within a Team

Improper or uncoordinated marketing and sales processes also can lead to the failure of a product (Figure 1.4). Take, for example, the failure of online grocery and furniture stores the first time they were launched in early 2000. Although 40 percent of their budget was spent in marketing, they missed out on two critical customer shopping behaviors: (1) customers like to touch and feel before they buy; and (2) walking into a store and buying groceries or furniture is not so negative an experience that people would flock to an online store. In fact, in the case of furniture, it was sometimes a family outing that stimulated the purchase. Similar examples exist for huge marketing blunders such as the introduction of Coke in China (in Mandarin, Coke translated as "female horse stuffed with wax"), and the unsuccessful launch of Nova by General Motors in Mexico (which meant "goes nowhere"). These companies spent millions before realizing their mistakes.

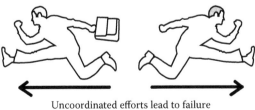

Uncoordinated efforts lead to failure

Figure 1.4   Lack of coordination.

Although projects are executed flawlessly, with good sales and marketing strategies, and there is customer demand for the product, companies may forget to plan for the right logistical and delivery systems. Online grocery stores went out of business because they did not sort out their delivery systems. For example, they had a difficult time managing deliveries on congested roads, to a widespread customer base. Their costs never came close to their theoretical efficiencies, and they were not able to maintain promised delivery schedules. Other E-commerce companies became successful only when they collaborated with local delivery establishments. Internet shoppers dropped in number after receiving delayed or poor service from online retailers at the turn of the century. Cases of customers getting a battery delivered to them on Christmas and the toy a week later were commonplace.

Natural disasters (e.g., floods, earthquakes, fires) and man-made problems (e.g., terrorism, war) can cause logistical issues and should be taken into account in making disaster recovery plans for critical applications. Most customers understand and are realistic in their needs during such abnormal times, as long as they see the company has things under control and is working to provide them with service free of interruptions.

Changing Playing Fields Cause Unprecedented Failure

Sometimes, parameters external to a business can have a detrimental impact on its products. As a software architect, one should always have an eye on the changing technology landscape (refer to McLuhan in Chapter 2 on systems). Technology changes can turn an offering obsolete overnight. When cell phones overran pagers, it took Motorola — the leader in pagers— a long time to catch up with Nokia in the cell phone market.

Other things, such as economic sanctions between countries, due to politics, can affect the success of software products, especially if they have an export-oriented market. All one can do is hope that political leaders maintain amicable relationships with the rest of the world.

Faulty Leadership Causes Failures

This facet may be out of one's control but leadership is a good indicator of the future success of a software project. Fickle-minded leaders, lacking the vision or the mettle to drive their ideas, hold back an otherwise successful company. Good leaders know when to stand firm and when to give in. Often, project managers are not strong enough to say "no" to a customer. Acceptance of changes late in the software development life cycle leads to scope creep, cost overruns, long working hours, and a generally unhappy, unmotivated team.

Sometimes there is management pressure to rush through the release of a product. In such cases, it is advisable to guide management with regard to any compromises that one will have to make that may affect the safety of the system. Management can then make a collective decision on the software release dates. It is better to deal with bad information as early as possible. Keeping quiet under pressure will only complicate the problem. In fact, it is quite likely that the cost will multiply if the problem has to be resolved at a customer site rather than in the development lab.

Techno-political factors rear their heads more often when external consultants and contractors are involved. Because their involvement in the project is for the duration of the contract, there could be a tendency on the part of less than professional contractors to ignore long-term consequences of failure, as the contractors would have moved on by then. The project manager should create an environment in which each contributor is committed to success, irrespective of the length of his or her attachment to the project.

Cascading Failures

As the name implies, cascading failures (Figure 1.5) begin with the failure of a small component, which in turn triggers the failure of other components, leading sometimes to the failure of the entire system. Quite often, such failures are the result of faulty fail-over implementation strategies. With fail-over, there is an effort to redistribute the load from a failed node, which results in an excess load on other components beyond their capacity. This may cause them to fail and may further aggravate the situation. The effect snowballs and soon the entire network may also fail.

Failures can cascade

Figure 1.5   Cascading failures.

Detection of such failures, at their very onset, is the key to preventing cascading failures. There are complex algorithms in distributed computing under Byzantine failure and Byzantine fault tolerance.

Monitoring Systems

Systems are created to deal with any number of things. Sometimes they deal with extremely dangerous situations, for example, nuclear reactors and space shuttles. It is very difficult to test these systems for failures because the failures in either case would have catastrophic impacts. Thus, these systems must be run through hypothetical failure scenarios and recovery mechanisms. Essential components in these systems include monitoring systems for the detection and reporting of failures, and emergency control functions that will make intelligent decisions by switching control to safe zones when faults are detected. In some cases this may even include human intervention.

Software systems should learn from this. Routine checks of the system should be mandatory. Browsing system logs periodically, even when users have reported no critical or serious failures, is a good exercise. It is also helpful to have monitoring software built into all server components to automatically check the health of the component periodically. It is important to remember that detecting failures, on a few server components, can prevent the spread of those failures to the entire system. Some techniques used in networking include checksums, parity bits, software interlocks, watchdog timers, and sample calculations. Sample calculations are beneficial when writing code for some critical function that may or may not require mathematical operations or multiprocessor systems. It involves doing the same calculation twice, at different points in time on the same processor or even building software redundancy by writing multiple versions of the same algorithm being executed simultaneously and verified for identical results.

Reliability in Software

Dimitri Kececioglu introduces a formal definition for this:

> "Reliability engineering provides the theoretical and practical tools whereby the probability and capability of parts, components, equipment, products and systems to perform their required functions for desired periods of time without failure,

in specified environments and with a desired confidence, can
be specified, designed in, predicted, tested and demonstrated."

In material product engineering, reliability is extremely important. Manufacturers want to reduce their costs as much as possible, sometimes taking
the route of using inferior quality raw materials, or not adhering to
approved production standards. This may not be the right strategy because
it can increase the cost of supporting the product once it gets out in the
field.

Although the above may have been used in the context of purely
mechanical systems, it also has relevance to the software industry. Conscious
efforts must be made to weave reliability through the life cycle of the
development by incorporating reliability models in one's software right from
the product planning stage. The architecture and design (scalability, performance, code reuse, third-party components, etc.) set the stage for the
reliability of the product. Further along, coding styles, adherence to good
software engineering practices, and adequate developer testing help in
creating reliable code. Subsequent testing, using meaningful in-house data
and field data (if the customer is using a system already), helps in ascer-
taining how reliably the software will work in a production environment.

An analysis of bugs discovered in the software, which requires proper
documentation of all bugs found in-house or at the customer site, irrespective of their severity (see Chapter 12 on quality), is another valuable
tool. Reliability engineering is known to use various distribution models
— Weibull being the most widely used — to get a good handle on the
success rates of manufactured products, and ensure that they balance the
business goals of the customer.

Accountability for Failure

Systems fail due to human error. Typical errors are often the result of
incomplete information to handle the system, or the failure to follow a
long set of procedures while using a system. Failures can also occur when
accountability has not been properly established in the operational hierarchy of the system. If users or operators are not fully aware of their roles
and responsibilities (especially those who are monitoring the behavior of
the system), they tend to assume that reporting a potential problem may
not be *their* job. They assume that the other guy or the manager will
ultimately spot it. Critical problems can easily be missed this way. The
following is a good checklist to ensure that no part of the system is passed
over:

- Consider all critical components in a system.
- If a component has more than one mode of operation, each of these should be considered individually.
- Estimate the probability of failure based on:
  - Historical data for similar components in similar conditions
  - QA bugs analysis
  - Experience of one's earlier projects
  - Documentation by industry experts in their usage scenarios
- Remember that failures in a particular operation can take a number of forms.
- Assign good people (refer to Chapter 8 on process) to these critical components — during development, QA, and their eventual operation.

Liability of Failure

Pilots will refuse to fly an aircraft if they have the slightest suspicion of a technical snag, and a builder will always be held liable for not following construction norms. Who is liable for the failure in a software system? If the customer does not have a maintenance contract, chances are that it will be expensive to get the services of the software company. It is this lack of liability that has contributed to the lack of serious analysis of failures in software systems.

Getting out of Failures

Two approaches are used: (1) fail-over and (2) fail-safe (Figure 1.6). Fail-over means detecting a system failure and migrating the functionality of the failed system to a backup system. For example, in most infrastructure networks (e.g., power grids or telecom lines), the loads carried by each substation or node are dynamically redistributed. The strategy states that that if a node is unavailable due to failure, the load it carries is rapidly distributed to the other nodes on the network. Similarly, in fault-tolerant machines or redundant servers, there is more than one intelligent controller connected to the same device. In the event of a controller failure, fail-over occurs and the survivor takes over its I/O load.

The fail-safe approach, on the other hand, deals with prevention. Such systems have the in-built capacity that any component failure triggers an action, or set of actions, that will always bring the system to a safe situation. Sometimes this is achieved through a process that uses controls and logic to prevent an improper operation or transaction from occurring and produces an error condition or defect instead of failure. Checks for

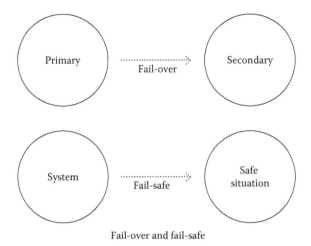

Fail-over and fail-safe

Figure 1.6 Avoiding failures.

boundary conditions (array bounds, divide by zero) are examples of such fail-safe mechanisms.

Product and Project Failures

Product development involves one or more projects, each of which has its own life cycle. A failure of the latter — that is, project failure — could be the result of inaccurate initiation, choosing a wrong life cycle, inadequate resourcing or funding, contractual disagreements, etc. An important observation to remember is that products may fail due to inadequacies in the projects driving them. Interestingly, these inadequacies do not cause project failures themselves. More details on product and project failures are discussed in Chapter 7 on life cycles.

Summary

Failure as a field has been studied extensively ever since machines and mechanical devices were created. There are many degrees of failure: the software could become inoperable; it could be operable but not deliver to its desired specifications; it may have been built to specifications but become unreliable to a point that its use is being impacted. Some of the reasons why software applications fail include insufficient R&D (research and development) processes during development and the natural tendency of humans to oversimplify complex interrelationships among the core entities in a system. Just as products can fail, so can projects. Project failure is often due to inadequate change control management. Fortunately, failure has its patterns. The probability of failure can be reduced through better design and engineering. As a designer, one should incorporate reliability models in one's software. As for handling failures, one can take the fail-over and fail-safe approaches.

To manage a system effectively, you might focus on the interactions of the parts rather than their behavior taken separately.

—**Russell L. Ackoff**

Chapter 2

Systems

I must create a system, or be enslaved by another man's.

—William Blake

For a profession that deals with systems, it is a matter of some perplexity that little attention is paid to *Systems Science* by those who build software systems.

That practitioners tend to ignore theoretical underpinnings of their professions is not unexpected. Good actors do not necessarily attend acting schools. Many managers are successful without being students of management science. Good software has come from people without a formal background in computer science. It is also possible that in the case of systems science, which has existed for many years, the concepts are being used by people without them being aware of using such concepts.

Software has become a profession for millions of people around the world, a majority of whom learn on the job. Careers often begin with programming, later evolving into systems design, architecture, or project management. Some in the field get formal training; others do not. Many still believe, and not without some validity, that design, architecture, or software management requires skills that are "more art than science." If two different designers were designing a school admission system, it is quite likely that the software system that would be delivered would be different in terms of its screens, its design, interfaces, data model, and its workflows, although both automate the same business process.

When it comes to building systems, there is no ready-made plan that can guarantee success. A common approach is to form a team of a few intelligent people and throw them at the problem. With such an approach, results obviously vary. While it does not necessarily solve the problem of varying results, utilizing systems science or the systems approach can be considered a valuable addition to the toolset used by such teams. Designers and architects stand on firmer ground when they recognize the underlying basis for some of the solutions they recommend. While designers and developers consider causal and temporal relationships between interacting entities, the systems approach adds more variety and conditionality to the process.

This book does not advocate systems thinking as a general-purpose solution that will improve your systems. We also understand that, similar to Operations Research or Management Science, practitioners often ignore formal systems thinking. Software development, as in the old guilds, involves mostly on-the-job learning, which is a good thing. However, we recognize that it is necessary to have some kind of conceptual framework to understand and organize what one is learning, to categorize and catalog one's mistakes and failures, and to recognize what carries over from each project that one works on. It is a learning and thinking framework.

Application of Systems Thinking in Software

The systems approach teaches us to take a holistic view, to look at things beyond the sandbox in which they appear to operate, and consider them as part of the ecosystem around them. The relationship between the whole and its parts is key to systems thinking.

The word "system" has its roots in the Greek *sústēma*, which means "brought together," or "combined or organized whole, formed from many parts." Today we use "system" to describe a set of entities that act upon each other, toward an objective, for which a logical model can be constructed encompassing the entities and their allowed actions.

Systems consist of many interacting parts, each with its own entities and events, which are not treated as isolated entities. These entities interact with each other to facilitate the flow of some element through and between them, such as information or energy. Examples can be found in the solar system, our own blood circulation system, in a government department, or in a factory. Some systems are physical — can be seen and touched — while others are virtual. A flood control system might consist of dams, canals, overflow areas, levees, and evacuation plans, whereas the legal system is a set of laws, rights, codes, and jurisdictions. One thing common to all systems is that they are expected to meet specified objectives.

The IEEE-Std 1220-2005 defines systems engineering as "an interdisciplinary approach to derive, evolve, and verify a life-cycle balanced system solution that satisfies customer expectations and meets public acceptability." It involves the application of efforts to:

1. Transform an operational need into a description of system performance parameters and a preferred system configuration through the use of an iterative process of functional analysis, optimization, detailed definition, design, test, and evaluation

2. Incorporate related technical parameters and assure compatibility of all physical, functional, and logical interfaces in a manner that optimizes the total system and its design

3. Integrate performance, production, reliability, maintainability, supportability, and other specialties into the overall engineering effort

---

Software engineers have used the systems approach to create a structured and requirements-driven process to development. The appeal lies in its ability to take an inherently ambiguous and complex set of requirements and apply a structured process to derive an efficient solution. This process is repeatable, can be uniform across analysts, allows implementations to be traced to customer requirements, and considers their implications beyond implementation.

Systems thinking is a vast field, together with a culture of active debate. We have selected a few thinkers from the field and present what we feel are their important ideas. They are powerful thinkers from varying backgrounds, whose ideas can be put to good use by system designers. The usefulness of any idea is often indirect as it works in the designer's consciousness to bear fruit at the appropriate time. We, therefore, do not attempt to draw immediate practical benefits of knowing about such ideas, many of which, at first glance, may seem irrelevant to software.

The Law of Requisite Variety

The term "variety" represents the number of *distinct* "states" in which a system can exist. An electrical switch has a variety of two: on and off. A cup of tea may have three distinct states: hot, tepid, and cold. Over time, the cup of hot tea may have only two states — tepid and cold — and then only one state — cold. The variety of the cup of tea has decreased with time. Still, for some other purposes, the cup of tea could be considered to have a variety of two: strong and weak tea. As such, fundamentally, variety is not an intrinsic property of the cup of tea. It is driven by the ability of the receiver or regulator to distinguish between the states. Not all possible combinations must be considered — only those that exist and can be distinguished need to be taken into account. If a car is categorized by a vector age, power, color, each of which can take two values old/new, high horsepower/low horsepower, black/white, but of the eight possible combinations, only four are actually manufactured, then the variety of the set of cars is four, not eight.

William Ross Ashby (1903–1972) was a pioneer in the study of complex systems. William Ross Ashby's Law of Requisite Variety states that "only variety can destroy variety." This law is one of the most general systemic-cybernetic principles. It is useful in understanding any type of system. Simply stated, it means that for any system to regulate (manage) another system or its environment, it must have at least as much variety (complexity) as the system it is trying to control. In the aforesaid car example, once the variety is known, the manufacturer would recognize the need for four different kinds of trucks to transport the cars, or four different sales strategies to sell them. Similarly, if an appliance such as a laptop computer is expected to work with both 110 Volts and 230 Volts input in two different countries, it must have a voltage regulator that works with 110 Volts and also with 230 Volts.

Consider a project as a system that needs to be regulated, and the project management team (architects, designers, managers) as the regulators. Ashby's law implies that the regulators must have the requisite variety to tackle its counterpart variety that exists in a project for certain vectors such as time, budget, scope, and quality. A project manager may wish to manage the budget of a project taking its variety as only two: over-budget and under-budget. That is, he or she is interested in the budget being in only two states — over or under the budget. He or she may then put in place control plans for each of these two states ("Escalate to management when project goes over budget"). Another project manager may, however, decide that the budget has a variety of three: 0 to 80 percent, 80 to 100 percent, and over-budget, with a separate control plan for the 80 to 100 percent state (e.g., "Call a special review meeting when the project has consumed 80 percent of the budget."). Finally, how the project manager would see variety in a project ultimately determines the management and control mechanisms that will be put in place. Good managers choose sufficient variety to control what needs controlling, as per Ashby's law. However, this is easier said than done, as we will see.

Variety Is Relative

Although it may appear simple, in theory, to determine the variety in any system, it is not so easy in practice. Various estimation approaches such as COCOMO, FPA, and ESTIMACS have been proposed and are used selectively by software managers. Ashby's law, in a way, simplifies the model because the regulation of variety focuses on "relative" parameters of complexity rather than "absolute" ones. For example, if you add new functionality to your application, it must be met with increased variety on the Quality Assurance (QA) side. QA acts as the control system for Engineering, deciding whether or not the delivered code is acceptable for release. For example, if your application must be enhanced to work with mobile phones, your test plans must be enhanced to test that it works with mobile phones. If you increase the variety in Development, then you have to increase corresponding variety on the QA side. If such action to "destroy variety" is not taken, then the QA system will fail to uncover some problems due to lack of proper testing. This seems obvious to any development team that takes it for granted that they would introduce new functionality with corresponding changes to their testing plans. The reason we do that, or need to do that, is explained by Ashby's Law of Requisite Variety.

Matching Variety

In information processing terms, the Law of Requisite Variety also implies that a system's information processing capacity should match its information processing requirements. If the information processing capacity is less than the processing requirements, then crucial information may be left unprocessed. Conversely, if an organization's information processing capacity far exceeds its requirements, the organization has room to meet new needs.

Any regulation can be attempted, or achieved, in two ways: (1) either the variety of the environment can be reduced or (2) the variety of the controller can be increased. Both approaches can be applied to software design and development. Using the first approach, one can decrease the external information processing requirements to match the available capacity (time, money, resources) for creating a functional and manageable software system. One could:

1. Focus only on certain areas of user needs, either ignoring other areas or else leaving them un-automated.
2. Develop policies and rules that reduce the scope of the application to be delivered.
3. Phase the delivery.

For the second approach, one could increase the information processing capacity to match the outside variety. For example,

- Employ more or better qualified resources.
- Train the resources specifically for the project.
- Use more effective technologies.
- Contract with other firms to integrate their product offerings, instead of building them oneself.
- Get team members to deal with more problems themselves, through self-management and employee empowerment. This reduces the variety required of managers on the project to manage individual team members.

Choices and Constraints in Software

If one asks whether destroying variety is one of the objectives of regulation, the answer is yes. Regulation requires constraints on a system. Although the term "constraints" sounds negative or restrictive, constraints are actually necessary. Most "laws" of science are constraints on the way nature behaves. Constraints help us in at least two ways: (1) as an organizing influence and (2) as an enabler of predictions. They are an organizing influence through the reduction of variety. Ashby gives the example of a chair whose four legs, when unconnected and separate, have six degrees of freedom, each for a total of 24 degrees of freedom. When they are joined, however, they have only six degrees of freedom, which are the six degrees of freedom of the chair. The reduction of 24 to 6 reflects the creation of a chair — an object that is its own entity, which is a whole and is more than the sum of its parts — a basic premise of systems thinking.

Constraints serve two purposes:

1. They enable us to make predictions.
2. Without constraints, there would be chaos.

Ashby gives another example of an aircraft. An aircraft can only move in a constrained manner; it cannot jump to any portion of the sky instantly. It is constrained by its speed, power, position, technology, etc. Only because there is this constraint, another system — an air traffic control system — can hope to manage or regulate the aircraft.

Software gets enhanced with new features when the variety in the software system (the regulator) tries to match the increased variety in the environment (the business). More variety in the regulator is good. A rigid system will fail when it encounters a situation that it cannot "match." In software, design constraints are sometimes applied early in the life cycle that drastically reduce the variety of the delivered system. For example, one may decide that only IE (Internet Explorer) browsers will be supported. If the variety in the market is higher (i.e., many customers use other browsers), then the early choice has reduced the variety of the software delivered in a manner that may make it unacceptable later on.

Ashby's work provides an excellent and underutilized approach to systems design. System designers should view information systems as regulating systems, with the requisite variety designed to match the environments in which the systems will be deployed. The Law of Requisite Variety encourages one to take a total systems view. While simple models can be powerful for the purposes of design, the underlying assumptions should not be too simplistic. They must have the requisite variety in their range of actions to match the variety required in real-world applications.

Most See, Very Few Observe

There is a vast difference between desires (wants) and requirements (needs). Customers usually have desires. The observant business analyst converts these desires into requirements. Architects and designers use the most suitable technologies to satisfy these requirements. They should have a keen sense of the prevailing trends in the surrounding environment, while proposing a solution that meets the requirements. This sense is the key to success in software, an effort that one must undertake keeping in mind that the up-front investment is sizeable, development is complex, time to market is long, and barrier to entry for competition is fairly low. As a creator of software, one would like to look ahead and deliver solutions that meet future, perhaps unanticipated needs. Architects and designers need to recognize new trends that could be leading indicators of some important changes that may become evident later. Radio waves and cathode-ray oscilloscopes signaled the advent of television. Similar examples are strewn throughout the history of computing. Microsoft and Apple were the first to observe the need for greater power and flexibility in the hands of end users, and thereby created the desktop era. ARPANET, DARPANET, Ethernet, and the WWW (World Wide Web) all existed prior to 1990, but were not seen as leading indicators of the way information systems would be delivered, until the launch of the Web browser.

Herbert Marshall McLuhan (1911–1980) was a Canadian educator, philosopher, and scholar, professor of English literature, literary critic, and communications theorist. McLuhan's most widely known work, *Understanding Media,* published in 1964, is a pioneering study in media ecology. In it, McLuhan proposes that media itself, not the content carried, should be the focus of study. He points out that all media have individual characteristics that engage the viewer in different ways.

McLuhan's most famous aphorism begins his groundbreaking work. He writes that:

> In a culture like ours, long accustomed to splitting and dividing all things as means of control, it is sometimes a bit of a shock to be reminded that, in operational and practical fact, the medium is the message.

The "shock" in this statement is that the message has been equated to the medium itself. We are accustomed to thinking that the message is what the medium delivers to its intended audience. For example, when considering television, we are mostly concerned with what is on television, that is, the programs. We examine the content of a particular show, interpret it, and judge its value. We may conclude that certain "messages" on television are harmful while others are beneficial. But, for McLuhan, it is the television medium itself, not its programs, that is the message. It is a message of structural change in society, occurring slowly.

The significance of such structural changes that occur or take effect slowly can be missed or discounted. Their effects on society, and productivity, work over long stretches of time. Thus, how can one recognize such a message? By looking for a change in "scale or pace or pattern" in interpersonal behavior. That is a message that something new has been introduced. We see that most recently in the case of the Internet. Even in its early manifestations, it has affected work and social relations. Note that we are not talking about anything and everything that is newly introduced in society. Every day, new gadgets are introduced and new inventions come into play. Unless these new technologies or devices change interpersonal and social relationships, we cannot treat them as the arrival of a new message, which might be signaling the arrival of some new medium. Recognizing such change is not always easy. We may have to depend on experts in media ecology to study and interpret them.

Eric McLuhan, son of Marshall McLuhan, describes it by saying that:

"Each medium, independent of the content it mediates, has its own intrinsic effects which are its unique message. The railway did not introduce movement or transportation or wheel or road into human society, but it accelerated and enlarged the scale of previous human functions, creating totally new kinds of cities and new kinds of work and leisure. This happened whether the railway functioned in a tropical or northern environment, and is quite independent of the freight or content of the railway medium. What McLuhan writes about the railroad applies with equal validity to the media of print, television, computers and now the Internet. 'The medium is the message' because it is the 'medium that shapes and controls the scale and form of human association and action.'"

Why do such changes concern a software designer? Because systems that we design today must work in the socioeconomic ecology in which it is implemented, which in turn gets affected by the changes about which we are talking. Our systems are expected to be functional for many years to come. If there are fundamental changes taking place due to the emergence of new media, as happened in the case of the Internet, designers can go wrong recommending a solution that will fit poorly in the new world. This happened with many software applications that had to be redone to work in a more interconnected, information-rich Web environment as that environment took hold in business and society. Is it always necessary for designers to think that deeply? Perhaps not always; but when large investments are at stake, it behooves one to pay attention to what McLuhan says.

Hot and Cold

In *Understanding Media*, McLuhan generally divides media into hot (high definition of information) and cool (low definition of information). The two terms have specific meanings. A hot medium is one that extends one single sense in high definition. High definition means the state of being well-filled with data. A cool medium is one with low definition. Because of the lack of information, much must be filled in by users. Therefore, a cool medium generally requires a higher level of participation of users than a hot medium. When looking at the two different kinds of media, it can be interpreted that the hotter the medium, the less someone needs to interpret what is being presented to them; whereas the colder the medium, the more someone has to uncover and engage in the media. For example, in comparing a high-definition photograph with a sketch, the photograph is "hot" because the viewer can glean a lot of information while a quick sketch is "cold" because the viewer has to "fill in the blanks." Note that cold is not necessarily bad. It has its advantages because it forces the viewer to get involved and engage some of their other senses and faculties, such as thinking. Within software systems, when one selects the media or channels for users to interact with — the screen, the report, the manuals, training slides — one must keep in mind such concepts. Wherever applicable, good interactions engage the users, not merely inform them: low definition is not bad, just different.

System Dynamics

Jay Wright Forrester is a pioneer of computer engineering and the founder of System Dynamics, which deals with the simulation of interactions between objects in dynamic systems. System Dynamics is a strategy for studying the world around us, something that all systems analysts do when designing information systems. The central idea is for one to understand how all entities in a system interact with each other; the concept of "feedback" is the differentiating factor in the field of System Dynamics.

Systems Dynamics is based on three broad and interrelated categories: (1) systems thinking, (2) dynamic modeling, and (3) simulation and modeling tools. This approach views system entities and people as interacting through "feedback" loops, where a change in variable A affects other variables B, C, or D over time, which in turn affects A, and so on. One cannot study the link between A and B in isolation, and then study the link between D and A, to predict how the system will behave. Only the study of the entire system, as a feedback system, can lead to some good predictions.

Any regulator (extending the Ashby example) can be used to explain a feedback loop. Consider the volume controls of the audio system in a car. At various points during the car ride, one may need to adjust the volume: when one starts from home in a residential neighborhood (quieter), then when one rolls up the windows as one enters the freeway, and then, once again after exiting the freeway. It is a cascading feedback loop, based on the surrounding ambient noise, leading one to regulate the volume with smaller and smaller adjustments, until one reaches the desired sound level.

This example can be used to illustrate the difference between systems thinking and systems dynamics. Systems thinking would dictate that a certain sound level, say 15 decibels, is good for residential areas and another sound level, 30 decibels, is good for freeways. One can hardcode such values in the software. One can make it more flexible by making it table driven. System dynamics, on the other hand, would use a model that would show that the level would have to be adjusted based on dynamic factors such as the speed and the type of the car one is driving (sound insulation), the traffic on the freeway (external noise), or the condition of the road (e.g., asphalt versus cement surface).

If one is attempting to understand the basic structure of a working system and its associated behavior in its entirety, system dynamics is a good approach. In fact, Forrester postulates that most real-world systems are nonlinear with multi-loop feedbacks, which is why models based on system dynamics can be better representations of real systems.

You can use the concepts of system dynamics in building software in the following ways:

1. Identify the customer problem or situation that needs to be changed.
2. Ascertain the behaviors of interest in the problem area and the associated information base (policies, structure, regulations, rules, users).
3. Develop a hypothesis based on the dynamic conditions of the environment that explains the situation.
4. Build a computer model (prototype) that best reproduces the behavior seen in the real world.
5. Create alternative behaviors (information base changes), and use the model to see how it affects the situation.
6. Propose the solution that best matches the desired situation.

These steps probably do not look very different from the software life-cycle process. Closer examination draws attention to the following:

■ System dynamics teaches one to use feedback loops to adjust one's progress for each of these steps. A model that "best" reproduces real-world behavior can only be determined after multiple iterations of coding and testing.
■ One continuously needs feedback across steps. For example, while building Step 3, one needs to keep an eye on Step 2; for Step 4, one must constantly reevaluate Steps 2 and 3.

System dynamics offers a few unintuitive suggestions:

■ When a solution does not meet the requirements, it is advisable to invest in reviewing the hypothesis on which the solution was built, rather than retaining the existing hypothesis and jumping in to tune the solution to match it. This is an important point.

■ Quite frequently one may notice that the solution one has developed does not correctly match the real-world structure, requirements, and policies with which one started. The obvious would be to tune the solution and iron out any deviations from the hypotheses on which it was developed. System dynamics, however, says that the real discrepancy, in such situations, is more likely between the understanding of the policies and the derivation of the hypotheses from them. It shows that the business analysts have, possibly, not understood the system's environment and scope, due to which the hypotheses prepared for further use become incorrect.

To take an example, a retail store has a return policy stating that goods can be returned within 30 days of the date of purchase. A system gets built with a business logic embedded in it that checks for the date and rejects transactions that are invalid. Such a system fails to work when rolled out to the stores. It turns out that when the requirements for a return policy were drawn, the analyst ignored other requirements that were dynamically linked to it, such as the policy for exchanging items, or for handling damaged goods, or for handling goods recalled by the manufacturer. The return policy, therefore, is a policy with many dynamic elements and, based on what Forrester says, the requirements should consider the larger dynamic model. The right thing to do is not to treat the return policy as a "business rule in software" problem but rather to reevaluate the return policy itself for completeness, making sure that it is corrected first.

■ Forrester recommends that you look inside for problems. He makes an interesting and impressive point about data and information by saying:

"There seems to be a common attitude that the major difficulty is shortage of information and data … The problem is not shortage of data but rather our inability to perceive the consequences of the information we already possess. The system dynamics approach starts with the concepts and information on which people are already acting. Generally these are sufficient. The available perceptions are then assembled in a computer model that can show the consequences of the well-known and properly perceived parts of the system. Generally, the consequences are unexpected … In many instances the known policies describe a system which actually causes the troubles. In other words, the known and intended practices of the organization are fully sufficient to create the difficulty, regardless of what happens outside the company or in the marketplace."

—Jay W. Forrester,
Counterintuitive Behavior of Social Systems, Technology Review, 73(3), 52–68, 1971

That is, before one starts looking for external reasons for failure or external sources for problems, look inside. There may be enough that is wrong to cause the problematic outcome.

Going Beyond the Analytical Approach

Charles West Churchman was an American philosopher in the field of management science, operations research, and systems theory. His thinking about the systems approach can best be summarized in his words:

"The ultimate meaning of the systems approach, therefore, lies in the creation of a theory of deception and in a fuller understanding of the ways in which the human being can be deceived about his world and in an interaction between these different viewpoints."

Thus, according to Churchman, the best way to approach a system is to look through someone else's eyes. The world is ever-expanding, so no single view can be "complete." In fact, Churchman scoffs at the arrogance of the narrator of the "four blind men describing an elephant" story in believing that partial views are useless, by saying that it is not necessary for every wise man to always get on top of the situation.

A designer should view a system "top down," but build it "bottom up," staying conscious of the environment (human nature, morality, politics, and aesthetics), and the organizational and technical aspects that surround it. Most world systems are open systems. Due to the interactions of the components, the overall impact can be very different from the effects of the individual components. An open environment is characterized by continuous exchange of matter, energy, and information.

One of the fundamental postulates of the systems approach is that the problems of most organizations (and organisms for that matter) are essentially stochastic in nature. This is different from the deterministic system view of many management scientists, where chaos is not an accepted phenomenon. As such, analysis and design approaches to systems should incorporate internal flexibility to accommodate changes in the environment.

Churchman studied various aspects of planning. He maintains that the planning activities, followed by most organizations that are based on a scientific approach (mathematical, economic, or even behavioral), are essentially reactive because the inputs are assumed to be external to the system (organization). Instead of being reactive, by using the systems approach, one can continuously monitor the environmental conditions around the system (organization) and elicit proactive responses because the objectives of the organization are under his control. They are internally determined.

Planning relies heavily on thinking and intuition. The initial phases of planning are very important. They should be undertaken with people from actual operations. Such planning often leads to the discovery of hidden or new goals. The finding of new goals is the correct use of the planning process of a project. For the new goals to be accepted or have any impact, one needs key persons, with influence in the organization, involved. Planning helps the managers themselves get good ideas, while the project team gets better plans with which to work.

The scope of the planning need not be curtailed by what is feasible presently. Planning should not be limited to current situations, but pay equal attention to how the situation may change by the time the final system is delivered.

Yet another lesson from Churchman is the importance of using technology for the sake of solving a problem — as a means, not as an end in itself. In particular, with respect to the information aspects of the system, his position was that a system should be designed to provide individual freedom with organizational flexibility — privacy with ethics, without compromising security. Systems exist for both organizations and individuals.

Management by Exception

Anthony Stafford Beer (1926–2002) was a theorist in operational research and an international consultant in management sciences. He published his first book in 1959; *Cybernetics and Management* built on the ideas of Norbert Wiener, Warren McCulloch, and William Ross Ashby, and argued for a systems approach to organizational management.

Beer is best known for the Viable Systems Model (VSM). It was inspired by his study of the human form, the muscles and organs and the various internal systems of the human body. It was based on systems theory and cybernetics. It identifies and analyzes the mechanisms that sustain the viability of complex systems, at several defined levels. Beer claimed that any organization could be considered in light of the way humans "manage" themselves by responding to the vagaries of a changing environment.

Beer looked at the human form as three main interacting parts: (1) the muscles and organs, (2) the brain and nervous systems, and (3) the external environment. Accordingly, he recommended that we should look at our own organizations (or projects within them) as having interacting parts that handle day-to-day activities, the coordination functions, the accounting and scheduling functions, etc. It is essential to identify systems that are vital to the viability of the organization, and thereafter resource them adequately.

In the VSM approach, Beer classified everything into the following three categories:

1. *Operational units (organs and muscles)*. These are the main functional units. They do most of the work. It is essential to create the right conditions for them to function with as much autonomy as possible. This can be achieved through adequate budgeting, well-defined missions, plans, metrics, and rules of intervention.
2. *The metasystem (brain and nervous system)*. These parts ensure the integrated and coordinated activities of the various operational units. The job of the metasystem is to hold the entire organization together. The metasystem can be subdivided into three main functions:
   a. *The internal eye — inward looking*. It looks at the entire collection of operational units and deals with ways of getting them to work together in mutually beneficial ways, by setting up rules and resolving conflicts when needed.
   b. *The external eye — forward looking*. It assesses the opportunities, risks, dependencies, and threats to the organization, and makes plans to help the organization surf the tide in the changing external environment.
   c. *Policy systems — rules of intervention*. This establishes the ground rules that govern the functioning of the entire organization. It is important to be democratic while constituting these rules, to ensure their widespread compliance.
3. *The environment*. This includes those parts of the outside world that are of direct relevance to the system under consideration. The environment affects the working of the organization directly or indirectly.

An important fallout of the VSM was its novel approach toward information systems. A VSM requires a thorough and up-to-date information system. It should have a real-time feed from *all* parts of the organization. Because this may be difficult to achieve in practice, a compromise could be the use of daily performance indicators. These indicators measure, with a predetermined periodicity, only that which is seen as vital within each operational unit (sales, cost, productivity, employee levels, and others). The figures can be analyzed for important trends and early warning indicators. Having knowledge about essential parameters that have changed away from the "norm" is more important that having data and information about everything in the organization. If everything is going as "usual," it is not necessary to spend time on it. These alerts are called *algedonics* in VSM.

This form of information gathering (based on alerts or exception) was probably the root of the "management by exception" mantra popular in the 1980s. This is a leadership style wherein managers intervene only when those they are managing have failed to meet their performance standards (e.g., a sales target). If personnel are performing as expected, the manager will take no action.

Management by exception is an efficient way to manage multiple large or complex projects. Instead of managing everything, one looks for items in the project that are not performing as planned and investigates these items. Before the project starts, one sets thresholds to define acceptable tolerances for vital parameters based on customer goals and what the customer feels is "critical for success." One can then focus on exceptions and opportunities that would probably have been missed because one was drowned in reams of nonessential detailed information.

The most important factor for success in this approach is the ability to identify an actual exception. Furthermore, at what level of detailed information should exceptions be detected, and how frequently should they be detected and transmitted? There are various tools and methodologies that organizations can deploy to identify exceptions.

Types of Systems

Systems can be classified in many ways. Those who build software should understand some of those types, including the following.

Open systems are those influenced by stimuli outside their known boundaries. A *closed system*, on the other hand, is one that can function by itself and is not influenced by external stimuli. Mechanistic systems can be open or closed. An automobile engine is an example of a closed system; many animals have circulatory systems that are open. Similarly, all social systems are examples of open systems.

Then there are *static systems* and *dynamic systems*. As the name implies, the latter have components or characteristics that change over time. Most dynamic systems will settle into a state of dynamic equilibrium. Due to a malfunction of their parts, they may, however, become static. A running automobile engine is a dynamic system until it runs out of fuel.

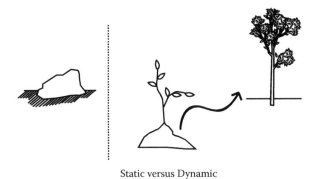

Static versus Dynamic

Figure 2.1   The Static versus Dynamic curve.

Physical systems are systems based on matter and energy. *Logical and conceptual systems* consist of ideas, often referred to as models. A social system based on morals and ethics may be considered an example of a conceptual system. Scientists strive to create models of systems that allow them to understand the systems, and predict what they will do in the future or when certain things are changed.

Linear and *nonlinear systems*. Determining the complete input-output spectrum of a system by exhaustive measurement is practically impossible to achieve. A system is considered linear if it is possible to use the outputs to a small set of inputs to predict the output to any possible input. To see whether a system is linear, one needs to test whether it obeys the two basic characteristics (of linearity):

1. *Homogeneity.* As one increases the strength of a simple input to a linear system, say double it, then one can predict that the output function will also double. This is sometimes called the scalar rule of linear systems.
2. *Aggregation.* Suppose one has an input X to a system, and one measures the responses X′ coming from it. Next, one presents a second input Y that is a little different. The second input would also generate a set of responses Y′ that one measures. Then, one presents the sum of the two inputs X + Y and observes the responses. If the system is linear, then the measured response will be X′ + Y′.

Systems that do not demonstrate these properties are nonlinear. Needless to say, the latter are definitely more complex to build, regulate, and manage. For example, errors and bugs in a system pose problems that are essentially nonlinear in nature; that is why there is so much stress on

debugging and the need for thorough QA. An innocent syntactic ("="
instead of "==") or semantic (incorrect placement of parenthesis in a
mathematical expression) construct that is overlooked during coding and
subsequent QA can result in bringing the entire accounting system of an
organization to a grinding halt, affecting payrolls of all employees.

- The system is an entity that maintains its existence and functions as a whole through the interaction of its parts. The behavior of different systems depends on how the parts are related, rather than on the parts themselves. Therefore, you can understand many different systems using the same principles.

- The properties of a system are the properties of the whole. ...These whole system properties are called emergent properties — they emerge when the whole system is working.

- Detail complexity means there is a great number of different parts.

- Dynamic complexity means there is a great number of possible connections between the parts, because each part may have a number of different states.

- Systems thinking is thinking in circles rather than in straight lines. The connections between parts form feedback loops. Feedback is the output of the system reentering as its input, or the return of information to influence the next step.

- Expect time delay between cause and effect in systems. The feedback loop takes time to complete. The more complex the system the longer the feedback may take to appear. Time delays, if not taken into account, can lead to overshoot and oscillation.

—From *The Art of Systems Thinking,* Joseph O'Connor and Ian McDermott

Complexity of Systems

We must have an understanding of the concept of complexity in systems. It is safe to assume that the construction and possibly maintenance costs of complex systems are higher than simpler ones. Before embarking on the building of any system, one must be able to judge to some extent whether one is dealing with a complex system or a simple one.

Organizations are complex systems based on a combination of mechanistic, as well as social systems that are organic and self-organizing. Because of this plurality, one must apply a combination of thinking approaches. Mechanistic subsystems, such as manufacturing or distribution, benefit from linear thinking, analysis, and the dissection of processes into smaller steps. Systems thinking helps one understand the dynamic nature of relationships. Thus, to assess the complexity of any organizational system, one must not only look to the outside environment for observable external behaviors, but also understand the basic assumptions, beliefs, and value systems that sustain the organization, its structures, and these behaviors.

The pertinent question that now arises is whether there is any rule of thumb to follow in an effort to determine if a system one is trying to create is simple or complex. One rule is that simple systems are based on simple processes. Of course, as with any rule of thumb, there will be exceptions. If there are a number of interacting subcomponents, one cannot consider a system simple. A possible exception occurs when the subcomponents are homogeneous and are governed by uniform laws. For example, we associate properties (density, pressure, mass) to various kinds of matter (solid, liquid, gas) without having to deal with constituent particles at the atomic or subatomic level.

Simplicity is sometimes associated with determinism. It is natural to expect that nondeterministic systems, or those systems that cannot be modeled by standard mathematical methods, are complex. But the converse may not be true. The famed Rubik's Cube is deterministic, but not simple by any stretch of imagination.

Another way to classify complexity, and one that software professionals are familiar with, is on the basis of whether the system is centralized or distributed. Complexity experts maintain that distributed systems can do all the things that centralized systems can do. In fact, they feel that the centralized system has some pitfalls:

- They need a central intelligence to manage them.
- The central intelligence is susceptible to infiltration and interjection.
- It may be difficult to get accurate and timely information to a central point.

■ Concurrency issues may cause delays that affect the overall performance of the system.

On the other hand, distributed systems are more difficult to assess in entirety, and difficult to test once they are developed.

In software industry parlance, "complexity" refers to the difficulty of the problem being solved by software. Most methods for determining complexity are specification based and focus on the "size" aspect like Function Point Analysis (FPA) and those based on Use Cases. Intuition may be useful for determining software complexity based on the complexity of the tasks required to create the software. The use of task complexity and cost models is also encouraged. Software process literature and commercial software management tools have suggested that such cost models can be combined with historical data on development times to predict the development times of future projects.

It has been proven that program size and complexity cannot be determined *a priori*. Similarly, well understood is that the productivity of intelligent developers, and hence development time, cannot be adequately predicted. There are, however, vectors that can be used to judge the relative complexity of a system that is being designed and developed. They include:

■ *Organization complexity.* This is based on the perceived maturity of the business and the maturity of the processes being used.
■ *Domain complexity.* Another good indicator is the "domain" in which the system falls. Some domains are inherently complex, such as those dealing with financial and economic markets, or scheduling and logistics. Software systems for such domains usually will be complex.
■ *Physical and geographical constraints.* While these may not be evident, multi-site development, or development where physical access to the customer organization is not available, makes the system development complex. Software for aviation, or offshore oil exploration, could be good examples of this category. These days, offshore development adds its own kind of complexity.

Summary

Systems science is a vast field. This chapter touched only on a few thinkers who are mostly talking about control systems — Ashby, Forrester, Churchman, and Beer. Their ideas help if we subscribe to the viewpoint that information systems are a form of control systems, controlling actions and situations within organizations through the use of information by managers and other users. Increased knowledge of various concepts addressed by systems science — feedback, emergent properties, concepts of complexity, for example — can only improve the quality of the information systems that we design.

Such principles or ideas must be implemented in practice. If they have to succeed, they must be part of a successful strategy.

Perception is strong and sight weak. In strategy it is important to see distant things as if they were close and to take a distanced view of close things.

—**Miyamoto Musashi, Samurai**

Chapter 3

Strategies

What's the use of running, if you are not on the right road.

—German proverb

The concept of strategic thinking, and strategies in general, has been in existence for a long time, much longer than the emergence of computers and computer-based information systems. The term is familiar from its early use in military strategies. Nowadays we frequently come across its usage in investment strategies, election strategies, treatment strategies, chess strategies, etc. Such strategies are planned with a view to help us win.

Strategy has many definitions. Peter Drucker states it best by saying that:

> "Strategy is about choices and it is about focus. Whenever scarce resources have to be allocated certain choices have to be made. If choices are not required or choices are not available then it hardly matters what the strategy is."

One's options are often limited although one may appear to be in an environment of free and varied choice. To understand one's options, one must look at the drives and the constraints (Figure 3.1). George Friedman, an expert on intelligence and international geopolitics, explains this limitation thus:

> "In a game of chess, it appears that there are many moves available. There seem to be twenty possible first moves, for

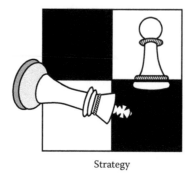

Strategy

Figure 3.1   Strategies are important.

example. In fact, there are perhaps six. The better you understand chess, the fewer options you have. You come to realize that most of the apparent moves are disastrous, and the good moves are limited. The better the players, the more predictable and understandable the game is...".

In IT (information technology), the existing or legacy systems, the reliability of new technologies and vendors, the skills of the staff available, etc. limit one's options. Good moves are limited. The flip side of this, which is sometimes ignored, is that today's decisions and actions shape the options available for tomorrow's strategies.

The True System

Before discussing strategy in software, software must be put in its proper place within a long stream of progress. Quoting Drucker once again:

"What has made it possible to routinize processes is not machinery; the computer is only the trigger. Software is the reorganization of work, based on centuries of experience, through the application of knowledge and especially of systematic logical analysis. The key is not electronics; it is cognitive science."

For example, what is remarkable about an "accounting system" is the system of accounting itself, and not the accounting software that automates it. The thing of value in "automation" is not the automation but what is being automated. How did double-entry bookkeeping come up to revolutionize accounting systems, way before there were computers or software? Pacioli explained this in 1494. This is the "true" system.

Luca Pacioli, a Franciscan friar wrote, Summa de Arithmetica, Geometrica, Proportioni et Proportionalita in 1494. This book included the first published description of the method of keeping accounts that Venetian merchants used during the Italian Renaissance, known as the double-entry accounting system. Although Pacioli codified rather than invented this system, he is widely regarded as the "Father of Accounting." The system he published included most of the accounting cycle as we know it today. He described the use of journals and ledgers, and warned that a person should not go to sleep at night until the debits equaled the credits! His ledger had assets (including receivables and inventories), liabilities, capital, income, and expense accounts. He demonstrated year-end closing entries and proposed that a trial balance be used to prove a balanced ledger. Also, his treatise alludes to a wide range of topics from accounting ethics to cost accounting.

—"Luca Pacioli." Wikipedia, The Free Encyclopedia. January 24, 2007, Wikimedia Foundation, Inc., <http://en.wikipedia.org/>

Technology, of course, works hand in hand with the "true" system to deliver expanded systems that are reorganizations of work and knowledge, in simple to complex ways. Trade and retail systems have existed since ancient times. E-commerce extends certain aspects — location, time, search, etc. — in brilliant ways. This thread of thought — separating the "true" system from its automation — is a key point. This distinction is necessary and important because, when one talks of *information strategy*, one should strategize about the "true" system as well as its automation.

For those who have already dismissed "true" systems as nothing more than "business requirements," there is a word of caution. The business requirements that most IT personnel deal with are business requirements targeted at IT personnel. "True" systems are rarely discussed because of domain issues, or because it is taken as well understood. Major strategic changes work at the level of true systems. Revolutionary ventures such as Amazon (.com) affect retailing more than the development of retailing software.

Aligning Information Strategy with Business Strategy

IT managers are often told to align their information strategy with the company's business strategy. What in fact does it mean? How does one do the alignment? Does the alignment happen naturally if the systems are delivered according to proper business specification? To give an example of such an alignment, take a look at the auto insurance industry. Studies have shown that when there is an accident, a quick settlement of the claim is to the company's advantage. This results in lower amounts for settlement because "extraneous" influences, which tend to enhance the settlement claims, have not yet acted on the customer. At the same time, a quick settlement makes the customer happy with the service provided, and makes them appreciate the responsiveness of the insurance company. An IT strategy of investing in CRM (customer relationship management) for improved customer relationship aligns well with the business strategy of reducing costs through quicker settlements.

IT managers need to have a keen understanding of the larger strategies driving their projects to align their deliveries better with business strategies.

Everything Important Is Not Strategic

The fact that a project has a business impact does not necessarily mean that it is strategic. Every IT effort appears to have some business impact, directly or indirectly. The number of strategic projects or initiatives in any IT department is small. They may be large, long, and expensive but they are few. These are the ones that should be well-aligned with business strategies. If there is a business strategy that requires one to strengthen the security of one's information assets for competitive, liability, or other reasons, then spending a lot of money making applications secure is a strategic initiative. Otherwise, it is one more improvement to existing systems, similar to other business enhancements and system upgrades — important, useful, but not necessarily strategic.

What Is Strategic?

How does one identify strategic requirements? As discussed previously, everything important is not necessarily strategic. Attaching the term

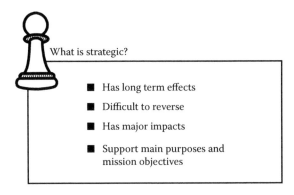

Figure 3.2   What is strategic?

"strategic" to everything important is as bad as calling every important activity in a project "critical," without knowing that project planners use the term "critical" for activities, important or trivial, that are on the critical path of the project's schedule.

Strategic requirements (Figure 3.2) have a few characteristics, including:

■ *They have long-term effects.* Selecting enterprise software is a good example. Making a choice to go with a particular enterprise software means making a long-term commitment — these packages can take years and lots of dollars to implement. Sometimes, smaller decisions also can have long-term effects.

■ *They are difficult to reverse.* Big technology decisions are often difficult to reverse. Because everything is interconnected, the costs of exit or change can be enormous. As standardization increases, some of these decisions become less strategic in importance.

■ *They clearly support main purposes and mission objectives.* A strategic project substantially helps the organization move in meeting its mission. One might be able to do something important that one was not able to do earlier, which could make a substantial business difference. An E-commerce project set up to sell products directly to customers is a strategic decision, if the organization always wanted to go direct to the customer but could not afford to build a direct sales infrastructure. It is also strategic because such a move would, of course, impact existing sales channels — distributors, dealers, and sales people. The harm in relations or credibility may be difficult to recover from if the E-commerce site does not deliver as promised and one has to revert to the regular sales channels.

A Few Common Internal Strategic Decisions

There are at least two facets to IT strategies. One deals with technologies, enterprise architectures, applications, and IT management models. Think of it as "internal" to IT. The other is "external" to IT and often more difficult it is how the company can use its information assets to deliver on its business strategies.

Now take a look at a few internal strategic issues with which most IT managers have to deal:

- Insourcing and outsourcing
- Architectures and technologies
- Build versus buy

Insourcing and Outsourcing

Insourcing is the use of consultants and contractors who work along with employees to deliver on projects and assignments. The assumption is that contractors are, in the long run, less expensive and easier to let go than employees. It is a valid and popular strategy to use consultants. At times it is driven by the need to get quick access to new technologies or to support peak loads. Some companies have active policies to have a certain percentage of their resources as consultants instead of employees. Managers often go around head-count restrictions by hiring contractors. IT departments have always had a large share of consultants and contractors working within them, often for longer periods of time, in comparison to other industries. The fact that some of these consultants continue for years shows that the peak load argument gets forgotten once the work begins.

Not every decision to hire a consultant is strategic. However, some companies use consultants strategically. A strategic use of consultants occurs when there is a need to handle a discontinuity that the company cannot manage through conventional retraining and slow improvement models. Web technologies represent one such example, when many companies used consultants to give them a jump start. As discussed previously, strategy is about focus.

Certain strategic initiatives (e.g., enterprise implementations) are better implemented through consultants because they can work in parallel with existing staff who will not lose focus on maintaining and supporting existing applications. Doing it otherwise would, most likely, put the enterprise implementation strategy in jeopardy.

Consulting also can be used strategically when a company wants to stick to its primary work and considers IT as too much distraction from its revenue-generation activities. A company may be located in a place where it finds it difficult to attract the level of technology skills required to do a good job. Consulting companies can deliver the skills more easily from central pools.

Organizations, and for that matter employees, often have a love–hate relationship with consultants. They sometimes are seen as gurus and lifesavers; at other times management sees consulting as merely cash going out the door. Employees may resent the higher rates given to consultants to do something "that they could have done equally well." Some organizations have become overly dependent on consultants for their operations, with employees playing more of a coordination and management role. The extent to which such a dependency poses a strategic risk depends on the nature and strength of the dependency. Management, however, should be evaluating that risk periodically. It may make perfect sense not to have any of those skills in-house or it may not, but it must be evaluated and controlled by choice and not allowed to unknowingly develop into such a situation.

There is an increasing trend, in recent years, to outsource "offshore" the development and support work of the company. To do this is, obviously, a strategic decision for company management to take. It is not easily reversible if the employees who were doing the work previously have been released. It is not easily reversible for other important reasons as well. If development work is done offshore, then the knowledge — both technical and business — accumulates there. What might begin as a cost-saving measure could lead to a lock-in based on the contractor's knowledge and experience.

Going offshore is not always about outsourcing. Sometimes it is part of the normal growth of offices and facilities to newer geographical markets — a development center in Brazil, India, or China. The management and control systems in place in such situations may be merely local variations of the central corporate systems.

If the majority of the responsibility for delivery shifts to an outside party, then the work has been outsourced. It does not matter that the supervision is retained, because the customer must always maintain a certain amount of supervision and coordination. There is an important point to consider about outsourcing. When something is outsourced, there is a shift from a *command* structure to a *contract* structure. When resources are internal — employees or contractors — work gets done through a command structure: workers are part of a command hierarchy and know it. When work is outsourced, getting the same work done involves going through a contractual relationship between two businesses. This contractual nature of the relationship may be hidden from day-to-day transactions but it exists and can be invoked. However obliging the vendor might be — he works within the scope of a contract. This can make getting things more difficult or expensive than in a command structure. Because a contractual structure replaces a command structure, is the reason that an outsourcing model may not be suitable for many kinds of projects and companies.

Architectures and Technologies

In software, technology choices can lock one in. Both vendors and customers recognize this lock-in. It makes one's choices strategic, perhaps unnecessarily, because to back out of it is difficult. For most of us, the choice of a particular make of car may be an expensive choice but it is hardly strategic. In software, selecting routine components such as database management systems, reporting solutions, operating systems, or hardware may end up having strategic implications. We discuss more on this in Chapter 5, Architecture and Design.

Build versus Buy

To build or buy is a strategic choice. Both can be expensive in different ways and lead to different outcomes or levels of satisfaction. Some organizations prefer one to the other. We look at this issue in detail in Chapter 9, Off-the-Shelf Software.

Using Strategies

For most IT personnel, the work they are doing seems far removed from the external strategies of the company. The internal strategy may not be easily appreciated by many in the IT department itself. As for external strategies, even the managers may have little idea of how their work contributes to larger business strategies. This situation may be the result of a lack of flow of information within the company, or it may be due to a technical–business split in the minds of IT personnel, akin to the mind–body split in philosophy. Technical folks are not too interested in the business aspects, and vice versa.

Many developers often feel that they do not need the big picture to do their work, this based on the assumption that the "business" aspects, including strategy, are reflected in the business requirements (Figure 3.3). This assumption is not valid. Further, there are business managers who do not share their business strategies with project managers or analysts, preferring to provide them only "requirements" without any further explanation. Good consultants and analysts try to up-level the discussion to

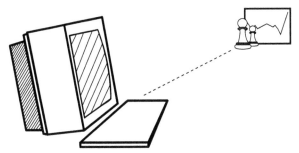

For most personnel, the work they do seems far
removed from issues of strategy

Figure 3.3 Feeling strategic.

understand the strategic implications of an initiative, although ultimately they too may prepare "requirements" stripped of any strategic content. As a result, most layers of IT work on little pieces of a larger mosaic whose design is not shared with them.

Is that lack of interest or knowledge a real problem? For IT managers, it could be. Because funding is based on higher-level strategies, an IT manager must necessarily be aware of the prevailing strategies so that he can influence them if necessary. Knowing and understanding strategies helps in anticipating new work and in evaluating the risk of a current project being shelved. No manager should ever be caught off guard on their projects, by a change in high-level strategy.

Some examples will help to clarify this:

- A company shifted its sales strategy from selling directly to business customers, to reselling their services through a few large companies. This obviated the need for elaborate CRM and billing systems, and consequently these projects were abruptly cancelled.
- A company had not put up an E-commerce site to avoid alienating its existing sales channels. Only when this issue was resolved did such projects get initiated, and quickly became important to top management.

Knowing the Big Picture:

Gerald Weinberg has a story of a minister walking by a construction project and asking two workers what they were doing. One replied that he was laying bricks. The other said he was building a cathedral. The second worker obviously knew the larger picture, knew the project's objective. (Weinberg's story has a twist — the second worker gets fired because the contract was to build a garage!)

Failed Strategies

Incorrect IT strategies can cause tangible harm to larger business strategies. Poor application architecture strategies can derail larger organizational strategies by limiting the available options at a higher business level. Poor execution strategies can cause harm to the bottom line by not delivering on expectations, thereby making the company miss important windows of opportunity. Do not assume that a strategic project will always succeed. Always consider what the impact on business would be if it were to fail.

The question naturally arises as to how a project or IT manager determines which strategic choices are riskier than the others. One model that can be applied is similar to the risk model in information security. Security breaches often are classified by their levels of impact on business: "it can bring down the company," "it can interrupt some aspect of the business," "it can cause some revenue loss," "it can cause some inconvenience," etc. One can use such levels to evaluate the impact of the failure of a strategic application development project.

Reducing Failure

A project might have been strategic when it was initiated. As time goes by, its importance might shift. Such classifications should be reevaluated. Organizations tend to give higher priorities and resources to everything that is classified as strategic at the cost of depriving resources to others. Similarly, an application that may not start out as being strategic may very well become so later.

Not everything that one builds software for is strategic, but those that are have business impacts that are larger than many technical personnel realize. Great care must be taken in all aspects of such work.

Summary

Strategy is about making choices and ensuring focus. Whenever scarce resources must be allocated, certain choices must be made. The kinds of strategic choices that must be made in IT are often related to enterprise technology choices, outsourcing, build-versus-buy decisions, and senior staffing. Due to various factors, the choices available may actually be quite limited. IT managers should be aware of the company's strategies because IT investment and corresponding projects are driven off such strategies. While developing strategies, it is essential to understand the "true" system: the system that lies behind the automation being envisaged — for example, the accounting system that lies at the core of the accounting package. Because everything important is not strategic, the strategic requirements must be recognized by a few salient characteristics, such as their ability to support mission objectives and their potential to have long-term impact.

Having selected the right strategy, execution of the strategy then becomes important. Key to success is a proper understanding of the requirements against which one is working. These requirements begin at a high level but can quickly get detailed.

There was a definite process by which one made people into friends, and it involved talking to them and listening to them for hours at a time.

—**Rebecca West**

Chapter 4

Requirements

"It's not a good idea to introduce the uncertain linguistic sub-tleties of English verbs into system development documents."

—Michael Jackson,
Software Specifications and Requirements: a lexicon of practice,
principles and prejudices

One builds to requirements. This fact is so ingrained in the software development process that it can be called a foundational assumption. Requirements are an agreement between the developer and the customer on what will be built and delivered. For custom application development, the requirements are given by the customer, who is funding the development. In the case of products, these requirements may come from marketing, which represents the intended customer. Requirements, in general, are a description or delineation of the expected behaviors of the application being developed. It is expected that such behaviors will meet a larger business need. For example, the preparation of a tax return is the behavior expected of a tax preparation application, which meets the business need to file tax returns for an individual or business.

The requirements, if met, are meant to solve problems. From a systems point of view, one needs to distinguish between "true" requirements, which would solve the problem being addressed, and the "requirement specifications" that two parties have agreed to deliver and accept as part of a commercial agreement. To the extent that the true requirements are reflected in the specifications, one is working to the requirements. If the specifications do not meet the true requirements, then the deliverable may still be according to specifications, yet the problem may not get solved as it should have been. We accept common usage in this chapter, and use the term "requirements" to refer to the requirement specifications that we use for building software.

Requirements are an agreement between the developers and the customers. Developers include all the groups, both business and technical, that are on the design and delivery side. Customers include those who are funding the work, and also the actual users of the applications being delivered. Together, the parties involved are called stakeholders. We discuss stakeholders in more detail in later sections.

It is quite apparent that in this matter two sides are involved — one side specifies the requirements and the other side delivers on those requirements. Between the two, there is a communication process that leads to the development of requirements. Whenever there is a communication process involved, there is a chance that the communication does not occur properly. When requirements turn out to be "incorrect," one often blames "poor communication." Consider a theoretical situation: what if there was only one party involved, where one was developing the application for oneself, and to one's own requirements? The communication problem would decrease, but still not go away. One would still find that the requirements were arrived at through multiple iterations. There could be a possibility that the requirements are wrong for the problem being solved. So the issue with requirements goes beyond solving communication problems between multiple parties. It has to do with the nature of requirements itself, the way they emerge, and the process by which they get developed and, of course, communicated to others.

Language is the primary means of communication between parties while gathering requirements. (The word "gathering" is an interesting choice; it conveys an image of someone walking about picking up what one needs and putting it in a basket.) We also employ formal tools when there is a need to express precisely what we mean. These could be diagramming or modeling tools, such as dataflow diagrams, ER (entity relationship) diagrams, interaction diagrams, and many others. Structured systems analysis and design techniques have been around for a few decades now. There are a number of good books on such diagramming and representational techniques and this book does not go into their details. The increase in precision of communication that these tools offer does not preclude the fact that the diagrams and models may get interpreted wrongly. The solution is not to make the tools more complex, trying to nail every ambiguity, but to combine good representational techniques with sound processes for validating that one understands correctly what is represented.

How to Specify a Problem

It is true, as the saying goes, that a problem clearly stated is already half solved. It is also true that a problem cannot be efficiently solved unless it is *precisely* described.

The (paper manufacturing) plant was working well when suddenly it was discovered that small pieces of wood were coming through in the dried, finished sheets of paper. It was immediately assumed that something was wrong in the pulping process, that one of the huge stainless steel screens had broken. ...

However, one man was not blinded by his papermaking experience. He did not take the "obvious" explanation. Instead, he closely examined the troublesome pieces of the paper and found that these were not softwood chips but hardwood splinters; moreover, they had never been cooked or chemically treated. Then he spotted a hardwood pipeline used to transfer the pulp to the papermaking machine. He told his colleagues that the lining of this pipe must be breaking up on the inside and let the hardware splinters get into the pulp mixture. ...his explanation was finally checked out and found to be so, proving that the problem had nothing to do with the pulping equipment. This might have been determined at the outset if the problem had originally been precisely specified as "uncooked hardwood splinters in finished paper" instead of simply "pieces of wood in the paper."

—From *The Rational Manager,* Charles Kepner and Benjamin Tregoe

---

When systems fail, one often finds that either the requirements were wrongly specified or that the application was not built to specifications. There are, therefore, two possible problem areas that one must watch out for:

1. The requirements are incorrectly or incompletely specified.
2. The requirements are interpreted wrongly by those building to the requirements.

It is the joint responsibility of the customer and the analyst to identify the requirements correctly and capture these in a requirements specification, to minimize the chances of incorrect interpretation by themselves, or by others. As discussed in Chapter 13 on communication, it is the sender's responsibility, in a communication process, to ensure that the message is "coded" in a way that reduces the probability of error. Proper requirements are the cornerstone of successful development.

Requirements for Products and Projects

Successful delivery requires managing two sets of requirements: (1) product requirements and (2) project requirements. One refers to the product being delivered, and the other to the requirements of the project that is delivering the product. Our SEE (Solution, Engineering, and Execution) framework draws attention to the fact that one must identify both sets of requirements. Requirements analysts deal with the first set of requirements. For them, the requirements is about getting specifications for the design and the development to begin. The bulk of these "business" or "functional" requirements will come from a few stakeholders. In terms of resource allocation, it makes sense to devote more time to these stakeholders. The project manager has to deal with the second set of requirements. These requirements may come from a wider range of groups and persons. We can treat them as separate sets of requirements but must recognize that any successful delivery requires managing both sets of requirements.

Stakeholders

Who is a stakeholder? A stakeholder is anybody impacted by the application when it is being built and when it is rolled out. This is a wide-ranging definition that includes many parties. These go beyond the "customers" who are funding the development, or the "business users" who are specifying the requirements. The number (and types) of stakeholders is often more than what a project manager or an analyst normally takes into consideration while preparing requirements. This variety must be recognized properly and, according to Ashby's law, be destroyed properly (see Chapter 2 on Systems). Anything else leads to requirements that will be incomplete.

Common stakeholders include:

- The sponsors (who are funding the work)
- The business user (the department for which the application is being developed)
- The actual users of the applications
- All persons who will build the application
- All persons who will support the application (customer support, technical support, training, roll out, etc.)
- All persons who will be impacted by the roll-out of the application (those displaced, those users who will not have the old version of the application or the "other" application to use once the new application is rolled out, etc.)
- All regulators (security, audit, legal, etc.)

It helps to view stakeholders as those who have a role to play in ensuring success. This can be a long list. It is better to err, initially at least, on the side of considering more parties as stakeholders than fewer parties. Some can be dropped once initial discussions on scope and deliverables are held.

There is an understandable fear in increasing the list of stakeholders. If each of them comes up with their own requirements, then the requirements can become unwieldy. The solution to this problem is not to ignore any of the stakeholders, but rather to have an auxiliary process to reconcile and prioritize requirements. Ignoring a genuine stakeholder is fraught with risk because he or she will, at a possibly inopportune moment, insist on their requirements being met.

It is common to miss out on those stakeholders whose role is fleeting. For example, certain E-commerce projects have scrambled at the last minute, trying to get legal approval for opening-page disclaimer verbiage to be put on the sites before they can roll out an application to customers, because they had not identified the legal department as a stakeholder. In large organizations, many projects lose precious time in the beginning during setup, waiting for security clearance for user IDs because they have not identified the Security department as one of the stakeholders for the project requirements.

Stand-Ins

It is a common situation where access to one of the important stakeholders — the end user — is denied. The stakeholders, whom the analyst gets to talk to, are stand-ins for the "real" users. This often happens when a business or product department, which deals with the end users (the external customers), refuses or minimizes access to the end users. The business office assures the analysts that the product office understands the real users' requirements, that they have all the information required for the design and development of the application, and that they will sign off on the requirements and accept the deliverable. This reluctance to allow access to end users is not always a territorial thing. It sometimes arises from a genuine concern that technical teams lack the level of communication and customer-handling skills that the business office possesses, thereby forcing the business office to minimize such direct interactions and encouraging them to step in as middlemen in the process.

From an application design point of view, not getting access to end users increases the risk of failure. There have been many situations where the end user sees the application only after it has been completely built, and is surprised at what is delivered. Operating in a stand-in mode can lead to an increased level of risk that the requirements are incorrect. This could happen because business offices may have little experience with formal analysis and often struggle with their own issues about understanding the end users. One must recognize such situations and attempt to observe some risk reduction tactics. Some of these are:

- Insist on access to the end user. This may require some escalation on both the delivery and customer sides. If there is concern about communication skills, address those.
- Have detailed questionnaires, asking for supporting documents for all key answers. This may require that the end users get involved in answering questions considered important from their point of view.
- Arrange demos of partially complete work during development, and try to get the relevant users invited. Observe the discussions between the business office and the end users during the demo for signs of confidence about how well the business office is reflecting end-user needs.
- Start a pilot with the end users early. Plan for an early release of partial functionality as a pilot. Pilots, if implemented properly, can sort out many end-user issues, including those of look and feel, that impact requirements.

▪ Set the expectation with the stand-in parties that there will be substantial rework costs if the end users ask for changes on seeing the application very late in the process. It is to the business office's advantage to encourage access early.

Prioritizing Stakeholders

Some stakeholders are more important than others; these include:

▪ The sponsors, who are either funding the project, or will become the deployment champions
▪ The subject matter experts (SMEs) who understand the business
▪ Those who will be involved in user acceptance testing

It is also to be carefully understood that software delivery is a techno-political process and stakeholder dynamics change with the dynamics of the organization. There is neither a textbook approach to identifying the stakeholders, nor is the list of stakeholders constant throughout the project.

Using Policies

In reality, it is difficult to talk to all stakeholders. In good process-driven companies, there would be policies that stand in for the need to talk to all stakeholders. For example, there may be a well-defined policy regarding security requirements. If these are treated as "applicable" requirements (or constraints on requirements), the policy can be said to represent security stakeholders with a reasonable degree of accuracy. Good policies reduce the communication overheads involved during requirements development.

The Nature of Requirements

Formal Requirements

Whenever speaking of requirements, we invariably refer to formal requirements. But requirements need not always be formal and explicit. They can be implicit also. For example, when a company wants to purchase something, it invariably raises a formal purchase order. But when one goes into the grocery store, one expresses an intent to buy something by bringing it to the register. This is a more simplified process of purchasing. Occasionally, the requirements are embedded in the work order itself. When you bring in your car for servicing, your requirements (whether or not the windshield wipers need replacement) are there in the work order. Similarly, when a customer wants something to be delivered as software, he or she could use more simplified methods of communicating. Do not assume that formal, heavy requirements documents are always necessary.

What does this mean? It means that requirements can range from "no explicit requirements" to very formal requirements where every detail has been spelled out. It is not that one is better than the other. The difference depends mainly on the type of project and the risks involved.

The Element of Trust

In software development there must be an element of trust between the customer and the developer when it comes to specifying and interpreting requirements. The customer must recognize the business imperatives of the developer, and the developer must make a fair attempt to interpret the requirements to the benefit of the customer.

If there is a lack of trust between the parties, then the solution is not to go down the path of more and more detailed requirements in the hope that, by doing so, all ambiguity will be destroyed and requirements made absolutely clear. That will not happen. A better approach is to take a fair shot at the requirements, have good management and risk reduction processes to support the implementation of the requirements, and maintain a reasonable level of trust.

The Technical–Business Divide

One of the divides that exists in the world of software is the so-called technical–business divide (Figure 4.1). Certain aspects of the deliverable are clearly technical, while others are purely in the business domain. Yet a practical solution always straddles both aspects. To maintain this distinction as seriously as some people do is to do a disservice to the way problems get solved, and solutions get delivered. Because one is delivering a business solution through technology, both skill sets are equally essential.

Analysts are expected to bridge the divide, acting as translators and go-betweens. That world view itself needs a little tweaking. All business requirements need not come from the business folks, and all technical requirements are not the prerogative of the technical delivery people alone. Because the end result is a techno-business solution, the dialogue should be more intense and direct than it is in many environments today. Without the proper intermix of the two, the future will always remain uncertain.

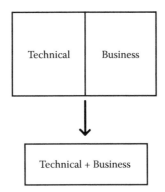

The technical business divide is artificial

Figure 4.1   Technical-business divide.

Phasing of Requirements

Requirements can be complete only in a relative sense. The requirements for the entire life cycle of the application are rarely complete but the requirements for the next release may be complete. In some development models, such as the waterfall model, there is a separate initial phase called "requirements." This phase is expected to end, sometimes referred to as the exit condition of the phase, with a set of complete requirements (or a complete set of requirements). There are other development models where one begins with an initial set of requirements and iterates through development and user feedback. In such models, the requirements must be complete for the current iteration.

Requirements and Scope

Projects have scope while products have requirements. A product may have a long list of requirements. Only through prioritization and phasing, a few of the requirements may get picked in a project, or a phase of the project. What gets picked up defines the scope of the project.

When a list of requirements is being drawn, we must classify them as *in-scope* or *out-of-scope*. Out-of-scope requirements do not cease to be requirements. They should be revisited periodically. They may have been taken out of scope for various reasons; but from a systems point of view, that item remains linked to something else that is very much in-scope.

Scope, therefore, is an artificial delineation, more to be used for planning. A designer or an architect must look beyond it.

Looking Back

Over the life cycle of the application, one finds that a lot of requirements have been addressed. Looking back, we may find that there was some logic to the order in which the requirements were picked up. Such phasing of requirements may be driven by business or technical reasons, resource constraints, product roadmaps, or based on the whims of the development groups. At times, this is necessary because later requirements cannot be fully understood or specified, until some earlier ones are designed or rolled out. For example, one can leave internationalization requirements of an application to a later phase.

Roadmaps

While such phasing is unavoidable, it is advisable to prepare a roadmap for the application or product. The design and architecture of the product should be driven by the roadmap, although the delivery of the features and functionality is phased. This approach is reflected in the oft-encountered statement, "We should design top down and build bottom up." This is another reason why architectures transcend projects. Architectures must look at the larger set of requirements and design for that even if one builds it up slowly. Local and short-term mindsets should be avoided — they will only add to the cost of the projects. This is similar to a situation in building a house where it is designed to be a multi-story building although only the ground floor is being built at the current time, or in the first phase.

Insist on getting the long-term picture when gathering requirements. One need not get into the details of the long-term plans. It would be enough to identify and recognize that such requirements will be coming down the line. It is the analyst's role to encourage such thinking through good questions and suggestions.

Types of Requirements

Functional and Nonfunctional Requirements

We have already mentioned the two categories of requirements: (1) functional and (2) nonfunctional. *Functional requirements* is what is generally meant by the use of the term "requirements." The application is being built to deliver some functionality — inventory management, hospital admissions, tax returns preparation, etc. The requirements related to the business processing logic are embodied in the functional requirements.

Nonfunctional requirements can also be termed "auxiliary requirements." In the examples discussed above, nonfunctional requirements would be related to performance, and support for various browsers. In a sense, this is a catch-all category. Nonfunctional requirements can have a direct impact on the design and architecture of the solution. Others affect the delivery of the solution, and may be a project deliverable rather than a software deliverable. Some of the nonfunctional requirements might be related to the application's implementation. There could be, say, a nonfunctional requirement that technical support for the application needs to be available from 6 a.m. to 6 p.m.

Wants and Needs

In addition to functional and nonfunctional requirements, two other terms are often encountered: "wants" and "needs." A customer may have many *wants,* but a system must be designed that meets his *needs.* The customer may not be able to distinguish clearly between the two; what he calls requirements is often a mix of the two. A good analyst, however, knows how to distinguish between the two.

Wants and needs are closely related. Wants may contain real requirements that will have to be sifted out. For example, a customer may "want" all historical data online. A little investigation might, however, reveal that what he needs is a year's data to be accessible should there be any disputes. The point to be noted is that wants, and wish lists, reveal needs that warrant further investigation.

There is still another reason why an analyst must separate wants from needs. It may be dangerous to assume that the customer always knows his requirements. It is possible that the analyst or the project team has more experience in building and implementing such applications. If so, they can suggest many requirements that the customer might not have thought of.

Classifying Requirements

There are various ways of classifying requirements. One is to separate them into:

- Essential
- Nice-to-have

The other is to classify them as:

- High
- Medium
- Low

Any classification scheme used must be simple and have clear rules for deciding how to classify the requirements. These rules must maintain a chain of clarity. For example, one might adopt a classification criteria saying that a requirement is critical if its impact on customer satisfaction is high. This leads to the need for defining customer satisfaction itself. For example, a need to provide online help could be classified as having a medium impact on customer satisfaction, thereby classifying the requirement itself as medium.

A Hierarchy of Requirements

Application requirements can also be organized as a hierarchy of requirements (Figure 4.2). If we begin from the user end, these can be seen as:

- Business requirements
- Systems requirements
- Functional requirements
- Detailed requirements

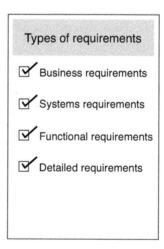

Figure 4.2 The four types of requirements.

Business Requirements

As the name suggests, these identify the business drivers and behaviors for which the work is being initiated. For example, the need to submit tax returns annually, or raise appointment letters for new hires, could be a business requirement, which requires building a new application, or making an enhancement to an existing application. Although these requirements are called business requirements, they are business requirements directed at systems personnel by the business user. The business user might have created a different set of business requirements, directed at other business users, to make a business case for those requirements.

What should a good business requirements document contain? First and foremost, it should identify the business end state that one wants to achieve — file the tax returns, hire the employee, and work backwards. A business requirement often stays at the "true" system level.

Systems Requirements

These are the business requirements that have been converted to application and system functionality. The business need to file tax returns annually converts into a systems requirement to create or enhance a tax preparation system. A business requirement to provide 24/7 support becomes a systems requirements to implement an online self-service Web site.

Systems requirements correspond to the "S" layer of the SEE (Solution, Engineering, Execution) model. There may be multiple solutions that can satisfy the business requirements. Some of these solutions may involve non-software solutions. All, however, must be considered.

Whose responsibility is it to consider all the options? If the responsibility was assigned to the Information Systems department, there would be a natural tendency to propose or prefer an information systems solution. Businesses need a *Solutions* group that is at a level above Information Systems. At times, the Strategy group, if there is one, can play this role. Others who could take this mantle are the business users themselves or a combination of business users and solution analysts. Solution analysts are different from requirements analysts, who would be interacting with business users to gather detailed requirements later in the process. These roles could be played by the same person as long as the roles are well understood.

Functional Requirements

Functional requirements are those that take the systems requirements and bring out detailed functionality. Functional requirements are followed by detailed requirements. It therefore requires a judgment call as to the level of detail that should be embraced. The functional requirements document is directed at the business users and the technical leads, and should be at the level of detail required to (1) satisfy the business user for whom the requirements are being covered and (2) to allow the technical leads to think of a technical solution to meet those requirements. For example, functional requirements for a customer support Web site might outline whether self-service tickets can be created and status tracked, whether online chat help is available, and whether users can access knowledge bases.

Detailed Requirements

Detailed requirements must carry enough details for the various designers. For a business application, this set of designers could be UI (user interface) designers, the program designers, or the data modelers. Detailed requirements are required at the "engineering" stage of the SEE model. At this stage, certain engineering decisions must be made and there should be sufficient details in the requirements to enable this. For example, if self-service tickets must be created, there should be a numbering scheme, a workflow associated with routing that ticket, and some integration, perhaps, with a different back-end ticket management system, with bi-directional flow of information.

This set of requirements — business, system, functional, and detailed — is a fairly decent stack, and is achievable with reasonable efforts. It is necessary to put all the documents together and see that there is a natural flow and elaboration between them. This stack also works well for enhancement requirements.

Requirements and Process

The fact that a process is being followed to gather requirements does not itself ensure that the requirements being gathered are correct. The requirements gathering process might, however, add a lot of value. It is sometimes more valuable than all the artifacts that are the outcome of the requirements process.

Weinberg has an important observation to make: if the user wants something to be part of requirements, the user must explicitly ask for it.

This is a simple yet profound observation about the requirements process. Users may assume that there is something about the requirements gathering process that will allow analysts to determine "true" requirements, even if they do not spell it out. In the end, however, it may turn out that the requirements are what the user tells them are the requirements. What the user does not tell the analyst may not get "discovered" and included in the requirements.

Approaching Requirements

If a problem can be put in a form — an equation, a model — for which a solution exists, then there can be drastic savings in terms of the time required to arrive at solutions. This is a popular, general problem-solving approach: look at a problem and try to convert it to a form that has a known solution. Similar approaches are possible in applications development. If the analyst can bring the requirements into a form or framework that allows reuse of available work, and the use of available solution frameworks, then development can be speeded up. Accordingly, analysts, architects, and development team leads have to work as a team. And successful teams often stay together and are more productive than teams formed on-the-fly. This also strengthens the argument as to why the three should be more actively working together during the requirements phase, instead of their roles emerging sequentially in the development process.

"…the architect must be the one who develops requirements. Even though the user may have provided a preliminary set of requirements with the RFP, it is essential that the development team and the architect conduct their own requirements study to identify and analyze the logic, the way the system is used and the operational requirements.

As the project moves through the requirements phase, design concepts begin to emerge based upon early perceptions of functionality and performance. These design concepts are essentially theoretical models. They help the system architect to "floor plan" the elements of the system and help both the design team and the user team to understand the relationships and dependencies between each and every module.

The whole point of doing an in-depth study is that the people who will design and build the … system must have an intimate understanding of what is needed, why it is needed, who needs it and exactly how it should work. Having any other group perform such work defeats the purpose of the analysis.

Sometimes sales engineers or sales support groups will aid the user in preparing the RFP and sometimes these people are even independent consultants will be called in to develop the requirements. This makes no sense; it doesn't save money and it doesn't save time. Nor will it ensure greater integrity. In fact, it produces the reverse of these worthy goals since it forces the architect to design with hands tied."

—From *Production Software That Works*, by
Behuniak, Iftikhar, Ahmad, and Courtright

Oversight

Most requirements gathering processes depend on the skills of the requirements analysts. Much has been written about how good requirements can be gathered and there is little else to add here. Because this important activity depends so heavily on the skills of an individual, or a few individuals, there should be a control process in place to oversee it. Normally, the way the process works is for the analyst to write the requirements, which the business user signs off. That is not sufficient because the business user is only one of the stakeholders and he or she may be satisfied with the requirements as long as they reflect his or her views. There should be a review of the requirements by a more complete set of stakeholders. This external review process can stay at whatever level of detail the project and individual bandwidth limitations allow. Political dynamics and the desire to avoid getting caught in an endless cycle of reviews often discourage this oversight, yet it is an essential part of the process, especially for critical initiatives.

Sign-Offs

Sign-offs matter from a legal standpoint. From a practical point of view, they matter less. A sign-off does not make a requirements document any better. It is as good or bad as it is. It still has all the problems of interpretation of the requirements. A sign-off by itself does not affect the probability of a change being requested after sign-off.

Sign-offs are useful in other ways. A sign-off is a milestone in a project and also signals the achievement of that milestone. A customer thinks before signing off, especially when he or she realizes that everything post sign-off is under change control. For the same reason, the user may be reluctant to commit, delaying the sign-off interminably, refusing to commit.

Sometimes the sign-off is left to a signing authority who may not have been involved directly with the requirements at any level of detail. Insisting on high-level sign-offs for requirements only causes delays. One must assume that there is a larger business contract under which the requirements work is being done, and the sign-offs at the requirements level could easily be left to those who have been involved in working out the requirements. This will also reduce avoidable delays. Sign-off authority must, however, be determined at the start of the project.

Requirements and Development

Conventional wisdom, as espoused in the waterfall model, dictates that design and development should follow requirements; it is sometimes more practical to start design and development before the requirements are complete. Starting work without waiting for completion of the entire requirements can be a real schedule saver. Of course, it requires identifying what is definitely going to be required, and taking a calculated risk. There are many structural elements, such as online help, error messages, log-ins, and even some processing flows that can be similar across applications, that the team might have built earlier. There is risk involved in this approach; yet when schedules are tight, it is something that must be considered. The trade-off is between the time saved and the costs of throwing away or reworking some of the work done preemptively.

Revisiting Requirements

Requirements, and the assumptions underlying them, should be revisited periodically. There is a fear that revisiting requirements will only lead to changes. The way to address this is to make the customer understand that the work being done is according to the signed-off requirements. The revisiting is to give the customers an opportunity to revalidate the requirements and trigger change control, with all the costs involved. Even if genuine changes in requirements are called for, this would still be cheaper than going ahead and building a product that does will meet customer needs.

Design and Architecture

Design and architecture of the system being built should be driven by the requirements. There is a school of thought that says that, when requirements are being gathered, one should not worry about how they will be met. The argument in its favor is that these are two separate functions, and more than one way could be found of meeting them. If one were to consider how something will be implemented, it would ruin the process of gathering the correct requirements. We disagree. The terms "requirements," "design," and "architecture" denote categories that delineate certain functions in a fairly continuous solution-building process. They are not rigid boxes that one cannot peek into until some magic words are uttered to get out of the previous box.

Not all requirements have a direct impact on the design and architecture of the application. Those that do are more important. In that same vein, some changes to requirements are more important than others. As change becomes necessary in the requirements world, one must consider investing in an architecture that is flexible at the start. Some architectures better address such flexibility in dealing with changes to requirements. Such architectures — for example, the MVC (model/view/controller) architecture — try to insulate changes to requirements to the user interface. Proper modularization of functionality may allow for easier handling of enhancements. Certain technologies may also make it easier, such as object-oriented technologies that would allow one to create classes with local variations using inheritance.

Lack of flexibility can become a constraint on the enhancements that can be supported in the future. Flexibility must be actively built into the design. Making the business logic data driven is one way of allowing flexibility, the cost of adding or changing data being less than the cost of making and deploying software changes.

Should the analyst look ahead and include such flexibility in the specifications, even when the customer does not ask for it? The preferred answer would be in the affirmative, particularly when the costs and risks are affordable. For example, the customer may specify that the same application will be used unchanged by all regions. Later developments may require that each region should have its own interface and logic. Such changes might have been easily handled if the architecture and the data model had been designed for regional changes although the customer did not specifically ask for it. This is a key judgment call.

In fact, one of the nonfunctional requirements that the customer should insist upon is flexibility in the architecture. Business users must insist upon an architecture review before it (the architecture) is finalized. Such a review should include architects from groups outside the project. Such reviews can be completed in a short period of time and could add considerable value to the solution building process.

Requirement enhancement requests should be handled through proper change control procedures. They can be classified along many vectors, one of them being the impact the change has on the design and architecture of the application. Of course, this impact is a function of where one stands in the life cycle of the project. Early requests can, probably, be accommodated with less impact than later ones, just as post-deployment enhancements requiring architectural modifications are likely expensive.

The analyst needs to have a good understanding of the design and architecture of the application so that he or she can modulate requests for future enhancements. This is a dialogue that is sometimes missing, with the analyst sticking to "providing requirements" and leaving the design to the designers. In fact, there should be active sharing of information about the requirements, design, and architecture between the analyst, the business user, and the designer. Users sometimes stay away from details of the design and architecture because they are too "technical." However, users who understand the architecture, including its limitations, can come up with more feasible requirements. This again appears to be a violation of the rule that requirements must be drawn in pristine isolation from other ground realities, but that a practical approach is generally cheaper and more efficient for the organization.

Changes in Requirements

Requirements change. A good delivery system handles such changes smoothly and efficiently, recognizing that the SEE model (solution, engineering, and execution) remains at work even for handling changes. A well-thought-out solution must be selected for the changes requested, proper engineering decisions must be made, and all aspects of handling the execution or implementation of the change must be carefully planned (Figure 4.3).

Reasons for Change

Why do application requirements change? The most obvious reason is that the business requirements have changed. As there is a close relationship between the two, a change in the business requirements must result in a change in the application requirements — unless these new business requirements can be handled through other non-software means.

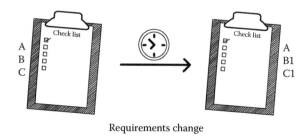

Requirements change

Figure 4.3   Manage changes in requirements.

Other reasons why requirements change include:

- Something was misunderstood by the user or the development team in the original requirements.
- Something in the original requirements was not thought through or specified in detail.
- Something was missing.
- There was a communication problem. For example, the customer assumed certain things about the delivery based on the agreed-upon requirements. This often becomes an issue at the time of user acceptance testing (UAT).

Recognizing Change

It is important to recognize a change as such. Costs are involved in handling any modifications to software already developed. Who bears this cost depends on the classification of the modifications requested. If it is a change from the original specifications, then the customer has to bear it under the rules of engagement as specified by the change control processes. If it is a "bug," then the developer may have to absorb the costs.

Any change agreed to becomes part of a new baseline, and can by itself become an issue in future cycles of discussions.

Changes and Releases

There is a development lead-time involved between when the requirement is identified and when it is implemented. For the same reason, what is in production at any time reflects the requirements finalized earlier. This lead-time is often determined not by the complexity of the change involved, but by an external release schedule. New versions of the application may be released only three times a year, or a major version upgrade is scheduled only once a year. Users who want their changes implemented must begin by understanding the release schedules in place. Calculating backward from the release date and allowing for development, QA, and UAT, it often does not leave much time for the requirements step. New requirements get incorporated into new releases, by which time more new requirements might have emerged. Thus a continuous catch-up goes on.

Requirements and QA

QA activities often derive from the formal requirements specifications. The requirements form an important input to QA. They are used to drive test plans and test design. This is an accepted, normal process.

The larger issue is that the QA group is a stakeholder in the project, yet is often ignored during the requirements development stage. This leads to situations where the requirements committed to result in onerous testing burdens. Development techniques that draw out requirements by preparing test cases for them have an advantage on this.

The need to involve QA personnel during the early requirements stage is an important example of why stakeholder coverage should be as complete as possible.

Uncertainty in Requirements

As previously discussed, requirements are never complete. Even to the extent that they can be said to be complete for a particular phase, there may be, in the minds of the business user, some uncertainty associated with what has been agreed to. If the requirements are uncertain, then it is quite likely that change requests will arise to reduce that uncertainty. One way of handling such uncertainty is to provide for a contingency in the budget allocated. This will benefit both the customers and the developers. It allows both to accommodate "missing" requirements or unanticipated complexity without having to, perhaps, go through a funding process. This use of contingency should remain under the change control process.

How large this contingency allocation could be is a function of the uncertainty that exists. Experience suggests that it should be reasonably large, if circumstances permit. Estimation of software development and delivery costs is still an art rather than a science. The reason why contingency is sometimes kept low is because the mainline estimates are well buffered for handling the uncertainty. That, although common practice, is a less advisable practice than providing proper estimates and then

The ship built has to float

Figure 4.4   User acceptance tests.

asking for contingency. It at least allows for the possibility that the numbers reflect some aspect of reality and can be used reliably for future analysis.

User Acceptance Testing (UAT)

User acceptance testing (UAT) is when the rubber meets the road. This is the point where a lot of the efforts expended up to that point are validated as acceptable. Often, it is also one of the more painful experiences for the development team.

UAT (Figure 4.4) is the step when the deliverables are validated against the requirements. It is not QA because the customer is not expected to have an understanding of software testing methods and processes. It is the customer's opportunity to confirm that the application is in a state that it can be released.

The problems arise due to differences in opinion about:

- The interpretation of the requirements (what is a bug and what is a feature)
- The implicit scope assumptions ("I always assumed help meant context-sensitive help and not a 200-page user manual in PDF")
- The state of completeness of what has been delivered
- The importance of the nonfunctional requirements

UAT gets complicated:

- When the people change on the customer's side between the time the requirements are prepared and the application is delivered; there may be disagreements within the customer teams about the requirements themselves
- If the time given for UAT is inadequate
- Because some customers treat UAT as yet another opportunity to improve the deliverable

- Because the UAT plan is not properly drawn and becomes open ended
- Because there are issues with the data, which the software developers do not see as "their problem"

Considering that the requirements will end up being the baseline for UAT, always plan for the UAT when preparing the requirements. As already discussed, certain development methodologies give higher priority to testing. However, testing and UAT are two separate processes. Both require considerable infrastructure setup, especially when it comes to data preparation. Data requirements for UAT must be an identified nonfunctional requirement in the project requirements document.

Summary

Requirements are the cornerstone of development. Delivery requires the management of two sets of requirements — one for the deliverable itself and the other for the project that is the vehicle through which the delivery is made. It is difficult to specify requirements — it has to do with the nature of the business processes themselves, the nature of the communication processes between people, the limitations of language and tools, and the "divide" between technology and business folks. One must solve the right problem, and that has always been a problem in software and other domains.

Gathering requirements is a term that captures well the process of identifying the stakeholders and finding out what they need. Over the life cycle of an application, the requirements are invariably delivered in phases. Changes to them are managed through change control processes.

However imprecise the process of gathering requirements is, good software gets built and it gets done through a combination of decent requirements, good processes, and a degree of trust.

Requirements must be converted into actual systems that have to be delivered. As discussed in Chapter 5, the architecture and design of such systems form the foundation of a successful system.

Because we do not understand the brain very well we are constantly tempted to use the latest technology as a model for trying to understand it. In my childhood we were always assured that the brain was a telephone switchboard. ('What else could it be?') I was amused to see that Sherrington, the great British neuroscientist, thought that the brain worked like a telegraph system. Freud often compared the brain to hydraulic and electro-magnetic systems. Leibniz compared it to a mill, and I am told some of the ancient Greeks thought the brain functions like a catapult. At present, obviously, the metaphor is the digital computer.

—**John R. Searle,**
in Minds, Brains and Science

Chapter 5

Architecture and Design

> See first that the design is wise and just: that ascertained, pursue
> it resolutely;
> do not for one repulse forego the purpose that you resolved
> to effect.
>
> **—William Shakespeare**

Architecture and design are essential to good software. They are foundational aspects of software development. As in the case of many foundations, they are not always visible or explicit. The advantages of good
architecture and design are often realized much later, especially when one
needs to deal with enhancements and growth. One of the major causes
of the failure of software applications and projects is the use of poor
architecture and design.

Architecture and design are different. One is not more important than
the other, yet both are difficult activities requiring a good understanding
of many domains and approaches.

Background

The discussion regarding the need for managing large software systems,
and integrating disjoint subsystems, began in the 1970s with DeRemer and
Kron. They emphasized the need for a language that could tie modules
together, citing the distinction between "programming-in-the-large versus

programming-in-the-small." In 1986, Prieto-Diaz formally extended this idea in the form of module interconnection languages (MILs). MILs are used to formally express the structure of a software system in the form of a module assembly with definitions of interconnections between them. In 1992, Perry and Wolf first introduced the formal notion of software architectures; they developed "an intuition for software architecture by appealing to several well-established architectural disciplines." On the basis of this intuition, they presented "a model of software architecture that consists of three components: elements, form, and rationale." The work of Garlan and Shaw is, however, considered seminal in the field of software architectures. They accept that "as the size of software systems increases, the algorithms and data structures of the computation no longer constitute the major design problems. When systems are constructed from many components, the organization of the overall system — the software architecture — presents a new set of design problems." They stressed the importance of architectural styles and representations, and how these different styles could "improve our understanding of complex software systems." Since then, there have been numerous contributions in software architecture, including architectural definition languages (ADLs), CASE tools, and RUP (Rational unified process).

Architecture versus Design

People engaged in the software industry often find these two terms confusing. Tom DeMarco perhaps wrote one of the best distinctions between the two:

> An architecture is a framework for the disciplined introduction of change ... Design is always concerned with capacity to accommodate change. This is true even of the extreme example of a system which is to be run once and then thrown away. It still makes sense to design such a system, because it still has to be able to accommodate one change, specifically the change that is the implementation process.

That is, *architecture* describes the properties of an entire system, while *design* specifications pertain only to a local or limited part of the system. To explain it further, one has the architecture of an entire house, but the design of the kitchen inside it. In software, architecture involves modeling a system into layers, partitions, components, and subsystems, along with the definition of the interfaces between them. Design is the step toward practical implementation and involves making decisions about technologies, languages tools, and their representation.

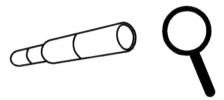

Architects and designers

Figure 5.1   The level of detail.

When dealing with enterprise applications, having to build systems using existing (sub)systems, even if one were to deal with specific technologies, is regarded as architecture. In case one were to build a new component, one would be stepping into the realm of design — just as the interface description would become design if you change the existing implementation.

Quite often, the distinction between architecture and design is made on the basis of the level of detail in the specification (Figure 5.1). The architecture is considered a high-level description of the design. This is fallacious because the content, and the purpose of an architectural specification, is very different from the design. To elaborate, in software, the architectural document would discuss system and network topologies, operational needs and goals, interfaces with other systems, and the justifications for each. The design specifications would involve constraints of programming languages, differences between two databases, and the coding standards. The distinction is thus qualitative and not merely quantitative. Frances Paulisch differentiated these in terms of focus: while design focuses on addressing the functional requirements of a system, an architecture covers both the functional and nonfunctional aspects (scalability, performance, usability, etc.).

The difference can also be brought about by the implications of each when DeMarco says that:

> The absence of a thoughtful architectural act assures that there is no initial accommodation to the changes that will propel the product from version to version, or the change that allows the essence of one product to be carried over into other members of a product family.

Design focuses on a particular embodiment of the requirements in the selected architecture.

Now take a look at the various aspects of software architecture before moving on to discuss the details of designing software systems.

The Importance of Architecture

A software architecture is explicitly needed to handle the complexity of the application. It helps designers and developers understand the application better, by defining the components (and their associated behavior), which together make the application and the interfaces used for communicating across these components

A software architecture document lays a solid foundation for the project. Not only does it serve as a foundation for the project — by illustrating the conceptual path from the requirements to a possible solution — but it also addresses the concerns and constraints imposed by the various stakeholders. It becomes the fundamental starting point for planning the execution of the project — design, development, and testing. While it establishes a foundation, one must also realize that the architecture document is not static — as it is not cast in stone. It is indeed a pity that most projects create a document, probably as an obligatory deliverable, and never revisit it as the development proceeds. Perry and Wolf say that as "the project moves to the implementation phase... the code or low-level design migrates, but the architecture is lost. This is often referred to as architectural drift." It would hence be advisable to decide on some tool to maintain the document when it is being created. Because the architecture document is usually required to address complexity in a system, such documents tend to be large and "unwieldy." One may want to select CASE tools or something similar to manage the architecture.

Software Architecture Document

Many good approaches that have been proposed to formulate a good architecture specification, like Kruchten's 4+1 views; Bass, Clements, and Kazlan's views; Booch, Jacobson, and Rumbaugh's UML; Buschmann; and Rohnert and Stal's pattern-oriented approach. As practitioners in the field, we have read and used elements of each of these approaches; we do not believe that there is any need to formulate a new architecture strategy. We would at the same time leave it to the readers to decide which approach they find more suitable. This section discusses the important elements of an architecture specification — the absolute "musts." They are sufficiently generic to use in any approach one chooses.

Apart from the usual scope, intended audience, definitions, abbreviations, and overview, the architecture document should necessarily have the following details.

Architectural Goals

This section describes the goals of the system, especially those that will have a significant impact on the software architecture, like security, any third-party software components, portability, scalability, and need for reuse. The goals may not necessarily be explicit in the requirements document — they will have to be derived from it. It is imperative that goals are listed in their order of priority. Prioritization requires assigning proper weighting; the architect will have to use his or her prudence in allocating this weighting on the basis of the user requirements.

Constraints

This is possibly the most important section of the document because it has implications on the shape and the future of the system under development. Consequently, it would be desirable to be as exhaustive as possible. Architects should cross-reference these constraints at various places in the document, where an architectural choice is mentioned. This helps future generations of the team who may want to evolve the system. Constraints (Figure 5.2) can be of two kinds:

1. *Imposed by user requirements.* Users can specify their choice of operating system, scalability, response time, and user interaction needs, delivery timelines, and the like. These may become constraints while developing the architectural blueprint for the system, and may force the architect to make some choices. The architect should review such overarching constraints with the business analyst (or the customer directly, if, as we recommend, the architect

Figure 5.2   The reality of constraints.

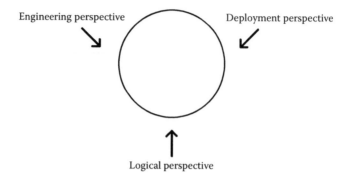

Engineering perspective   Deployment perspective

Logical perspective

Figure 5.3   Architectural perspectives.

has been involved in the requirements gathering process) to ascertain their criticality. Customers are often open to making compromises in their needs if they understand technology constraints, or the resulting financial implications.

2. *The result of architectural choices made by the architect.* Architects can decide on certain network and deployment topologies, or choose third-party components that they think are appropriate to the needs of the customer. They are, however, aware of the constraints each of these choices will impose on the system and its evolution.

Architecture Perspectives

Most approaches to creating a software architecture are somewhat similar, yet some tend to be more comprehensive than others. Architects have a tendency to be exhaustive in their creations, and even delve into design- (and occasionally even coding-) level details. We do not encourage this practice. Using SEE principles, we believe that there are three perspectives that should be treated as *musts* to create a architectural description of the system.

Logical Perspective

It is important that the architect dons the "systems thinker" hat at this stage. Use this to describe the architecturally significant building blocks — software and hardware components (or subsystems) — that together constitute the system. It would be nice to show usage scenarios, and use-cases and logical classes/structures for these components, but it is not necessary, especially at the onset of creating the document. It is imperative that the interface definitions between these components, only from an interoperability and expectation-from-either-party perspective, are clearly brought out.

This *logical architecture* sets the stage for the other two perspectives, so be careful with what is proposed. Keep an eye on the engineering (team composition, technology awareness, etc.) and execution (timelines, budget, resource availability, etc.) aspects of the SEE framework. Realize that the Taj Mahal was built over the course of 12 years and used the services of more than 20,000 persons!

Engineering Perspective

This is the place to show the physical organization of the logical components — the concept of the "n-tier architecture" surfaces here. One will also describe the data and control flows between the components. Most of the constraints of the system should get addressed — performance, scalability, security, portability, etc. A high-level organization of the persistent data store adds completeness.

Deployment Perspective

This is one of the few places in the life cycle of the application to consider the deployment scenarios for the system. This perspective addresses the network topology, the physical deployment of the system in terms of machines and servers, and their size and capability. The deployment architecture must tie in closely with the engineering perspective, as it directly affects the constraints.

Kinds of Architecture

Enterprise Architecture

An enterprise architecture defines the structure and behavior of an organization. The intent is to describe how the organization's constituent people, processes, and systems can be made to effectively align with its current objectives and future strategic direction. Given its comprehensive nature, it helps to weed out inefficiencies and redundancies, and focuses resources on things that are most crucial to the main goals of the organization.

An enterprise architecture contains four categories of definitions:

1. *Business.* This includes a discussion of the policies and standards used in the operation of the organization. The various organizational setups (functional and service) and the business processes

that drive these functions, along with the stakeholders — vendors, suppliers and service providers — are also discussed.

2. *Application*. This defines the interfaces between the various functional and business processes discussed above. The software inventory in the organization is also maintained under this heading.

3. *Information*. This categorizes the data and information resources of the organization. It includes the raw data, metadata, documents, databases, images, and all similar artifacts.

4. *Technology*. This covers the physical elements in the organization — hardware, servers, networking, phone systems, and operating systems (legacy artifacts).

The *process* of developing the enterprise architecture is considered to be, perhaps, *more* important to the organization — it helps improve overall decision making, especially for growing organizations, in volatile markets.

Service-Oriented Architecture (SOA)

Service-oriented architecture (SOA) is a concept that postulates how layered systems should be built using a set of services. A service is typically associated with some unit of work, or a defined set of functionality. In SOA, it is relegated that these services will be performed on behalf of another entity (e.g., another program). The main advantages of an SOA-based system include:

■ *Separation of tasks*: the functionality offered by a computing entity (provider) is encapsulated in the form of a service.

■ *Loosely coupled*: where there are no dependencies between the service seeker and the service provider, and all interactions are stateless (each interaction is independent of any other interaction).

■ *Formally defined interfaces*: where the services interoperate, based on a well-defined set of rules (protocol) that are independent of any implementation (J2EE, .Net, etc.).

An implementation of SOA, which is often found is in Web services; WSDL, SOAP, UDDI, etc. are acronyms commonly used in this context. Credit card approvals while shopping online, airline reservations, and tracking shipments on the Internet are all examples of Web services in action, based on an SOA framework.

Information Architecture

Founded in 2002, The Information Architecture Institute has more than 1000 members in 60 countries. It defines information architecture as:

- The structural design of shared information environments
- The art and science of organizing and labeling Web sites, intranets, online communities, and software to support usability and findability
- An emerging community of practice focused on bringing principles of design and architecture to the digital landscape

Basically, information architecture is the set of ideas about how to philosophically treat all information in a given context, and, in a general way, how to organize it.

System Design

There used to be a time when most software applications were modeled on existing manual systems. It was much easier to visualize the system and decompose it into functional modules, components, and classes. GUIs (graphical user interfaces) were made to look similar to paper forms, and most processing was an automation of the manual environment. Things are rapidly changing in the software industry. Most software built today is an advancement over an existing automated system — in an effort to make it more powerful, usable, freely accessible, interconnected, responsive, etc. These advancements are a result of the changing technology landscape, with new inventions and discoveries such as faster CPUs, larger on-board RAM, the Internet, wireless, RFIDs, and the like. For example, when Amazon (.com) was initially conceived, it could have been viewed as an automation of a warehouse, an inventory management, supplier relationships, and front-end sales for books. However, over the years, Amazon has graduated into a large resource pool of all kinds of artifacts, including books, reviews, sales and marketing tools, ratings — like a barometer of buyers' interests. These changes are making the work of a designer even more difficult.

Design Document

Like the architecture document, this section discusses three important elements of a *design specification* — the absolute "musts." Once again, they are generic enough that they can be used in any design approach.

Class Design

The class design is based on the use cases or the module deconstruction best suited for the application being built. Various approaches can be used in representing the design, starting with HIPO (Hierarchy plus Input-Process-Output), OO (object-oriented) diagrams by Yourdan, or some language such as UML (Unified Modeling language). The common design patterns, or module building blocks, are represented in detail. Any implementation details that should be kept in mind are also cited here.

Data Access Design

This not only describes the logical and physical representations of persistent data used by the application, but it also includes descriptions for constraints, stored procedures, triggers, scalability criteria, etc. Details of OR (object-relational) mappings (if any), data access rules and restrictions, database (DB) library interfaces (ODBC/JDBC), and any technical implementations such as resource connection pools may also be included.

User Interface Design

This part is often missing in many design documents. It is important to design the GUI (graphical user interface; or presentation layer) in such a way that one can manipulate it (customize or personalize it) without affecting other parts of the application. It is also advisable not to focus on the colors and description of screens alone, but also on user navigations and control flows. Many a beautiful product has been unsuccessful because users had to make *just one* additional click. The argument was that that one click per record could add up to a million additional clicks per year — time better spent elsewhere.

GUI screen mockups are used to show an achievable user interface design that fulfills the requirements, while helping close the gap between what is required (expressed through requirements document) and what is feasible. The main purpose is to demonstrate its look and feel, and its usability to a certain extent, before the real graphic designers step in. This is especially important when users are migrating from one system to another; for example, from a desktop system to a browser-based system, users may see it as a loss of usability and, possibly, performance.

The purpose of the navigation aspect is to express the main interaction paths of the various kinds (roles) of users throughout the system. The use cases come handy here. Pick the most crucial ones and demonstrate their navigations — how a particular type of user would achieve the use case through the proposed screens. Most decision makers want to see how many clicks it will take to get to the data they need frequently.

The Process of Designing

While designing systems, there is often an urge to put the best or brightest resource on the job. Although a technically sound person is imperative, we feel the designer should have a good understanding of the business domain in which the system is being built. The best designer from a communication and networking background may be a misfit while designing a mortgage or loan application.

At the start of the design process, a designer has the requirements, and possibly the architecture documents at his or her disposal. It is imperative to have a very good understanding of the former — to understand and imbibe all that the author of the requirements document meant to communicate (the real customer needs). It is best not to make judgments and overlook details that one might consider trivial, especially in the initial stages of the process. In projects with aggressive deadlines, or where the size of the project does not warrant the use of the regular software life cycle, it is possible that requirements are not very thorough, or the requirements, architecture, and design phases have collapsed into a *specification* phase. We prefer the latter, although it may not seem appropriate. Our philosophy of SEE dictates that the latter approach can help in looking at the various aspects of the system, which would otherwise have been neglected for want of time. If each of the phases had been given inadequate attention, as a designer, one could do the following:

- Insist on more customer meetings to get further details before closing on one's design.
- Build a design based on one's understanding of the application, and get it approved by the customer. The latter is quite important.
- Choose to adopt a prototyping phase in the software life cycle (refer to Chapter 7 on life cycle for details), even if it is a straw man that one is able to build.

Any software design should incorporate all of the following:

- A structural decomposition of the application into modules and components — a top-down approach
- Detailed definition of each module and component, and their data processing capabilities

■ The order of operations performed in the overall application, and the flow of control across the modules

Irrespective of which design methodology one decides to pursue, we have found the concepts under Hierarchy plus Input-Process-Output (HIPO), in fact HIPO-II, to lay a very good foundation to the design. Although HIPO was developed during the 1970s for systems analysts and designers, it never gained popularity as a tool for designing software. At the core, it contains:

■ *Hierarchy.* This shows the decomposition and interrelationships between modules and components of a system. It looks like an org chart.
■ *Input-process-output (IPO) specification: for each module.* The designer can choose the level of detail for the specification, starting with just diagrams for the simpler modules, to even pseudo-code for the complex ones.

We do not say that HIPO should be used for application design. Our claim is that the concepts embodied in it with respect to decomposing and representing a system are very powerful and become a good organizing influence for the designer. Another advantage of HIPO is the diagramming and visualization aspect. We believe it is very important that a designer be visually oriented; that is, he or she should be able to visualize the organization of an application and how each module fits in with respect to user needs. Using HIPO, as one builds the hierarchy, one defines the associated IPOs. Each of these definitions will raise further questions, which will require one to break a module into sub-modules, if the IPO seems complex. Once one has a rough sketch prepared, one can move to creating use cases, sequence diagrams, class diagrams, or whichever methodology one chooses to follow.

A Note on Design Patterns

In 1991, Yourdan and Coad introduced the concept of *object-oriented design* (OOD). In 1994, Gamma, Helm, Johnson, and Vlissides, known as the "Gang of Four," wrote a book on design patterns; in it they discussed "recurring solutions to common problems in software design." Patterns have changed the way we design systems in today's world. One fact that most people do not know is that the Gang of Four's work was based on "patterns" that were introduced by Alexander, Ishikawa, Silverstein, et al.

in 1977, in their book about towns, buildings, and construction. The latter wrote that "towns and buildings will not become alive, unless they are made by all the people in society, and unless these people share a common pattern language, within which to make these buildings, and unless this common pattern language is alive itself." They define a pattern as an entity that "describes a problem which occurs over and over again in our environment, and then describes the core of the solution to that problem, in such a way that you can use it a million times over, without ever doing it the same way twice." Readers must note that the original definition of pattern did not imply *a problem and its solution* that could be used as it is (code reuse — as a parallel in software). It was a way to categorize and abstract problems (with possible solutions to them) by identifying certain peculiar properties and invariants for them.

Their fundamental concept is that "no pattern is an isolated entity" and "each pattern can exist in the world only to the extent that is supported by other patterns." This has elements of systems thinking in it. Any design pattern is made up of, and interacts with, other patterns around it. In this context, designers have a tendency to pick a number of patterns and try to fit them all into their design. Christopher et al. caution the "builder" against this practice — "it is possible to make buildings by stringing together patterns, in a rather loose way… an assembly of patterns. It is not dense. It is not profound. But it is also possible to put patterns together in such a way that many patterns overlap in the same physical space; it has many meanings captured in a small space." A good designer is one who can compress patterns — make the "cheapest possible building" yet have all the necessary patterns in it.

Zachman Framework

The Zachman framework is a logical structure intended to provide a comprehensive representation of an IT (information technology) enterprise. The framework uses a 36-cell table with six rows (Scope, Business Model, System Model, Technology Model, Detailed Representation, and Functional System) and six columns (What, How, Where, Who, When, and Why) to define rules for managing such enterprises.

The Zachman framework is designed so that people with different perspectives can communicate. Instead of a 6×6 table, it represents a multidimensional framework that helps enterprises plan, design, and create complex and evolving information systems. It defines a structure independent of any toolsets and methodologies used in it. There are different perspectives in any organization, and each is addressed in this framework. Each row's perspective is different. As one goes down the table, topics become more concrete and less conceptual, as do the associated perspectives.

The framework clearly understands and preaches that any enterprise IT setup goes beyond the realm of the architect, designer, developer, and QA group. There are more stakeholders, such as planners, business owners, and keeper, who may play a key role in the enterprise, and are often ignored in other framework models. Although most developers have probably never heard of Zachman, the latter has become the *de facto* standard for enterprise architecture within the data organizer and IT community.

However, the framework can be misinterpreted as a sequential approach to modeling the enterprise starting with the first row or column, and moving down. This is far from reality. The framework allows users to start from any cell and navigate through, keeping the basic modeling principles of stakeholders and perspectives in mind. It can also disintegrate into a process-oriented, documentation-heavy bureaucratic approach given the focus on organizing knowledge and data. Given its freedom from any particular toolsets or methodologies, it should be used primarily for identifying issues and gaps.

What It Takes to Be a Good Architect and Designer

Architects and designers are like coaches of a team. They are not the supreme commanders or the heads of the project; yet they are the "know-all" for the entire system being built. It is their vision that becomes the blueprint for the development team. In this capacity, both architects and designers should be able to visualize and see the "bigger picture." While keeping an eye on the user needs, they should be able to craft something that can take care of evolving business and technology requirements. While an architect should be more business and technology savvy, a designer should be properly grounded in technical details (horizontal versus vertical expertise). Simultaneously, both must be good communicators — to document their vision and gain acceptance for their work.

Mitch Kapor, the creator of Lotus 1-2-3, wrote a very good description on the roles of (architects and) software designers. He mentions that in both architecture and software design, it is necessary that the professional practitioner be able to use "a way to model the final result with far less effort than is required to build the final product." Kapor takes it a step further to explain that:

> "A design is realized only in a particular medium. What are the characteristic properties of the medium in which we create

	What (Data)	How (Function)	Where (Location)	Who (People)	When (Time)	Why (Motivation)
Scope Planner	Things significant to the business	Mission of the business	Locations of the business	HR strategies used by the business	Events important for planning	Business goals and vision
Business Model Business Owner	Language or Semantic Model used	Processes used in the business	Business logistics and relationships across offices	Relationships between organization structure and workflow	Schedule of significant events	Business policies and plan
System Model Architect	Logical entities and their relationships	Business functions and systems architecture	Roles in a distributed systems approach	Human interfaces between people	System events	Business rules
Technology Model Designer	Physical entities and relationship models	System design	Technology architecture and underlying framework	Presentation layer and UI design	Control flows	Business rule design
Detailed Representation Implementer	Implementation strategy and data definitions	Programs	Network and component architecture	GUI creation	Triggers	Rule implementation
Functioning System Keeper	Data, classes, objects	Functions, procedures	Network elements, hardware, third-party software	GUI, help files, documentation	Deployed jobs and processes	Software evolution

software? Digital media have unique properties that distinguish them from print-based and electronic predecessors. Software designers need to be able to make a systematic study and comparison of different media — print, audiovisual, and digital — examining their properties and affordances with a critical eye to how these properties shape and constrain the artifacts realized in them."

What both architects and designers need most is a depth of experience. They are not born as architects or designers — they graduate to that position. Theoretical knowledge of architecture and design principles, although important, is not a substitute for the experience one gains by learning on the job, creating new systems on an empty canvas.

Occam's Razor

William of Ockham (1285–1349) is credited with formulating the (logical) razor that bears his name, which is phrased "entities are not to be multiplied beyond necessity." The origins of what has come to be known as Occam's razor are traceable to the works of earlier philosophers all the way back to Aristotle in 322 BC. Like many Franciscan monks of his time, William was a minimalist in his life, idealizing a life of poverty. He argued that universals had no existence outside the mind and that we do not need universals to explain anything.

Occam's razor is also called the Principle of Parsimony. These days, it is usually interpreted to mean something like "the simpler the explanation, the better" or "do not multiply hypotheses unnecessarily." Occam's razor has become a basic perspective for those who follow science and analytics; it is a guide to choosing the hypothesis that contains the least number of unproven assumptions. It must be noted that Occam's razor never claims to choose the *best* theory, but only proposes simplicity as the deciding factor in choosing between two otherwise equal theories. It is possible that, given more information, the more complex theory might turn out to be correct.

In most projects, designers are required to base their solution on a conceptual model of a real-world system (or process). It often appears that a simple model best approximating the system will suffice. In practice, however, such solutions based on simple models fail to handle the problem and often cause a series of new problems. Designers often go through several complete redesigns before finding a viable solution. This is really not a violation of Occam's razor, which does not refer to the necessity of simple solutions as much as choosing simplicity in solutions. In this case, the problem lies with getting the right set of possible models (with the appropriate amount of detail) to choose the simplest solution.

One sees examples of Occam's razor in everyday conversation. When asked about the distance between, say, Los Angeles and San Francisco, one would say 450 miles. This distance is generally the direct driving distance. You do not think of this distance via Denver or via New York, which is obviously more than 450 miles. Why are those options automatically eliminated? It is because the mind always tends to choose the simplest distance model that satisfies the question. In the same vein, if one sees standing water on one's lawn in the morning, the simplest explanation could be that someone left open the garden tap. One does not jump to the conclusion that the town is flooded.

This principle is equally applicable in debugging. When encountering an error, the developer must test the simplest possible cause for it, before moving on to more complex causes. It would make sense to look for a programming error within the developer's program, then move on to other interacting functions or modules, then if necessary to other software layers such as libraries, rather than beginning with the assumption that the compiler, or the hardware, has some problem.

Summary

A good system builds on the foundations of good architecture and design. Architecture differs from design — one is global while the other is more local. If an application is complex, it should be built using a proper architecture. Proper architectures help manage the complexity of the system. Architectures exist at various levels; there are enterprise architectures and information architectures. These can be of various types: client/server, service oriented, and others.

The key to successful software design is to recognize and respect the media that is being used — digital, electronic in this case. It is understandable that initial efforts in software design imitated the manual systems that were being automated through software. But as software matures, one needs to take the design to a different, more potent level.

We also need to look at *data* and *information*, terms familiar to all of us. They constitute the basis for the existence of many computer applications.

Every gardener must have had the experience of hearing from some reputable and trustworthy gardener that a certain plant is miffy and uncertain, yet you have it all over the garden. Even more annoying is the comment that a certain plant is foolproof, yet you have utterly failed with it four times at least. The best that any gardener can do is to tell his own experience with a plant. If it grows like a weed he should say so.

—Henry Mitchell,
On Gardening

Chapter 6

Data and Information

From a bathing tub
I throw water into the lake -
slight muddiness appears.

—Hekigodo Kawahigashi (1873–1937)

Successful information systems depend on a good understanding of what one wants to track and why. A solution designer for such a system needs to recognize the differences, and the relationship between data and information. Thinking about data and information must include ideas about:

- *Recognizing the nature of data.* Data and information can be looked at in various ways — original or derived, formal or informal, raw or processed, data or metadata, complete or incomplete, to name a few.
- *Designing information delivery.* Designing information delivery is about selecting the right approach, representation, and organization. It requires an understanding of how the root of information processing lies in forms and workflows.
- *Managing data related tasks.* The management of data requires inclusion in the solution of many related tasks such as retention, tracking of changes, classification of data, reconciliation, migration, and others.

105

Nature of the Data

Data and information permeate the work of information systems professionals. Early ways of distinguishing between the two were simplistic: *information* referred to the contents of a report, while *data* was everything that resided in a database. We have not come too far away from such a viewpoint. For many, information is considered logical, and data is seen as physical (persistent).

Derived Data

Some users do not distinguish between data and information, treating data and information as two terms for the same thing. Many pieces of data appear to convey some information anyway. When given a piece of data, there is information right there. If one knows a person's date of birth, one believes one is getting the person's age as well. Some will disagree with that saying that the date of birth is only the data, while the age of the person is information, which is derived from the date of birth. The database designer would like to store the data, the person's date of birth, and not the age because the latter can (and should) be "derived" by the application. There is a derivation (processing) step that converts data to information. In this example, the derivation is so obvious and simple that this "processing step" can be taken for granted.

But why should one stop with a simple transformation? Some may say that the age (in the above example) is also data, and not information. It becomes information only if there is some value to that derivation — for example, if it is used to decide whether alcohol can be sold to a customer at a store, or to determine whether a person is eligible for social security benefits. Under this approach, everything remains data until it is put to use, and only at that point can it be called information. Only actionable data is information. Of course there is a subjective element as to what becomes actionable when information, like beauty, is in the eye of the beholder.

Internal versus External

By a corollary argument, in data processing terms, every transformation step is not a conversion of data to information. Although the data is moving toward its information delivery objective, it is unlikely of value or interest to someone outside that processing boundary. If the intermediate data or result is valuable to those monitoring the process, then it must be treated as internal information. System designers need to clearly distinguish between internal and external information delivery points. In use case terminology, these are different use cases.

Formal versus Informal Information

All companies generate and process large amounts of informal information. This includes everything from water cooler discussions, phone calls, meeting discussions that are not recorded in the minutes of the meetings, etc. Formal information is invariably preceded by informal information. Detailed discussions may lead to a formal proposal to a customer. The proposal document is treated as formal. Notes saved may be treated as formal or semi-formal. Invariably, written information, whether on paper or as e-mail, is recognized as formal or semi-formal. Oral information is treated as informal. This definition may not be correct legally. Oral agreements and commitments are often valid or acceptable although one is advised to record and file anything that is important in writing.

It is this informal information, which has gone missing from formal records, that makes the actual experience invaluable. One cannot learn all about a project by looking at formal documentation. The formal documentation is only the tip of the iceberg. There is a lot more — information and interpretation — that remains in people's heads. Good managers may begin with a review of the formal information but always add steps to get to the informal information.

Most of the information that one deals with, in information systems, is formal information. They are considered "formal" systems although they are, at best, a partial reflection of the "real world." In what sense are they formal? They are formal because they map to formal business processes directly or indirectly. A purchase is recorded when a purchase order is raised. An employee is added to the employee master when an employee reports for duty and signs his Date-of-Joining form.

A formal information system is often inadequate to capture all the information dynamics associated with a transaction. Yet, they are complete and sufficient for many operational or legal purposes. The systems professional, while recognizing the overall limitation, must discharge his or her responsibility to maintain accurate and complete information while using them.

Why should the existence of informal information affect the design of a formal system? Because both are essential for users. Users use multiple sources of information — both formal and informal — in their decision making.

Data Generators and Users

Who uses formal information? The intuitive answer is — the people most involved with it. Do not assume that is always the case. Let us take an example of a sales order that is recorded in the company's order database. Each entry in that database contains details about the sales order but not all that is known. The sales personnel know more information than is ever put into that database. They know the personalities involved, the difficulties encountered in getting the order, and the compromises made in the proposal. To say that the order was for 12 widgets at $100 each and is to be delivered to "this" address by September 1st, is to get a useful but incomplete picture of that order. (Adding notes fields to capture such "unstructured" information helps but they are rarely amenable to processing.) For those deeply involved, the sales personnel in this example, this order information appears partial and weak because the people know a lot more about each order than what the system can tell them. For those outside the sales department, the production or shipping departments, the formal information is very useful and probably sufficient. Having such a database is a great help in improving communications. This difference in perception between data generators and data users leads to a subtle error on the part of system designers who often assume that the persons most interested in the databases they are creating are the data generators.

The real users of formal information are often other users. Designers must communicate with data generators, and also with such users.

Data-Related Costs

There have been estimates that the information stored in formal databases is only a tiny fraction of the information that exists in the world. This is understandable. Formal information is a result of data capture and organization. There is a cost associated with doing that. Obviously, economic considerations drive what companies or individuals are willing to capture formally. The cost of data capture is driven by the cost of sensors (that helping data capture) and the capture-related processing. The cost of sensors at least is decreasing. As this cost of capture goes down, a larger proportion of informal information will become part of formal databases. Bar codes are a good example of low-cost data capture. Some companies, through self-service screens, are pushing data capture costs to the edge by getting the customer to fill in the data required for capturing, for example, the bill, in the supermarket checkout line. It is good for the system designer to understand data-related costs and incorporate that into the solution options.

Why is some information formally recorded and others not formally recorded? One needs to go back to the basic underpinnings of information systems to throw some light on at least one aspect of where the formal selection takes place, and how it emerges. At the risk of some simplification, as people needing the information get physically separated from the sources of information, information systems come into play. For example, the managers need to know what is in the warehouse without physically visiting the place. They need only turn to the inventory report. As long as the formal information presented in that report represents the reality in the warehouse, the system compensates for the separation. It must, however, be noted that this information is with respect to some agreed-upon vectors only — in this example, the stock levels. The report does not give the manager any information about how clean the aisles are, or which bulbs in the overhead lighting are not working. This choice must be made, that is, stock levels and not cleanliness of aisles. This choice results in attenuation. This attenuation must be recognized. That the company ends up with a database of stock levels and not a database of cleanliness of aisles is because this "choice" was made to address a certain requirement at a certain time. The data that is not captured is in many cases lost.

Raw Data

One often hears the term "raw data." It is not clear what it means. A trivial definition is that raw data is unprocessed data. It is the original data captured by a server or a device. Most systems do not deal with raw data. Some systems requiring higher degrees of proof about what they store, such as those related to criminal, legal, or pharmaceutical systems, may talk about raw data more than the normal business application. Access to raw data may also be required for data quality improvement reasons. In a system with data flowing across many companies and partners, trying to improve data quality requires clear trails of where the "bad" data was introduced. If one is informing or blaming any external (or internal) party for introducing errors, one must be sure that the error was introduced by that party, and not earlier or later, due to faulty logic in the processing.

If raw data loses its raw status on the slightest change or transformation, then most data that we deal with is not raw. For example, conversion of data from EBCDIC to ASCII could make the data "not raw." A screen that posts data to a database may not be sending through all the keystrokes (backspaces, overwrites) as entered. Any physical representation needs some form of delimiters. When dealing with "Joe, Smith, 123 Sesame Street, Box Town, CA," what is the raw data of the address? Is it the content or the entire string? If the raw data is of fixed length, then the delimiter can be considered "outside." Sometimes data sets have missing values, and if you represent missing values by putting in an asterisk or a space or a special code, that is processing of sorts and the data is not raw anymore. Ideally, every transformation should be traceable, preferably both in a reverse chronological order and an upstream/downstream order. This can be used for audit purposes or for improving data quality. Of course, while recording the entire trail, do not forget to record the changes to the metadata.

The concept of upstream and downstream gets merged with the concept of raw data. The intuitive assumption is that upstream systems have "rawer" data than downstream ones. Changes flow down. The point to keep in mind is that this does not mean that the most upstream system has the "rawest" data. The most upstream point may be downstream for another system. Some databases attempt to maintain both raw and enriched data in their schemas, allowing access to both. This is because users may want to see what "originally came through." The raw data in such cases may only be raw in the sense that it was on the input side of that system. Calling it raw does not mean that upstream systems have not touched it. The enriched data is the "cleaned-up" version. For example, one may wish to retain both the audio recording and the transcript of, for example, a hearing. However, unless one can prove that it has not been subsequently edited or transformed or manipulated, it cannot be treated as raw data.

Sometimes, raw data may actually exist outside the formal databases. The raw data for a payment transaction may actually be on a signed check. If one is scanning the check and storing it, then it is raw compared to the data entry transaction, but the physical check itself is the raw data because there could be scanning or compression errors.

How can one bypass the filters to get to raw data? Designers must allow for such possibility. One may want to send data to a printer more directly than through a particular printer driver. One may want to look at the image of the check rather than a listing of its posting in a database.

Getting raw data can be expensive. In any system when there is a demand for raw data, the designer must question the request and verify its necessity before running off to provide it. However, designers need to incorporate into their systems some transparency about the degree of rawness of the data for the benefit of the user. For example, NASA pictures are identified as computer renditions. Poems that are translated are clearly identified.

Metadata

Most data in a company's database is not scientific in the sense that it does not come from scientific observations or observations of scientific experiments. It may be objective and accurate, but it is driven by agreed-upon assertions or definitions. For example, the "duration of a call to a call center" may be picked up very accurately from the system clocks but the *definition* of start and end times, of a call is set by the designers. The knowledge that one draws from such data — through business intelligence or regular reports — lacks scientific rigor. Trying to compare the length of support calls across companies when they are operating to different definitions of duration is meaningless.

Right data can go wrong. Data must be understood in its context, which may or may not be the metadata in its conventional definition. This often happens with respect to codes. If one sees a record that says *Joe* belonged to "Dept 17" in 1982, then unless one has access to the Dept code table as of 1982, one cannot assume that the "Dept 17" today is the same as that in 1982. In *data warehousing*, this is the issue of slowly changing dimensions. Not recognizing and recording this change can render old data, which was accurate or right when recorded, useless or ambiguous at a later date.

When a data entry form changes, it could be driven by a change in the process or some other external factor. For example, a new legal requirement may be driving the need to get additional information. Such changes mean that the data in a database could have come through old and new versions of forms. If fields before a certain form version are blank, there could be a reason for it. Tracking the history of form changes is important. There may be metadata about the information reflecting this history. Most of this information is not captured properly or is difficult to determine.

Certainty of Data

Data does not have Platonic certainty. The data we store may be right or wrong. It does not become right just because it is recorded in a formal system. An employee may give his or her date of birth to a company and it could be recorded with or without verification. Unless this information (verified or not) was captured, one would not be able to say that the employee's date of birth was, in fact, correct. It is not sufficient to turn to documents defining verification processes because, while it is true that such a process existed at the time of capture of the information, there is no certainty as to whether the process was followed for this particular employee.

Determining Information Needs

It is a fair claim that information systems "convert data to information." Yes, this is why software and systems are built. The work of converting data to information is arduous, often expensive, and requires battalions of human resources.

In the early days, the term "data processing" was very much in vogue. Hardware was the main sales driver, and the use of computers to process data was a sign of modernization of the company. Data processing conjures images of glass rooms, batch processing, legacy applications such as payroll and billing, operators instead of users hovering over the machines, and printed outputs rather than screen outputs. From such practices emerged a simple way of distinguishing between data and information: Information was a report, and data was that which resided in a database. Information was seen as more logical and data as somewhat physical. We have not come too far from that approach.

There is a common-sense use of the word "information" where it is merely a synonym for data. There is a distorted use of "information," where "information" is used instead of "data" because it sounds more important and useful, for example, saying "information model" when one means the "data model." There are specific engineering areas such as information theory where the term "information" is used in a specific, well-defined, and mathematical sense — information systems personnel rarely use the term "information" in the sense of information theory.

Selecting the Right Representation

There is yet another important aspect of data and information. Data represented in one way can convey more information than when it is represented in another way. A table of numbers represented as a graph can make a better point of an upward or downward trend than just the table. It is related to the way the receiver processes data. Edward Tufte, noted Professor of Design at Yale, has a series of books and lectures that look at the visual representation of data, good and bad ways to clarify information. A good way of learning how to reveal information clearly is to study how to hide it. If one is tasked with designing a good screen or report, turn the problem around and try to design a screen or report that will hide as much of the information as possible. This counter-intuitive exercise will reveal what is involved in good representation. For example, to hide information in a report, as some financial reports do, one would use long, dull tables of numbers, jarring fonts, fine print, unexplained abbreviations, missing column headings or units of measure, mixed-up scales on graph axes, and the like. Now reverse the logic. If one had avoided such "mistakes," the screen or report would become clearer. In this vein, Tufte mentions magicians. One of the key ways they minimize the transfer of information to the audience is through the use of distraction — something is swirling in the left hand while the right hand switches the coin. Reversing this logic, if one wants to maximize the transfer of information to the user, one should minimize the distraction — that is why Web pages with revolving globes can be distracting and are considered bad design.

Determining the Many Uses

In one sense, data is neutral. It stands ready to serve many (information) masters. From the same data, different information can be drawn. One can use the end-of-day inventory to calculate daily sales, as well as make replenishment decisions. One can use the date of a person's employment to assign him or her to a particular performance review cycle or to calculate retirement benefits. The flow between data and information is "one to many." In such a situation, data design must anticipate the many uses. This is done through system requirements. This is also what makes enterprise data models difficult to design and implement.

Organizing Data

The conversion of data to information involves two basic activities: (1) organizing and (2) processing. Organizing data is reflected in the data models underlying the application. Applications are built on these data models. If both the data model and the application are designed at the same time, one would expect the fit to be there. Issues arise when an application is expected to use an existing data model "belonging" to another application. The data model may have to be modified. Any change to the data model can be expensive as "data serves many masters." There can be side effects and ripple effects.

Data models deal with data related to entities and the relationships between entities; for example, a customer can have many orders. Adding a new piece of data (e.g., cellphone number) is easier than adding a new concept related to customers such as "national customers" and "international customers," because the latter introduces new semantics within the data model and the applications residing above. Such changes are often required because the *variety* (refer to Chapter 2) involved is not recognized properly. What you thought was a single entity called "customer" turns out to be two differing entities.

Depending on the technologies used, the cost of handling such a change differs. It is safe to assume that some business logic, screens, reports, and workflows are likely to change. A project manager must treat changes to a data model as one of the more expensive change requests.

Recognizing System Boundaries

The conversion of data to information happens at system boundaries (Figure 6.1). Let us take the conventional example of someone asking us for directions to our home or office. If they were planning to make a trip to visit you, and you gave them the physical route only — take Freeway X, Exit Y, turn right and so on — you would be excluding at least a few additional pieces of information that would be required to make the trip successfully, that is, actual road conditions, parking locations, toll fees, other dependencies. In other words, if the user's "business" objective is to make the trip, then the route information is only partial information. Even if you do not have the other information, you could do two things: (1) inform the person that he or she needed to get those pieces of information before proceeding on the trip, and (2) point them to some reliable sources where the information could be obtained directly or indirectly. A satisfying Web page gives you the information it can provide and points you to the information it knows you need even if it does not provide it itself. The conventional reports that come out of IT departments look weak in front of these formats, primarily because they ignore the missing but required information. They are weaker than even this because IS reports continue to churn out views of data based on only what they

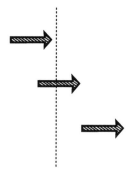

The conversion of data to information
happens at system boundaries.

Figure 6.1   System boundaries.

control in narrow swaths of real estate, driven by system or organizational boundaries.

Note that footnotes and fine print are formatting methods of presenting the excluded information. They are not often used that way, however. Footnotes are used for elaborations, clarifications, or qualifications of the information delivered in the main body of a report. Fine print meets the objective of presenting information in a way most likely to be ignored. They can, of course, be used to address the issue of "what we do not know."

Portals and dashboards are attempts to bring data from multiple places to one place for a more "useful" experience. For them to be more effective, they need to incorporate the "not-knowing" principles.

Designing Information

Forms and Formality

The concept of formal information comes from the concept of forms. Forms have been part of bureaucracies for ages. A successful manual process was invariably built on a succession of well-designed forms that moved the process along, doing what the information systems of today are supposed to do well — providing the required information at the right time to the right person. Even today in offices with considerable automation, forms, many of them manually filled in, continue to be in use, although many feed automated systems.

Paperless offices and societies have not been attained. Paper continues to be an efficient method of capturing information. It requires low setup and support costs (a pen and a paper), allows cheaper scalable and parallel processing (at a DMV office, for example, it is less expensive to have many people fill in paper forms in parallel than to provide an entry terminal for each person), and, in many cases, doubles as both an application and a proof of application because of the formal signature on it. Carbon copies can be retained by the applicant for his or her records. Paper, however, is less efficient in getting it processed downstream. Data entry can introduce errors and has a cost. Paper forms do not provide the intelligence and validation that electronic forms can offer. However, a system designer should consider paper forms as a valid design option. They are not outdated. (Many Web sites still basically serve up forms supplying them as downloads or screen forms.)

There are more graphics in Web-based applications but they appear to be present more in the opening lead in screens. By the time forms-based processing begins, Web-based workflows are a series of electronic forms.

Psychology of Forms

On the one hand, whatever people are filling forms for — an application for a license, an expense sheet, a medical background form — it has associated with it all the tensions of the activity that the form is the beginning of — the driving test, possible questions or disapproval of the expenses by the manager, the fear of what or what else the medical visit will reveal. Forms also have an association with paperwork that is for the benefit of someone else, not the person filling in the form, often a faceless and difficult bureaucracy. Forms have become associated with bureaucracies, not processes.

Forms affect one's sense of control. You are responding to someone's demand, and, yes, often it is a demand for particular pieces of information about yourself or your transactions. There is some authority figure — the boss, the doctor, the government — behind it. It is not a voluntary, friendly sharing of information. Of course, you are free to walk away from the process and not fill in the form.

Reveals the Organization

Forms are also edge points of not-so-transparent processes. This is obvious when one has selected or filled in the "wrong form." If it turns out that the form for out-of-state persons is Form 456 — not Form 123, then there was an implicit expectation that one understands that the way the processing is organized is that out-of-state persons are treated differently from in-state persons. It tells a lot about the organization. (This window into the internal, often administrative, organization revealing itself through edge items also happens on Web sites of large companies. If one sees the site divided into products and services, it is likely that the company is also organized with products and services as different departments.)

Forms Need Not Be Visual

Form design concepts are applicable to other channels. When one encounters "Press 1 for Billing, Press 2 for Technical Support" on the telephone, it is also a form. Obviously, some of the design principles are different but one is — through a mixture of audio and tactile (pressing keys) modes — filling in a form. It is as if one is filling in a form that says, "I want to talk to someone in Billing about my phone bill, my phone number is XXX-XX-XXX...." When a customer enters an office and selects a line to stand in, he or she is filling in a form: expressing an intention, making a choice, requesting a service.

> **❝** A man doesn't know what he knows until he knows what he
> doesn't know. **❞**

Figure 6.2 Thomas Carlyle.

Reveals Levels of Ignorance

Thomas Carlyle (Figure 6.2) said, "A man doesn't know what he knows until he knows what he doesn't know." The information systems that we design and build deliver "what we know." They rarely take the trouble of identifying what we do not know.

This omission makes our information systems incomplete — not only in some theoretical meta-information sense, but in their practical usefulness. By ignoring the information that is excluded, the reports that we generate from our systems, formal, well formatted, and correct as per some logic, remain incomplete in an informational sense. Although there may be valid reasons why some information is excluded, the most obvious being that it is not available, what is required, however, to satisfy Carlyle's dictum is that this exclusion or omission must be identified as such by the provider in a manner recognized by the consumer. The reader of the report must not only know what one *is* getting, but also what one *is not* getting. Take a look at the example below.

Managing Information

Reconciling Multiple Sources of Information

The first issue that comes to mind when one thinks of multiple sources of information is reconciliation. Attempts to reconcile data from two sources can be difficult. The problem is often at the metadata level. If one report shows the number of employees as 120 and the other as 118, then the difference is most probably in the definition of "employee" — it is possible that the latter does not count as employees those who are on extended leaves of absence. Data dictionaries and metadata repositories are attempts to tackle the problem at this level. Can we have one definition of employee throughout the company please?

Classification of Data

Companies have policies regarding the classification of data. This may be for security reasons, for retention reasons, to implement backup policies, and to support many other objectives. The classification and the action associated with the classification often are reasonable. If it is "Top Secret," one must do so and so. The problem seems to lie in recognizing the category of the data with which one is dealing. Making the rules for recognition more and more complex would lead to a self-defeating situation at some point as it starts getting ignored, simplified, or mostly subjective. One must consider the likelihood that the employees will choose the category that is safest or most convenient for them in terms of getting approvals or keeping things moving.

Classification is a judgment call. This means that any time data is classified as such, there must be some metadata about the classification itself — who did it, when they it, any reasons for selecting that classification, etc.

Classifications change over time. Classifications can also change if some minor adjustments are made to the data being retained. For example, the removal of a small piece of sensitive information — a particular table, a photograph, names of sources in an intelligence report — might allow a different classification. Such options also must be made part of the classification metadata for that document.

Systems of Record

Companies have multiple sources and stores of the same information. One of them is designated a "system of record" (SOR). What does this mean?

The most upstream source of information need not be the SOR. An SOR is information that the company classifies as the SOR. It could be processed, cleaned up, or enriched. It is the recognized proof point for the record of a transaction. If it does not exist in the SOR, then it did not happen. The SOR must be definitive and authoritative.

One must be careful to distinguish the need between a consistent source of information and an ultimate reference. The ultimate reference stands alone as the final authority. It is the official record. Others must be, one would assume, consistent with it. The SOR does not have to be consistent with the others.

Every database, although maintained to high degrees of accuracy and backed up regularly, is not an SOR. The legacy systems concept of a Master — Employee Master, Customer Master — appear to be likely candidates but they may not be so.

Considering the wide range of information handled by any company, there would be multiple SORs in a company. An SOR need not and cannot be a monolithic data store. The SOR can, of course, be an entire system. For many companies, its ERP (enterprise resource planning) system is its

SOR. The SOR need not be transaction based in the formal sense; it could be a system of record of eligibilities for a program, for example.

How unchangeable should SORs be? How long should data be retained? Do SORs have to be read-only? Can it be an SOR if data is being modified or dropped? These must be defined internally. For an SOR to have validity at a later date, access to it must itself be controlled and monitored with all modifications being recorded.

Changes must be made first to the SOR. That may not always be feasible. Local data stores may have more up-to-date information as they are closer to the edge or some aspect of the process.

And in the End, How Useful Is Information?

John Keegan, one of the best military historians of our day, in his book entitled *Intelligence in War*, comes to the conclusion that good intelligence has a limited effect on military outcomes. Similarly, information has a limited effect on the success of organizations. Information, by itself, cannot guarantee success or even its proper use without the proper management skills and the presence of other required resources and conditions needed for success. It is an important input but remains a secondary factor in management.

From the chapter entitled "The Value of Military Intelligence":

> "[I]ntelligence, however good is not necessarily the means to victory; that, ultimately, it is force, not fraud or forethought, that counts. That is not the currently fashionable view. Intelligence superiority, we are constantly told is the key to success in war, particularly the war against terrorism. It is indisputably the case that to make war without the guidance intelligence can give is to strike in the dark, to blunder about, launching blows that do not connect to the target or miss the target altogether. All that is true; without intelligence, armies and navies, as was so often the case before electricity, will simply not find each other, at least not in the short term. When and if they do, the better informed force will probably fight on the more advantageous terms. Yet having admitted the significance of the pre-vision intelligence provides, it still has to be recognized that opposed enemies, if they really seek battle, will succeed in finding each other and that, when they do, intelligence factors will rarely determine the outcome. Intelligence may be usually necessary but is not a sufficient condition of victory."

In an environment of information overload, this is a sobering thought.

Summary

Some users treat data and information as synonymous terms. It is better to treat only actionable data as information. Although there is a subjective element as to when data becomes actionable, the conversion often happens at system boundaries.

While information systems deal mostly with formal information, users deal with both formal and informal information in their decision making. Analysts must be cognizant of this. There is a cost associated with generating formal information. Data analysts need to help the customer make wise choices about what should be tracked. At the same time, they can help make information systems "complete" by identifying what is not known in any situation. Finally, it must be recognized that information has a limited effect on the success of organizations. Being in the information systems arena, this may be difficult to accept. Yet, information is only an important but secondary factor for management.

…how many stages has life? English Renaissance writers and painters took to the task of finding and enshrining an answer. Those who found three followed the authority of Aristotle, equating the stages of life with morning, midday, and evening. Four had a natural analog in temperate zones cultures, in the progression of the seasons from spring to winter. Five mirrored the number of acts in Shakespearean drama…

—**Tyler Volk**
Metapatterns

Chapter 7

Life Cycles

And one man in his time plays many parts,
His acts being seven ages.

—William Shakespeare

The concept of life cycles in the biological sciences defines "life" as an entity capable of eating, growing, transforming itself, and responding to external stimuli. The term "life cycle" has been borrowed by other fields and extended to "nonliving" systems, with the stress being on the cycle aspect of it rather than the life aspect.

In software, the "input–process–output" paradigm is the seminal life cycle of all information processing. Benington introduced the first concept of life cycles in software as early as 1956. The industry accepted the term after Royce introduced the waterfall life cycle in 1970. Since then, many categories of life cycles have evolved and are in use today — product life cycles, product development life cycles, "build" life cycles, software support life cycles. In fact, we have introduced a new field in "life-cycle management" — Product Life-cycle Management (PLM), Information Life-cycle Management (ILM), and the like.

Everything Sequential Is Not a Life Cycle

A life cycle is distinguished by three characteristics: (1) a unit developing in stages, (2) a process regulating the development, and (3) a transition between states moving the unit toward a predetermined goal. Although it may appear so, everything sequential is not necessarily a life cycle. The 18-hole golf course and the English alphabet set from "A" to "Z" are both sequential but they are not associated with a life cycle. For a sequence to be a life cycle, it must possess some of the distinguishing characteristics of a life cycle cited above. In our example, a golfers "game" over a period of time has the elements to be a considered a life cycle.

It may be noted that sequential should not be confused with a forward direction. Something can be sequential and yet take steps back, in a sequence. Similarly, the regulation mechanism in a life cycle may introduce conditional branching and feedback loops within the sequence of steps.

Coarse-Grained Process Models

Life cycle is a coarse grained process model. It allows one to get a good picture of the entire process but does not itself get lost in details. The details become (sub-)elements of the process. Boehm has given a good description of this concept in his introductory paper on Spiral Models in 1988. He says that a life cycle "addresses the following software project questions:

- What shall we do next?
- How long shall we continue to do it?"

He goes on to say that a life cycle differs from "a software method (often called a methodology) in that a method's primary focus is on how to navigate through each phase (determining data, control, or "uses" hierarchies; partitioning functions; allocating requirements) and how to represent phase products (structure charts; stimulus-response threads; state transition diagrams)."

A software product development life cycle can be explained as consisting of requirements analysis, an initial design, a proof-of-concept prototype, code development, QA (quality assurance), and delivery. Each of these steps can have sub-elements; for example, requirements analysis could include user surveys, feasibility studies, performance analysis, reverse-engineering, documentation, etc. Some of these sub-elements may be life cycles in their own right, if they possess the distinguishing characteristics of a life cycle.

Take the example of the QA life cycle:

1. Perform unit test
2. Log problems in bug tracking system Fix bugs
3. Perform system test
4. Log problems in bug tracking system Fix bugs
5. Develop regression test plan
6. Document known problems
7. Stress testing (if needed)
8. Preparation of capacity planning guide for HW/SW needs

Unit test life cycle or process:

1. Code, buddy/architect code review
2. Code meets documentation and unit test criteria
3. Module/integration test specifications reviewed
4. Review against specifications
5. Integration testing with automated test suite development
6. Follow SCM guidelines

Standard Software Life Cycles

The software (development) life cycle (SDLC) includes all those events that occur when producing a software product. Although life cycles have undergone a lot of change and evolved over a period of time, there are two fundamental SDLC approaches considered here: (1) waterfall and (2) iterative/incremental. Newer models such as RUP are also discussed briefly to set the background.

Waterfall

Proposed in the 1970s by Royce, the waterfall life cycle was used extensively until the 1990s.

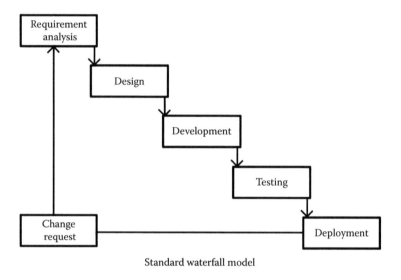

Standard waterfall model

Figure 7.1 The original waterfall model.

Standard Waterfall

The standard waterfall model (Figure 7.1) is divided into a set of non-overlapping, sequential phases that correspond to:

- Requirements analysis and specification
- Design
- Development and implementation
- Testing and quality control
- Integration and deployment
- (Optional) operation and maintenance

The waterfall approach works if there is complete, or almost complete, information at the beginning of the project, with little or no change during the development (of the project). There is no concept of going back between phases, something that happens all the time in practice.

Waterfall with Feedback

This model has the same phases as the standard waterfall but includes feedback between phases for the team to go back to a previous phase if a problem is encountered (Figure 7.2).

This model is still sequential. Although there is a feedback loop, it allows one to go back to an immediately earlier step only. The process

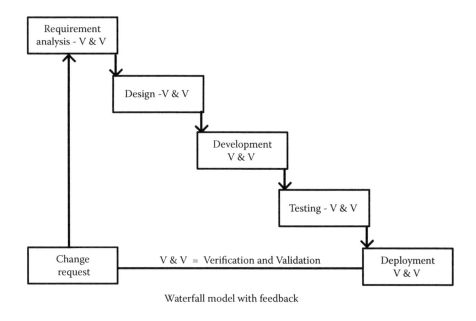

Waterfall model with feedback

Figure 7.2   The waterfall model evolves.

by itself does not help in avoiding, until late in the process, the discovery of defects that may take the project back many phases, and thereby force rework.

Iterative, Incremental

Most modern software development life cycles stress iteration throughout the process and add incremental functionality (Figure 7.3) within each iteration.

Spiral

In response to the deficiencies in the waterfall SDLC, Boehm defined this iterative life cycle — "spiral model" — of software development in 1988. This is the basis for most modern software development processes since then.

In the spiral model (Figure 7.4), the cycle starts with certain requirements. Projects risks, with respect to the requirements, are evaluated, and the implementation (development) of the product for that iteration begins. Once it is complete, customer feedback is obtained, and the next iteration is initiated. In this iteration, again, the highest risk items are addressed first. While the parts of this loop may change, the pattern of repetition and incremental delivery of product are repeated throughout the life cycle.

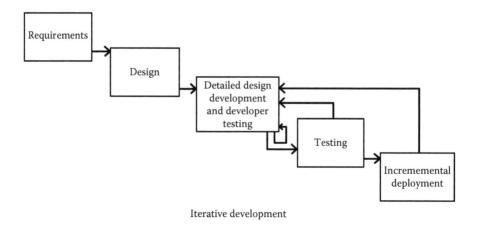

Iterative development

Figure 7.3   Incremental model.

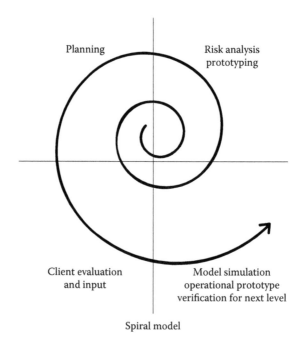

Spiral model

Figure 7.4   The spiral iteration.

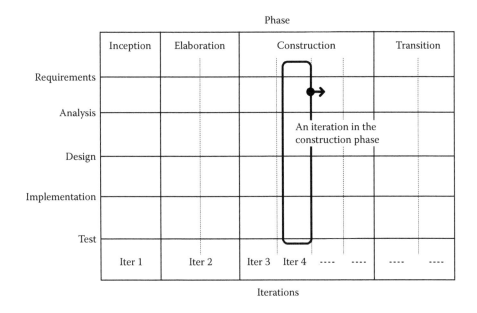

Figure 7.5   Rational Unified Process (RUP).

Rational Unified Process

The Rational Unified Process (RUP; Figure 7.5) is a commercial implementation of the Unified Process that was defined by Booch, Jacobson, and Rumbaugh in 1999. The main tenets of RUP have been defined by Kruchten as:

- Develop software iteratively.
- Manage requirements.
- Use component-based architectures.
- Visually model software.
- Continuously verify software quality.
- Control changes to software.

RUP describes the software development process along two dimensions.

Vertical Dimension: Disciplines or Workflows

The vertical dimension is a description of disciplines (classification of tasks) a software development team performs when implementing a software system. The main disciplines in RUP are:

- *Business modeling*: to understand the organization and the business in which the software will be used.
- *Requirements*: to understand the customer needs and analyze them to ensure that the right solution is developed.
- *Analysis and design*: to architect the system, design the components, build an object model, and define the solution specification.
- *Implementation*: to build the software programming code blocks that will realize the requirements.
- *Testing*: to ensure that the software is built according to the requirements.
- *Deployment*: to package, deliver, install, and train the customer to use the software.

There are other disciplines that are considered to perform a supporting role, such as configuration and change management, project management, environment, etc.

Horizontal Dimension: Phases

RUP defines four phases along a horizontal axis that is a temporal scale. Each phase is usually achieved through one or more iterations with software being produced (usually) at the end of each iteration.

The four phases are:

1. *Inception*: to determine what is to be created, for whom, and whether it is economically viable.
2. *Elaboration*: to address the key components of the system, identify various technical approaches, and assess the proper architecture.
3. *Construction*: to develop the system.
4. *Transition*: to deliver the system.

The end of each phase marks a milestone. This is a point in the development life cycle where one makes a decision whether or not to continue the project.

Using Life Cycle as a Model

A life-cycle approach is better suited to manage a relatively independent unit of work. Something that goes on forever, for example, running a nation, is not handled through life cycles.

A life cycle helps one figure out where one is. If in the requirements phase, whether it is a two-person-year project or a 200-person-year project, it says that one is in the early stages of the project. As in the human development life cycle, earlier stages require greater care and nurture than later ones. One should take extra time and effort with specifications and design before going on to the other stages. This is recognized in terms of rework costs, which are higher, particularly if a change must be made later. Uniform allocation of resources across all stages of a life cycle is neither required nor advisable.

Plans and Life Cycles Are Different

A life cycle is rarely detailed enough, which it should not be, to constitute a plan. Life cycles, however, can be used as a framework to develop better plans. If the life cycle is frozen *a priori*, it can define the starting granularity of a plan — requirements, design, development, etc. Each of these can then be treated as phases of the plan and expanded in more detail. A detailed plan may appear, at times, to be distorting the life cycle. For example, if the plan is based on the waterfall life cycle, some aspects of the testing, such as the development of a test plan, may be pulled ahead in the plan. Life cycles help in higher-level understanding of what is involved. Planning helps in working out the details. It brings into the life cycle an element of viability and realism.

To arrive at a proper plan requires one to select the appropriate life cycle. One of the reasons why plans fail is the "wrong" or poorly understood life cycle being used as the underlying framework. As they say in the military, "The map is not the territory." Similarly, in software, the plan is not the project — for that matter, the life cycle is not the project either. Life cycles and plans are models, abstract approximations that serve a purpose, but must not be confused with reality.

Planning Does Not Work in Firefighting Situations

Dwight Eisenhower said, "Plans are useless; planning is priceless." (*Source:* A speech to the National Defense Executive Reserve Conference in Washington, D.C., November 14, 1957.) While true in most situations, it hardly works in emergencies. There is a great difference because while planning for an emergency, you must start with the very definition of "emergency" — as it is unexpected, it will, in all probability, not happen the way you are planning.

Most IT and software support is about firefighting and heroics.

Choosing the Right Life Cycle

Even for similar activities, there may be different life cycles. The life cycle of automobile manufacturing in the United States is different from that in Japan because of the environment, availability of resources, and downstream activities of buying and selling cars. This should be expected.

It is an art to select a life cycle that will work in a particular environment. Sometimes the selected life cycle may need modification. For example, in some environments, QA (quality assurance) and code reviews may require additional resources. If offshore resources are being applied, there will be a need to add tasks to the life cycle to set up a distributed development environment. This may have to be added as a separate step before development begins in any conventional waterfall or spiral cycle.

Managers should be allowed to fine-tune a model to suit the needs of a project. Organizations that insist, in the name of standardization or process control, that only one methodology be used to manage projects do a disservice to the developers and managers.

Prototypes Are Important

The prototyping phase is perhaps the most important of all steps in the life cycle of a system development. A prototype is basically a working reproduction that best models the final system (Figure 7.6). There are different names for it: proof of concept, pilot, trial system, prototype, model, etc. There may be minor differences in the way these terms are used within organizations. It is best to ask for clarification when one encounters these terms.

A prototype can sometimes be expected to deliver too much: demonstrate the capabilities and potential of the final system to users, validate initial budget estimates for time and resources, evaluate risks and dependencies, plan alternative strategies, formulate procedures for full development, training, market delivery, and future evolution. Such anticipation may be fraught with risk. The reason is that a prototype cannot be expected to model the entire life cycle of the product. In fact, a prototype must choose a vector (such as functionality, or performance, or scalability) along which to compress. Automobile manufacturers run years of field trials on "concept cars" before a single production run. If one has that much time and budgeted investment, one also can do the same for one's software.

An acknowledged benefit of prototypes is that it helps senior decision makers get a feel for the final system, an experience that would be impossible to attain through a two-dimensional paper drawing or

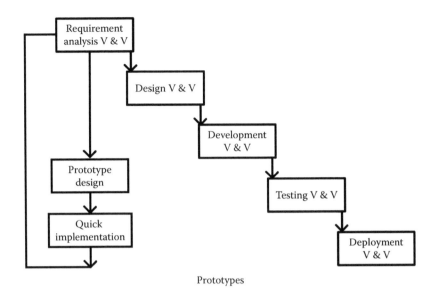

Figure 7.6   **Prototypes are important.**

chalk-talk. It may also help them choose among alternate designs. A possible side effect could be that if the prototype is seen as "too real," then one might walk away with the impression that most of the development work is completed and a little more work on the prototype will lead to delivery of the system. Building architects whose prototypes consist of physical scaled models do not carry such impressions or raise such expectations — the customer should not think that he can walk into the building soon.

Throwaway or Reusable Prototypes

Care must be taken to define the scope and intent of the prototype. Some prototypes may be created by simple configuration and customization changes to the original OTS (off-the-shelf) product. These are helpful in demonstrating the capability of the software in the context of the end users, instead of showing the vanilla OTS product with a lot of "we can build that for you" statements.

In your enthusiasm to cover all aspects of the final system, do not land up building it in entirety. As previously discussed, prototypes might be needed as a stage in the development life cycle of a new product, idea, or concept.

One could categorize them as "throwaway" or "reusable" prototypes. The difference comes from the approach one chooses in building them: horizontal or vertical slice. Throwaway prototypes are simple, quick, and (possibly) dirty implementations of a concept. They are used to give an overall feel of the final system, screen navigations, layouts, or the user experience. They can be discarded post demonstration, and development of the actual system will begin thereafter. Reusable prototypes, on the other hand, form the basis of the final system — in fact, its foundation in many respects. The idea is still to create a quick version of the system but something where most of the prototype code will be reused as building blocks. "Quick" in both cases is a relative word. It is not clear how much time should be employed in creating prototypes. There is a notion of percentages (similar to customizations) with respect to the time and resources needed to create the entire system.

Life-Cycle Phases

There are many software development life cycles and many programming practices in vogue. We believe that there is enough documentation regarding the benefits and shortcomings of each. The missing piece, however, is to determine how much weight should be given to each phase within the life cycle. How should one distributes one's time and resources in the most meaningful way, to get the maximum benefit? One way is through a cost-benefit analysis of the tasks one plans to undertake in a life-cycle phase.

To succeed, one should decide on the preset goals (not features) for each phase. It is imperative that the goals are clear and unambiguous. They should be specific for that phase, as well as to the point. For example, in QA one might start with a goal of "zero critical and serious defects in the system." The parameters on which one might do a cost-benefit analysis would be:

- Functionality that the customer believes is:
  - More important
  - More used
  - More visible
  - Has a bigger financial or safety impact

These parameters will help one narrow down one's goal and focus on areas of immediate importance.

Some Places in the Life Cycle Are Better Suited to Terminate a Project

If a project life cycle must be terminated prematurely (and perhaps restarted at a later date spearheaded by a different set of workers), are there points in the life cycle where it is better done, where there is least loss of work? One obvious conclusion is that any cutoff should occur at the logical end of a phase, rather than somewhere in between. Further, we believe that:

▪ User needs analysis
▪ Requirement specification
▪ Prototype
▪ Integration test

are the completion points that are better suited, and resource continuity after their completion is not critical. Note that we have tried to steer clear from any form of design, as a recommended place to break. This may be of significance in software more than in consumer product manufacturing where designs are usually created far from the manufacturing plants. So also with VLSI design and the actual chip fabrication. In software, however, the designer deals with soft issues of interpreting user specifications. Implicit calls are made about code structure, style, programming practices, organization tiers, and technology base throughout the process of design. In software, the designer outlines not only the "what," but also the "how" to a great extent.

Partial code blocks are also places where care should be taken while transitioning across teams. On the shop floor of a manufacturing company, one would not see workers transitioning their jobs, before finishing, to tighten the screw, or welding the joint completely. Unless coding styles and practices have been well documented and rigorously observed, following someone else's code is always difficult to understand and continue where they left off.

Software Shelf Life

How do built-in obsolescence (BIO) and planned obsolescence in various products affect a life cycle? Do they follow a different life cycle that takes these factors into consideration? Contrary to popular belief, the life cycle of such products does not differ much from those that do not take BIO into consideration. However, BIO is factored into the various phases of the life cycle. Automobile manufacturers introduced the notion of BIO in the early 1960s, by giving "model numbers" to their cars on the basis of the year of manufacture.

Software is released with version numbers. Manufacturers often force customers to upgrade their software to the latest version if they want continued support on their software. This software "replacement" strategy allows manufacturers to make technology and functionality considerations for a two- to three-year horizon, unlike "legacy" systems, which were created with a ten- to fifteen-year timeframe. It has become customary to give software patches, in the form of minor or major releases of the product. This can be done in software because the costs of replacements are low (in most software implementations — refer to Chapter 11 on migration). We could compare this with the enormous costs involved in cars being recalled for a seat-belt glitch or a tire problem.

Data Shelf Life

Related to BIO is the notion of data shelf life. One may be tempted to buy data storage devices that advertise lifetime guarantee of the data, or media that is guaranteed to last 25 years; but the reality is that it may not be possible to find a suitable data reader for the media after ten years. With falling hardware prices, and the ubiquitous use of the Internet and e-mail, data volumes in large and small organizations alike are increasing. Everyone seems to be dealing with terabytes of data now. In this situation, where do we store our data, and for how long? Some of it is answered by regulations and legislation that the industry follows. Beyond this, there is a need to provide guidance to the IT managers by defining best practices for the organization. Data should be kept for no longer than the desired purpose for which it was created.

Movies versus Software

Ever sit through the entire length of a movie, through the long list of credits at the end? Did you notice the granularity of the roles of the cast and crew? Crew, camera crew on location; editors, assistant editors, and continuity editors; different stunt coordinators for automobile wrecks and people; grips and 2nd grips — the list is unending. Is there something to learn from it and use in the software life cycle? We could do a better division of tasks than, for example, a manager, a technical leader, fifteen developers and six QA engineers.

Movies are announced three quarters (i.e., nine months) in advance. In fact, quite often, the previews of a movie end with the actual *date* of the release of a movie. In software, product organizations large or small are unable to disclose software release dates. We remain vague — "second half of next year" — to say the least. One reason could be that movie making has almost become a science, although software development is still an art. Furthermore, we should also have backups for our team players if we want to have a flawless (software) production. There are many roles in software that remain unrepresented, and we may just need to recognize the efforts of each and every person in the life cycle a little more.

Summary

The "input-process-output" paradigm is the seminal life cycle of all information processing. A life cycle is a coarse-grained process model. It allows one to get a good picture of the entire process but does not itself get lost in details. There are many software development life cycles. One needs to understand the benefits and shortcomings of each before using it. There is an art to selecting a life cycle that will work in a particular environment. A life cycle provides a good way to figure out where one is on one's way to completion. A life cycle is rarely detailed enough to constitute a plan. Understanding the life cycle is not a substitute for planning — yet planning without understanding the life cycle is not advisable either.

Planning requires an understanding of both life cycles and the processes involved at a more detailed level.

The goal of all civilization, all religious thought, and all that sort of thing is simply to have a good time. But man gets so solemn over the process that he forgets the end.

—**Don Marquis**

Chapter 8

The Semantics of Processes

> If you can't describe what you are doing as a process,
> you don't know what you're doing.

—W. Edwards Deming

There seems to be a process for everything: clinical trials, school admissions, impeaching presidents, and, of course, developing software. Such processes are closely linked to repeatability; they allow highly repeatable tasks to be performed with added efficiency. The emergence of the industrial age and the extensive use of machinery has a lot to do with the emergence of processes. There have always been methods, practices, and recipes, mostly used in one-off situations. When they needed to be automated, they had to be converted to a process. For example, the recipe for making a chocolate cake is good enough to make a cake at home. The same recipe must be converted into a manufacturing process to make hundreds of such cakes every hour. The recipe has not gone away — it still drives the "design" of the cake. The process is the implementation of that design. Software development processes also are attempts to capture the essence of software development, and make it repeatable, predictable, and scalable.

The word "process" has its roots in the 14th century Latin *prōcēdere*, meaning "to go forward." With its 17th century incarnation in English, "process" has now become "a set of operations done for achieving something." There is an important underlying notion of some "advancement" with respect to time. Process includes all that is involved, or that drives a transformation. It is a description of what is happening, at some level of detail, in terms of the changes taking place. Hovering around processes are similar sounding terms such as procedures, methodologies, best practices, checklists, etc. Some of these terms, such as "best practices," are recent, emerging out of management consulting domains. Another frequently encountered term is "procedure." Procedures are rules with expectations of compliance, and penalties if not followed. There is a degree of formality associated with procedures. For example, one needs procedures for conducting national elections — one does not need them for a casual hiking trip.

Because "process" is loosely defined, it has led to loose usage, especially when used as "business processes." For example, Thomas (1994) cites the case of one large bank, which estimated that it had three core processes, while another manager reckoned it had seventeen. In software too, we encounter "process" in many places. Information systems and computing are built on a simple model: input-process-output. COBOL programmers turned to it whenever they could not give a meaningful name to their piece of code: 1234-Process-Data came to the rescue. Programs in execution are also called processes. This chapter uses the term in the context of either business processes or processes related to software development.

Process and Entropy

The human body can be considered an almost perfect system: it behaves in a predictable manner, has seemingly innumerable processes that work in sync with each other, and constantly endeavors to be frugal in consuming resources. The laws of thermodynamics and entropy (a measure of the disorder in a system) explain most enzymatic processes in the human body — from diffusing oxygen into the blood, to the deterioration, decay, wear and tear, breakdown, and failure of cells in this perfect system. There is a lot to learn from a study of the processes within the human body and how that relates to the wax processes help maintain software systems.

Processes are built to bring order to chaos. Situations will tend to migrate a system from an ideal stable state of equilibrium to a state of chaos. This is common in software projects, as in other projects. Project management processes are used to restore equilibrium states. Multiple processes are required and are at play at any time: processes for escalation, communication, development, project management, testing, material acquisition, accounting, and others. All these processes are planned expenditures of energy to restore the system to equilibrium. If projects are failing in one's own organization, look at the processes at work — one may not have enough of them to begin with or not have the right ones for one's requirements.

Developing Good Processes

Most software companies do something well that makes them survive and thrive as a business. It can be safely assumed that underlying this success are good business and technical processes. These processes often are not captured and encapsulated formally. In fact, such smooth functioning may lead one to believe that one "does not need a process." However, one should look at it differently. If things are working well, there must be some good process, perhaps unidentified. Management must extract such processes and think of them as a valuable intellectual property, no less important than the technical processes used for manufacturing.

The converse of such an approach is also important. Some companies pick a process that might not have really worked too well in the past, and formalize it, just because they are familiar with it. Before concretizing (or automating) an existing method of working, one should review it for its soundness and applicability. One of the reasons why many software implementation projects fail is because existing manual processes are automated without such analysis. There is no value in simply investing in a bad process to make it go faster — it will still be a bad process. As Drucker (1986) says, "There is nothing more useless than to do efficiently that which shouldn't be done at all."

Understanding the Process Environment

There are a number of factors that one should consider when designing or selecting a process to use (Figure 8.1). These include:

- *The maturity level of the client organization.* Some organizations may not be ready to use certain processes because they require a degree of understanding and sophistication that the organization has not developed. For example, release processes defined for corporates such as Microsoft or SAP may not be suitable for start-ups.
- *The enforceability of the processes.* A process that is in place but is ignored by all sends the wrong message and undermines the

"Things always get better after they get worse.
So it's good to make things worse as quickly as possible."

Figure 8.1   The process environment.

case for processes in general. It is better to withdraw such processes. As an extension to this point, do not define a process for
the 20 percent of the team that will not follow it anyway.

■ *The complexity and criticality of the system being managed by the
processes.* There is a distinct difference between a process required
to select a new corporate CEO compared to the one to hire a
marketing intern for the summer.

■ *Project constraints related to schedules, resources, and quality
expectations.* Sometimes, the processes selected are overkill for a
project of that type.

Take Care of the Basics

A good process provides a predictable operating framework to take care
of the basics. This relieves one of the need to think and reinvent the steps
each time one embarks on a project. Coding standards, definition of IDEs
(integrated development environments) and toolsets, naming conventions,
and documentation styles or templates can be decided once, and followed
without further discussion at each stage of the development. Such processes allow one to focus one's energy on the creative and high-risk
aspects of the project.

Include Communication Mechanisms

Communication is the cornerstone of any good process. A good process
provides not just the mechanisms for this communication, but also

indicates the form, purpose, audience, and goal of that communication. For example, a process for Java development may recommend well-structured documentation within the source code, which can be extracted as a meaningful "Javadoc" later. Developers can relate to its need instead of feeling that they are generating "unnecessary paperwork." Processes must be sold internally.

Design Feedback and Improvement Mechanisms into the Process

No process can be perfect, especially the first time it is created. One must perfect it over a period of time. Always be open and actively solicit feedback about the effectiveness of a process. Remember that processes follow the same life cycle as a law in basic sciences. One starts with a hypothesis, and after much validation, formalizes a theory.

Keep Processes Simple

Having a process that is explainable and understandable is key. It is better than having a complex process that covers all aspects but is not understood by anybody. A well-known software design guideline is captured by the acronym "KISS," implying "Keep It Simple, Stupid." A process that is too complex is destined for failure. One should not add any tasks or activities to the process unless they are critically needed. Instead of trying to define steps for every condition that could possibly arise, one could have a "catch-all" step: for example, "For all other situations, please refer to the manager." In fact, like a beachcomber with a metal detector, do a periodic sweep of the processes to remove any legacy tasks that have no current significance.

It brings to mind the example of the purchase of a mainframe computer by a large organization, for which part of a building façade had to be destroycd to get the machine inside the building with the help of cranes. It was a one-off situation, although painful to all involved. Because of this one incident, it was stipulated that all IT (information technology) hardware acquisitions would need clearance from the building civil works department. This requirement remained in place for a long time — a major nuisance for people wanting to buy even a laptop. This is an example of a process that was introduced for apparently valid reasons but needs some serious beachcombing.

Build in Applicable Conditions

Processes are guidelines — not laws. Good processes should have some flexibility through "side" branches emanating from a main process, with members of the group empowered to take them if the situation demands. In the case of the example above, if the process requiring building inspector's clearance was required only based on the dimensions or weight of the acquired hardware, it would have been an improved process without burdening all those it does not affect.

Benefits of Processes

Process as Learning

The act of formally developing a process is sometimes its most useful aspect. For example, trying to develop a PERT (Program Evaluation Review Technique) chart for a project before beginning it has value even if the PERT chart is ignored later during project execution. In software development, one uses this concept implicitly in developing reusable code and modules. Developing a reusable piece of code requires one to think through many details carefully. Every piece of code that works is not reusable merely because it works. It is this thinking through the design, and future usage scenarios, that is probably as valuable as the actual benefits of reusing the code in other projects and products. This is the same idea in the proverb that it is better to teach someone how to fish than to provide him with fish.

Processes as a Growth Vehicle

One example where this is obvious is the concept of franchising. Franchising is one way some businesses grow. Franchising may have started in the 19th century through informal agreements, but modern-day franchising came into being with restaurants and fast food. It is now used as a growth strategy in manufacturing, wholesale, real estate, service, and retail businesses. Even the healthcare (hospitals, clinics), accounting, and education (schools, childcare) sectors have expanded in recent years with a lot of success. The number-one prerequisite for determining the suitability for franchising (marketing and financial need notwithstanding) is that the business and its working processes should be teachable. These systems and operating procedures should be packageable in a way that others are capable of replicating them. Only such modularity and replicability can ensure that a customer gets an identical experience with any franchisee — identical in everything from the marketing messages, to the look and feel, the actual "commodity," and the entire purchasing experience. If there are difficulties in articulating the processes that underlie the success of a business, the chances of success in franchising are greatly diminished. Software development environments that aim for reuse should study and use franchising as a model.

The same concept comes to the fore in outsourcing call centers, for example. The ability to outsource the call center is a result of the company's processes having reached a level of maturity where the steps involved can be identified and documented well enough to be understood by external vendors. Airline reservations is another area where this is very evident. Global systems such as Sabre, Galileo, and Amadeus can be designed because the ticketing and seat assignment processes are well known and similar across airlines. Because the processes are well laid out, these systems could be extended to travel agents so that they can print tickets and boarding passes for their customers. The same processes are now used for self-service on the Internet. Once processes are well formed, they can be moved around.

Learning as Input to Processes

Processes ensure exchange of information across teams and generations of teams. One's approach to a deliverable should not be limited to getting the deliverable working. It should include communicating what one has learned while building that artifact. The general assumption is that this knowledge is communicated through the documentation associated with the deliverable.

A better and more effective way of communicating what one has learned is through improving associated processes because the processes travel farther than documentation. Many software organizations miss this last step. The last step is not lessons learned, but rather processes improved. Organizations must work with an implicit assumption that processes will evolve and adapt as the situation needs. Goss et al. (1993) have argued that processes that undergo incremental improvement are not sufficient for most companies today because they do not need to change "what is"; rather, they need to create "what is not." Processes thus are also powerful agents of change.

Recognizing Processes

An important observation is that a process is not necessarily linear. There are many steps within each phase that overlap. Similarly, anything going forward is also not always a process. Which of these are examples of processes?

• A recipe
• Following directions to reach a place
• Time
• A checklist
• Flowing water
• An elevator going up
• Human growth
• The number system

Resistance to Processes

The term "process" often meets with unexpected resistance. It is as if developers and even managers are allergic to the term itself. This is probably because of its assumed association with restricting one's freedom and creativity. A process, especially someone else's process, is considered a tool of authority, used in constraining one's creativity and management style. The rational response is that the fear is justified because processes can be constraining. However, constraints can also be positive.

We have all done a good job in creating things under universal constraints (e.g., gravity). In fact, many feel that developing solutions under constraints is challenging and fun. Games are bound by rules; poetry and music have constraints of forms. Another good example of creativity under constraints can be found in growing trees. Espalier is a very old plant-growing technique. It involves careful training and pruning of the branches of a tree along a support — wall, fence, or trellis — to produce a two-dimensional tree. Espaliered plants are used in landscaping for both function and beauty. In an area where space is limited or where a plant is needed to decorate a large blank wall, espalier is most helpful.

True ingenuity comes from finding ways to exploit and overcome constraints (Figure 8.2). Espaliering is being used commercially for fruit trees, such as apple and pear trees. The technique allows more plants in the same space, enough sunlight for them, and tremendous ease of picking the fruit. Because the trees (the branches) are predominantly two-dimensional, pickers find it very easy to reach the fruit instead of having to constantly move ladders around the circumference of a usual tree.

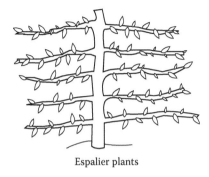

Espalier plants

Figure 8.2   Creativity under constraints.

Think about this when faced with the argument that the release management process in software is constraining. Getting the application into production differently for each developer is hardly a welcome scenario.

Processes Degenerate into Bureaucracies

There is a need for an efficient and formalized way of executing a project, especially when the team size is larger than four or five people. The downside of such formalization is the emergence of, in many situations, a bureaucracy. Not all bureaucracy is bad. A bureaucracy is a complex organization composed of nonelected professional administrators, marked by division of labor, hierarchy, rules and regulations, and impersonal relationships. It is rule driven, an after-effect of strenuous attempts to avoid corruption and misuse of powers. The problem with bureaucracy is due to the "fallacy of multiplication": each step of formalization can be individually justified, and therefore all formalization can be justified. They believe that if it is good to monitor a certain important aspect of a system, then they should monitor all of its aspects. Following the rule is no longer the means — it is an end in itself.

The reason why many are allergic to the term "process" is because some software companies tend to force all projects to follow certain processes, irrespective of whether doing so helps or hinders them. Such unthinking enforcement slows down the team and leads to a lack of confidence in processes in general, with many devoting their energies to work around them.

Do Processes Help?

It is an expected fact that software development depends heavily on the quality of the people involved. How much do processes help? There is some debate about the relative merits of processes versus people. Many are of the opinion that a good process is more important, that it can compensate for some lower quality on the part of developers. This is a real-world problem because it is likely that one's project has a mix of good, and not so good, people. The argument in favor of processes is that if an average developer follows a set of project guidelines (coding standards, naming conventions, use cases, and unit tests), and regular meetings are conducted to check the status and adherence of the process, then quality software is the likely output. There are, however, many followers of the opposing school who believe that processes are overrated in software and that there is no substitute for good people. Their contention is that there is nothing like a "good" process because no process can embody 100 percent of the project needs, or cater to all the risks.

Good people are good not just because they are experts in the business domain or that they have a good command over programming, but rather because they have internalized good processes that they have found to work most often for them (Figure 8.3). True professionals show a great deal of discipline (and patience) in following processes to handle mundane day-to-day stuff. They realize that 80 percent of most development will be around this — any carelessness here will only magnify as the process goes through its critical phases. Professionals see the intent behind the activities in a process. Even if they disagree with it, they can relate to why they are being asked to follow it. A big part of the problem is solved just because of this open attitude. If the process is really bad, they will give meaningful feedback to improve it, instead of rejecting or subverting it.

From a business point of view, it is critical to have a good process to guide the team because teams will have a mixed level of skills. It is difficult and expensive to staff the entire team with the best people available. It is more economically attractive to lower resource costs and have better processes. Keep in mind, however, that the processes must be good, because many in such teams will apply the process as is, without exercising further judgment. As discussed previously in the section on designing good processes, a good process has built into it ways to communicate objectives, goals, and desires to the people in question in terms of inputs, outputs, and transformations therein. From a management point of view, a process is good if it can make a positive difference in the performance of the entire team.

If forced to choose, we would recommend that you put your faith in the capabilities of people over processes. To believe that a process is

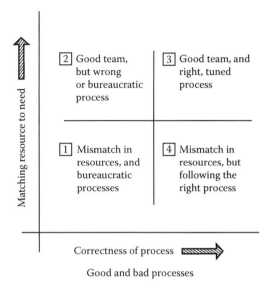

Figure 8.3   People and processes.

more important to the success of a project than the people who execute it is fraught with risk.

Introducing New Processes

The introduction of any new process is always viewed with skepticism. People start questioning what was wrong with the current process, or if their work should be monitored more closely, or if it will increase their paperwork. Why has OUR project been selected to use it? Some of the approaches to introducing new processes smoothly include:

- If the new improved process means a drastic change from the past, make it look like a "recommendation to follow" rather than "enforcement." People are opposed to change and will accordingly discover problems with the new process. A good process involves a lot to make it work. The process will need to be open enough to consider the unknown, and will need to be adjusted as lessons are learned. If one enforces a process, it will be difficult to change it periodically without making it look as if too many changes are being made. People may then reject it altogether.
- Introduce a pilot process in those areas of the organization where one believes people will follow them, even if these areas are not

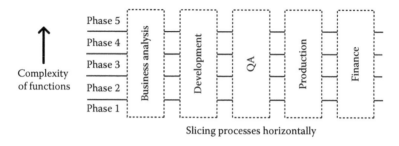

Figure 8.4 **Process rollout should be gradual.**

the most critical to the organization's success. Every success will add to the credibility of the process.

■ If people are difficult, use the sales broadcast channel WIIFM — "what's in it for me." Start by getting buy-in from the key people, by convincing them about the likely benefits of the changed process. One may even have to provide incentives to them to roll it out to their respective groups. This agreement and buy-in is very important for the success of any process — trivial or complex.

■ Slice the rollout of the process horizontally (Figure 8.4). Start with the simple changes and then get to the more complex and elaborate ones. People are prone to accept small deviations in their daily routine rather than entirely new starts.

Summary

The concept of process has emerged to allow us to perform highly repeatable tasks. We often define or select a process based on past experiences, sometimes institutionalizing processes that did not really work too well in the past. When things are working smoothly, management must look for the underlying process and see if it is replicable. Many, however, view such smooth functioning as a reason for "not needing a process." The introduction of any new process is always eyed with skepticism. When it comes to processes in general, resistance is natural. Processes are seen as stifling creativity, which, for badly designed processes, may be true although it is the act of developing a process that is sometimes its most useful aspect. There are a number of factors that should be taken into consideration when designing a good process.

Designers should keep in mind that processes interact with other processes and the environment around them. Designing a process in isolation can lead to failure.

When K'ang-tzu sent him some medicine he prostrated himself and accepted it; but said, As I am not acquainted with its properties, I cannot venture to taste it.

—*The Analects of Confucius,*
Translated and annotated by Arthur Waley

Chapter 9

Off-the-Shelf Software

A business is successful to the extent that it provides
a product or service that contributes to happiness in all of its
forms.

—Mihaly Csikszentmihalyi,
Noted researcher on creativity

There appears to be a software product for every business domain and
industry, so heralding the end of the era of bespoke development. However, such off-the-shelf (OTS) packages have not completely overtaken
custom in-house development. The economics are in favor of the OTS
product. Software is expensive to build — the fixed costs are very high,
and the development takes a lot of time and human resources. As long
as the needs are similar, spreading such costs across multiple organizations
should make a lot of sense to both sellers and buyers. We have seen
enterprise software implementations increase, especially among the larger
companies in the areas of manufacturing, finance, and human resources.
However, in many other areas of the organization, custom development
continues. Why is this so, even though there are so many OTS products
available? The following could be some reasons:

■ An available package may, in reality, be no better than a deliverable
from a small internal project within the company. Without some
initial commercial success and satisfactory early implementation

experience, vendors rarely find the opportunity to improve their products.

■ An off-the-shelf product needs an ecosystem for the "product" to become a "solution" for the customer. The ecosystem consists of integrators, sales and support channels, and also user communities and resource pools of people with experience in using the product. This ecosystem gets developed only with implementations. Naturally, if there are not enough implementations, the product has a weak ecosystem, which would not give any credit to the product.

■ It is difficult to develop affordable business applications for small and mid-market customers. The normal categories in which markets are divided — small, mid-market, and enterprise — can be misleading when it comes to creating or buying enterprise software. There is a core complexity that comes from the nature of the domain and does not diminish because the customer runs a small business. These are akin to setup costs in manufacturing, which often remain the same irrespective of the length of the production run. Taking another analogy, if one is throwing a party, one needs to clean the house irrespective of whether the guest list is four or forty people. Smaller companies do indeed handle fewer transactions, and code combinations, but still this will not reduce the design and development complexity for the vendor. That is, complexity does not automatically decrease because the customer is small or mid-market. Unfortunately, the affordability does go down with the size of the market, which creates a problem for both the buyer and the seller. This is one of the prominent reasons why many products targeting small business are unable to show good market penetration (except, maybe, for computing infrastructure or office automation-type, stand-alone applications).

The Involved Parties

Successful off-the-shelf (OTS) product implementations involve, invariably, three parties:

1. Vendor
2. Customer
3. Systems integrator

The partnership between the three is critical to any implementation's success. The vendor goes through the product creation and management activities to create a product that has a ready market and can stand competition. The customer, represented through its IT department, goes through technical evaluations and due diligence activities to pick the "right" product and make correct business decisions. The third player in the mix, the systems integrator (SI), is often the implementation consultant to help the customer in selecting the "right" product, as also does a gap analysis, build customization specifications, and then form the implementation team to begin the converting the product into a solution. Thus, all three bring different perspectives to the table.

Defining Off-the-Shelf Products

Look at the list below. Which of these would you consider an off-the-shelf product, and why?

■ House for sale
■ Land for sale
■ Furniture in IKEA that comes with "some assembly required"
■ Vacation package
■ Airline flights
■ Restaurant food, frozen food
■ Books, CDs, DVDs
■ Your DSL service package
■ A painting, museum

The definition or categorization of a product is not simple.

Buying Off-the-Shelf Software

If a "good" OTS product can be found, there are many advantages to using it over an in-house development. Let us compare buying an OTS software product to buying a preconstructed house (rather than getting it built). The advantages of a ready-made house include:

■ The house is most probably well designed and incorporates advanced thinking in architecture and living design.

- You can see and experience what you are getting (WYSIWYG), instead of hoping that your two-dimensional designs will turn out to be your dream home.
- The house is designed by professionals who probably know more about building codes and regulations than you do.
- In all likelihood, the house has been constructed by a team of engineers better than a team that you could assemble or manage.
- It takes less time to move into a built house.

The analogy can only be carried so far. There are critical differences between buying a house and buying software. In a house, a person can see most things that will affect them in their daily interactions with it — the rooms, the electrical fittings, the kitchen installations, the landscaping, etc. Most artifacts may be physically visible or accessible; others, such as wiring and plumbing, may not be visible but there are codes and certificates that reassure them that they meet basic quality and design guidelines. In an OTS product, on the other hand, there is a lot that is hidden or access to which is restricted. Such things are difficult to evaluate for most end users. A certified inspection regimen hardly exists, and regulation is primarily left to market forces. Consulting firms with years of domain expertise are frequently called in to help. One cannot assume that consultants are neutral. Some are in the business as business partners of the OTS vendors and are likely to favor specific offerings. For software, the unknowns at the time of purchase can be unreasonably large as compared to the purchase of a house.

This lack of transparency can be addressed to some extent by having a better acquisition process, more detailed RFPs (Request for Proposals), selection committees, service agreements, satisfaction warranties, etc., but it cannot be eliminated. In situations where this information-gathering or risk-reduction process itself goes out of control, which might be a leading indicator of a difficult implementation ahead, there might be a temptation to skip the OTS path itself and try to build one's own system. This may turn out to be a more painful alternative for many.

How far or close should managers be to the vendor?

Troy Anderson, in his book entitled *The Way of Go*, describes the concept of *ma-ai* in *aikido*:

"Its literal translation is space-harmonious... there were advantages and disadvantages to being in close and being far away... Too close in to the opponent and certain techniques don't work. A spear is not the best weapon to use in battle at very short range... Too far from the opponent and it is too difficult to say that your position has an effect. *Ma-ai* is the right distance from the opponent for attacking or defending."

Such thinking has relevance in business strategies, especially when it comes to vendors, as well as partners and competitors. One wants to maintain the right distance.

Preparing to Buy

When getting ready to buy OTS products, consider the following:

- Separate wants and needs. Divide requirements into Essential and Nice-to-Have. Also, qualify Essentials – essential for what?
- Avoid requirements that are vague; you may get a bad fit. Ensure that your requirements have the required *variety*. (We use variety as defined by Ashby and discussed in Chapter 2).
- Gather requirements from a cross section of users. The success of the implementation will depend on the users' ability to use it in their environment.
- However, do not drive the acquisition only through *your* requirements. It may prevent you from looking into features within the package that could be useful if you knew what they were or how they could be used.
- Remember that success depends not only on the base product, but also on its implementation. Neither one will stand alone.
- Expect resistance to change, especially when users are comfortable with the systems they are currently using (Figure 9.1).

Also consider who within the vendor's organization knows these OTS products. The candidates include:

- *The engineers who built the products.* They each know certain aspects: the internals, the APIs (application programming interfaces), the scaffolding, and the "piping." For a complex product, only a few may know the entire piping anyway.

"Whenever we upgrade our software, I see an
increase in productivity. Everyone finds something
to do so they don't have to deal with the new software."

Figure 9.1 Impact of a new introduction.

- *The architects and designers.* They concentrate on the formal base product, the underlying technology frameworks, and the customization tools, but few of them step over to the user side and use it.
- *Professional services and consultants.* Yes, they see the various customizations (dialects) and more ground-level reality but can still be surprised by the way the base product behaves.
- *Other players.* Other players, such as sales and support personnel, who, at best, have some partial views of the product.

It should not be surprising that, as a customer, you may sometimes have felt that the parties you deal with — sales, support, or professional services — do not know the product as well as you would have expected. It is difficult for them too.

Reducing Risk of Failure

As a customer, one probably understands one's existing system better than the vendor from whom one is planning to buy the software. Good ways to improve the fit and reduce risks include:

- *Identify key features that a package must support (along with the key functionalities that it should have).* These features could be support for some old hardware terminals, legacy software, data export requirements, etc. Do not look at business functionality alone. Sometimes, interfaces to such nontechnical infrastructure are showstoppers.

■ *Understand the implementation life cycle and the risk matrix.* For example, data migration is an important aspect of bringing in a new package, the complexity of which is often underestimated.

■ *Develop informal sources of information.* They can provide valuable input. Have your technical staff talk to their peer network who might have worked on such packages. Talk to reference customers who have used the OTS product in environments similar to yours. Talk to interview candidates whom you may be planning to hire for such projects; interviews are a good way to obtain information.

■ *Having trial runs is not simple, as most packages require some customization and considerable configuration; however, do not rule out the pilot (proof-of-concept) project — there is much to learn when you see it working in your environment with your data.* However, it is important to dedicate the right resources and time for such trials. If going for a pilot, do it right. If it is done for namesake only, serious impedance mismatches may be discovered after purchase.

■ *Avoid checklist-based requirements.* You are buying a solution, not a list of features. Checklists come up against the understandable reluctance of vendors to say no to any of your requirements as long as there is some wiggle room. Both you and the vendor could mean perfectly different things for the same requirement. The solution is not to go on being more detailed until every last nuance is nailed down, but rather to look for signs of evasiveness in the answers from the vendor and to demand clarity.

■ *Similarly, avoid checklist-based prioritization of the list of features* (Figure 9.2). Prioritizing vaguely worded requirements can be a recipe for disaster.

■ *Be aware of the constraints in your organization's environment.* Things that the OTS vendor may be taking for granted may be unheard of by you. They could be related to hardware or software infrastructure, networking bandwidths, user skill sets, or even climatic conditions. Most implementations of perfectly sound OTS software fail because certain key constraints are discovered too late in the delivery life cycle.

■ *Do not assume that the vendors have the required experience in implementing their own product.* They may know it better at an internal engineering level but the implementations could have been left to outside certified consultants.

Checklists

Figure 9.2 Checklists are not always good.

- *Avoid asking for things you do not need straight away or presume their need in the distant future*, for you might be rejecting a perfectly acceptable product.

There are other high-level factors to consider, including the culture of the vendor and the metaphor for selecting the OTS product.

The Culture of the Vendor

Think of OTS products as cultures, not in the sense that SAP® is a German product and Siebel® is an American product, but in the sense that the product is the outcome of a particular company culture. In any company where things are done in certain ways — some acceptable, some not — certain value (design) systems are adhered to, which in fact point to a deep-rooted behavior pattern. The product that one is purchasing is a product of some design and development culture. For example, one might be baffled by the way the same functionality is implemented in different products, or the way it differs from how one would have done it. Screen navigations, default values and processes, menus, toolbars and short keys, terminology, error messages, and data and tool interfaces can all be different, driven by the varying design cultures behind them.

Another reason why it is important to try to understand the vendor's culture is because it affects one's future relationship with the vendor. Some (vendors) believe in slower release cycles, ensuring that they take their time to introduce new functionality reliably. While working with such vendors, one needs to adjust one's expectations accordingly. On the other hand, one may be dealing with a company that puts out software versions frequently, and cleans them up as one goes along. In that case, one needs to recognize it and give it due importance.

Metaphor for Selecting an OTS Product

Select the right metaphor for implementation of enterprise software, which is often one of the strategic IT undertakings for many organizations — it can be a long and arduous journey. The metaphor we recommend is that of learning a new language. For the company, implementing a new OTS product is like learning a new language — albeit these are languages with non-natural language names such as SAP® and Siebel®. They have grammars and lexicon familiar to few, yet they must be learned consciously by an organization.

Now consider how one gets to learn a language. There is the formal element, the informal element, and the practical element. For example, one needs to know the formal syntax, query elements, nomenclature, and data elements used in the OTS product. These are best gathered through classroom sessions with an experienced trainer. It would be inefficient to try to understand these concepts only by "playing around" with the product. On the other hand, there is hardly any substitute for using the software in practical situations, to learn aspects that cannot be learned in the classroom. Most end users who have used an OTS product over a period of time can tell you of very practical and ingenious ways of doing things with the product.

The Dependency Factor

A frequent and normal fear while choosing an off-the-shelf package is that it makes one "dependent" on the vendor, possibly "forever" (i.e., lock-in). This fear is understandable. It is one good reason why products must be selected carefully, after looking at factors beyond functionality and price.

From where does this dependency arise? How is it different from a dependency on some other technology? After all, if one has developed a system in COBOL or Java, one is dependent on that. How different is it from, say, selecting a "corporate" database such as Oracle? In discussing dependency, one often mixes business and technology dependencies.

The business dependencies include economic factors; once one is "locked in" to a package, the vendor can raise prices. Exit can be painful, expensive, and risky, especially after one has captured a number of business rules in the package. To be fair, this exit barrier could be equally bad in an in-house development, in case the business rules are scattered, undocumented, and cryptic. There is still another business angle, especially in enterprise management software. The introduction of a particular product within the company introduces a strong gradient to use that product in other areas within the company even where it may not offer the best value. If one buys a product for its Finance and HR modules, one is under pressure to use its CRM (customer relationship management) modules because "data is integrated," the customization tools are familiar, the user experience is understood, etc. Under this argument, one ends up losing the right to go with the "best-of-breed" for different areas.

The technology dependency is clearer. One gets the technology that the vendor provides. If the vendor moves to a "better" technology and offers future upgrades, one must shift to that technology, even if one has some reservations about bringing that technology into one's company. If, however, the vendor does not move to the better technology in the timescale one would like them to, then one is constrained — one is a partner in a three-legged race.

Both selling and buying in organizations are semirational, technopolitical processes. The probability of making a good purchase depends on how well one knows what one wants, what is available on the market, what has worked in the past, etc. The best results do not come only from checklists and impersonal vendor evaluations.

To reap the benefits of an OTS implementation, the organization needs to learn aspects of the system, as they unfold, in daily usage. Many good OTS products have been dismissed prematurely because users often lack the patience and perseverance to invest the time and effort expected. This may seem like an unfair charge to those who have seen implementations go way over schedule and budget but all we would like to impress is that, even in a well-controlled environment, a certain time period is required for an OTS product to show its power and benefits. Learning to live with OTS products, and learning how to make good use of them, are essential in today's IT world.

Summary

Build-versus-buy decisions, especially related to enterprise applications and technologies, are strategic decisions that IT departments must take and live with for years. There are many advantages to buying off-the-shelf products as compared to building them, and the trend is toward using off-the-shelf products wherever good ones are available. Many factors go into selecting the products; an important one that should be taken into consideration is the ecosystem that exists around off-the-shelf products that have been on the market for some time. Avoid checklist-based requirements; they come up against the understandable reluctance of vendors to say no to any of your checklist items as long as there is some wiggle room.

Off-the-shelf products may require extensive customization before use; many product implementations have failed because there is a core complexity that comes from the nature of the domain that is often underestimated, especially by small and mid-market companies. Successful implementations involve, invariably, three parties in the ecosystem: (1) the vendor, (2) the customer, and (3) the systems integrator.

With off-the-shelf packages, there is the fear of lock-in. It is the reason why products must be selected carefully, after looking at factors beyond functionality and price, trying to work with what is called the total cost of ownership (TCO).

Most off-the-shelf products, especially at the enterprise level, require some degree of customization. Failure to properly customize them leads to unsuccessful implementations and unhappy customers.

There is nothing like returning to a place that remains unchanged to find the ways in which you yourself have altered.

—**Nelson Mandela,**
A Long Walk to Freedom

Chapter 10

Customization

You must be the change you wish to see in the world.

—Mahatma Gandhi

Customers have been moving toward nonproprietary shared solutions for quite some time. This trend is primarily due to increasing costs and the realization that there is "no economic benefit to having proprietary applications," as Professor Nicholas G. Carr, a former executive editor of the *Harvard Business Review*, says. In many business areas, applications exist that, with proper customization, can be made to work effectively and efficiently for any organization. This chapter focuses on customization and the customized approach to application development and implementation.

Customization refers to incorporating changes in the software that is already available as a product. While it may be true that only a few products offer genuine customization, many products allow some configuration, enhancement, or personalization — features that are useful and, at times, sufficient for the customer to get an improved fit to their environment. Often, the differences between customization and configuration appear to be a matter of degree. Remember that the scale, issues, and opportunities provided by a customized solution can rarely be achieved through configuration alone.

Customization is the ability to make *substantial* modifications to *pre-created* software *without access to the original source code* using the *customization tools* provided with the product.

Four important differentiators are:

1. Customization works off pre-created software. This software is, in most cases, off-the-shelf software, although it could be home-grown too. Home-grown packages are less likely to build the customization tools necessary to customize the application, only because the source code is under the organization's control.
2. Formal customization tools must be provided as part of the product.
3. Such tools must allow the customer to make substantial modifications, which will differentiate customization from "mere configuration."
4. Customization does not need access to source code. Home-grown applications can also be architected with the same rigor and quality of good products. Yet, if the changes are being made directly to the source, then that must be called enhancement rather than customization.

Customization versus Enhancements

In the authors' opinion, customization should refer to the first major modification in an off-the-shelf (OTS) product. Subsequent modifications to a customized package, however substantial or significant, should be called enhancement. This avoids being in a stage of endless or continuous customization. The reasoning behind this is that, once one has acquired an OTS package and made an initial set of modifications to suit one's needs, this package has become *one's* package because it now reflects one's needs and environments. Subsequent changes should be called enhancements — and not customization, which tends to indicate an "outside" base from which one has moved away.

Such shifts in terminology also appear in other domains. A writer who keeps editing what he has written is still "writing" as long as he is in the creative phase. After he sends the manuscript to a publisher and starts incorporating the feedback, he is "editing" not "writing," although this editing may share a lot with the "writing" done earlier. The formal act of sending the book to the publisher establishes a boundary for the terminology change.

Customization and Configuration

The difference between *configuration* and *customization* is one of degree. Configuration "tweaks a few knobs" and changes some settings to get the software to do what one wants. Customization, on the other hand, consists of more full-fledged changes that are difficult to reverse and invariably address substantial functionality.

Take a look at a word processor. If one were to change a font for a particular document, one would not call it configuration because it applies only to that document and does not apply across the installation. However, if one were to select a default font during installation of one's word processor, one would call it configuration. In either situation, one would *not* call it customization.

A user may get features that he or she wants through customization or configuration. Generally, configuration is cheaper than customization because it does not involve the use of tools or expensive development resources. For example, MyYahoo provides personalization through configuration, not customization. The user is limited to the options that Yahoo permits for a MyYahoo page. Some products, however, might go with the smallest set, offering some configuration but no customization. The issue of configuration versus customization looms larger in shared or managed application environments. There, the costs of supporting multiple customized instances of the product can be very expensive compared to supporting a table-driven, user-specific, multiple-configuration environment.

Would you call these customization or configuration?

- Changing the reclining angle of your seat's back
- Replacing the fabric of the chair
- Hanging a new painting on the wall
- Repainting the wall
- Adding a new field to a screen
- Moving a field around on the screen
- Replacing the speakers in your car with better ones
- Setting tuner pre-selects on your radio
- Setting up account codes in a GL (general ledger) package

Customization and Ground-Up Creation

Customization differs from ground-up creation in many ways. During customization, one is working off somebody else's body of creative work.

One is expected to build on that base. Working with someone else's less-than-transparent creation with the intention of modifying it can make one feel that one's hands are tied or that one is working in the dark.

Customization follows an authorization to make changes given to you (the customer) by the product designer. The nature and scope of changes that are allowed to be made are part of the product design. You, as a customer, can control customization's content but not its larger scope. You must operate within the playing field according to the rules set by the designer. This scope, however, may change over time as the base product evolves. Things that would have had to be customized in an earlier version may become part of the base product in future releases.

A question that often arises is: what is a "good" percentage for the degree of customization required? That is, what should the ratio be between what is in the box and what needs to be customized? The customer would like to get as much as possible out of the box. Vendors would like to suggest that the customization needs are minimal. There is an argument that if the percentage of customization required is too high, buyers will consider developing the application themselves. The talk of percentages is a red herring. The very nature of business precludes such generically applicable ratios even for highly structured domains such as accounting. Each product has a different degree of effort, expense, and benefits associated with it. Before one starts quantifying the efforts, expenses, and benefits, one must decide on the customization objectives, for example, saving time, avoiding effort, ensuring quality, bringing in new technology, etc.

Customization Requirements

Customization requirements (Figure 10.1) are fundamentally delta requirements. This delta is between what the package provides and what you require. Determining both is difficult. If one knows what one requires, then determining what the package provides may not be easy, especially in a pre-sale mode. Ironically, at times, knowing what one requires also can be the problem.

What are delta requirements? In one sense, all requirements are delta requirements. When developing an application from scratch, the delta is between what exists (nothing, something manual, or another package) and where you want to be. When you are customizing an OTS package, the delta is between what the package provides and what you want.

As in any purchase or sale transaction, both being two sides of the same coin, there is necessarily an unequal distribution of information about either side. The vendor knows the product but not the customer's

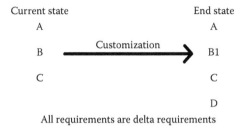

Figure 10.1   Customization requirements.

detailed requirements. The customer knows the requirements but not the product. Each tries to reduce the risk associated with dealing in an environment of imperfect information. The buyer can reduce his or her risk by engaging an expert consultant who is an expert on the OTS product. The seller can improve his case by getting the buyer to invest in drawing clear requirements. Hopefully, this improves the situation. There could be other approaches. The buyer might take an opportunistic approach and allow the features in the package to drive the requirements. This, at times, makes a lot of economic sense. For certain organizations, it may be cheaper to change their business processes to fit the package rather than fit the package to their environment. It may not only be cheaper, but also it may turn out better, especially if the business processes in themselves are not the "best practices."

Customization Facilities

Customization facilities vary from package to package and go from very basic facilities to advanced development and integration environments. Some products provide such powerful customization facilities that users, for all practical purposes, can ignore the base product and create applications that are far removed from the domain. For example, one can build an Event Management module using customization tools that came with a CRM (customer relationship management) package, incorporating new screens, reports, and business logic. In such cases, the base product is being used as a development environment. Such customization poses less of a problem for the customer because future versions of the base product would, if backward compatible, protect earlier customizations. They could pose more problems for vendors, in case major structural revisions are made where such off-domain customization may not be part of the new design. Furthermore, the vendor could run into opposition if, due to acquisitions or mergers, they want to replace installations of Product A with a similar Product B (e.g., replace one CRM package with another). The vendor's obligation is to protect the base product or domain functionality and its related customization while the customer also wants to protect the off-domain customizations.Areas of Customization: An Example

---

Areas of customization vary from product to product.

For a CRM product, these could be:

- Product definition — product information to be captured, complex product trees, product bundles, dependencies, prerequisites, configuration, up-sell, cross-sell, etc.
- Marketing — business rules, fulfillment methods, lists, etc.
- Promotions and campaigns — nature of, targets, channels used, etc.
- Quotes — one's creation and approval processes, templates, rules, etc.
- Order capture — sequencing, complex scripting, order-level discounts, jeopardy determination, back-orders, order qualification, etc.
- Order management — decomposition, multiple suppliers, dependencies, etc.
- Workflows — to match one's company's workflows
- Delivery and fulfillment information — specific to one's product and service, returns, etc.
- Customer service — registration, warranties, eligibility, customer configuration, etc.
- Customer profiles — the information about the customer that one would like to record
- Industry-specific regulations, terminologies, etc.
- Reporting — one's specific reporting and analytic needs, etc.
- User interface changes, etc.
- Integration with other in-house applications, etc.
- Data model related, etc.
- Data loading related, etc.

■ Partner management and programs, etc.

Handling Upgrades to Customization

Always keep in mind that the more one moves away from the base product through customization and enhancements, the more careful one must be about handling upgrades. While backward compatibility is possibly assured at the base product level, one's customizations need not be assured. Certain efforts might therefore be required to get the existing customizations back on track. Things that can go wrong include:

■ Screens that do not work after upgrade (e.g., XML/XSL transformations used earlier) may be replaced by components embedded in the browser container
■ Obsolete APIs that require replacement with new APIs
■ Data model changes (e.g., primary keys may change) attributes and internal representation of objects
■ Support for certain third-party tools may get dropped

A variation of the upgrade problem could be where one might have added functionality to a particular version of the product, that gets subsumed in the future release of the product (becomes part of the base product in the new release). How is this best handled? What can one do today if one thinks that the functionality being handled today may be part of the product tomorrow? Such functionality should be created in a loosely coupled fashion so that it can be replaced without too much trouble. For example, if one needs a warranty details screen, because there is no such screen in the original product, it should be implemented with minimal changes to the data model, perhaps through the use of temporary tables. In case the future release of the product already incorporates an acceptable warranty feature, one's screen and database changes can be retired easily.

Why Customization Projects Fail

Customization projects, both large and small, have not had a good track record of success. The larger ERP (enterprise resource planning) customizations have many times run into considerable cost and schedule overruns. Smaller companies trying to implement customize products have often underestimated the efforts required and have encountered serious customization limitations in small to mid-market packages.

Customization projects fail for many reasons, including:

- The delta requirements are not well understood:
    - This can happen because either or both sides of the equation — one's requirements or the baseline functionality — is wrongly assessed.
- Customization turns out to be more difficult than envisaged:
    - Sometimes the base product is complex and companies begin trying to customize it without an adequate investment in understanding it, thus leading to considerable rework.
    - Sometimes the customization facilities are just inadequate to get to the required end state.
- The base product has a fundamental incompatibility with your requirements in terms of the data model or the business logic employed:
    - This could be because one's requirements require a sophistication that does not exist in the product and cannot be added by the tools.
    - The product, although intended for your industry, is too generic.
- There are limitations to the customization allowed:
    - There may be limits to the amount of customization that you can do (e.g., the number of new screens or fields you can add, etc.).
- There are performance problems due to heavy customization.
- Management of the customization project does not use a model that is appropriate for such purpose.
- And all the other reasons why software projects fail.

The objective of any implementation is to solve a business problem. By buying a package that at the very outset was a bad fit, many projects are reduced to "getting the package to work," at massive cost to the company. Managerial egos and reputations can get involved. It would be a good idea to recognize that this is a likely development and constitutes "external" bodies to periodically review the situation.

Dominance of the Customization Model

As good OTS products emerge in many functional domains, it is likely that custom development by IT will be restricted to niche areas where such products are not available. It is a harbinger for change in the way skills are distributed within the industry's major players — product companies, consulting companies, IT departments, outsourcing companies, and others. Hard-core development would grow within product companies and reduce within IT departments. When that happens, IT departments would be staffed with delta developers and managers dealing with customization, enhancements, and support. The entire implementation stack will be rarely understood or controlled by one party. This is a natural progression toward specialization and shared environments.

Need for a Customization Framework

As more projects become customization projects, one needs a framework for describing customization itself. One needs a meta-definition of customization that allows one to model and define the customization abilities of a product. This would help with the comparison between the customization features of various products and allow for more effective sharing of customization technology and processes across products and projects.

Project management needs to work off customization life cycles, which are different from those for ground-up development life cycles.

The staffing requirements for customization projects can be different. Knowledge of the product being customized is important but it does not provide the entire picture. Depending on what one is shooting for, one may need to think as a product designer, trying to understand the constraints and choices faced by the base product architects and designers, if only to figure out where the pitfalls likely are. Sometimes, customization projects could also be migration projects in the sense that one is undertaking a customization project to migrate away from a legacy system. In such cases, the customization project staffing requirements overlap with migration project staffing requirements; in such cases, knowledge of the legacy system would be an asset.

Pros and Cons of Customization

Some dissatisfaction is inherent in a customization project. This often comes from the fact that one is dealing with somebody else's thinking and design. It also stems from the fact that when one builds one's own business application, some of the benefits actually come from the process of creating the system: that is, the process of discussion and debate that goes into designing the system can be very useful. Eliminating this exploratory phase removes an important experiential aspect of the entire project. It could also be argued that this experience is not totally lost as it does occur during customization, although it manifests itself in a slightly different (delta) manner, with different objectives.

Customization and Management

Management needs to recognize the implications and consequences of taking the customization route. It is incumbent upon management not to forget why they went in for the customized OTS product approach to begin with — to save time or money, and to compensate for the lack of internal resources. It is also important to remember that auxiliary commitments might have been made (e.g., business processes) to accommodate the new product.

Summary

Of the many products out there, only a few offer genuine customization although many products allow some configuration. The difference between configuration and customization appears to be one of degree. If configuration can meet one's needs, that is preferred because customization tends to be expensive. If it cannot, then either you, as the customer, must modify your business processes to fit the product or the product must be modified to fit your needs.

Customization facilities vary from package to package, and go from very basic facilities to advanced development and integration environments. Avoid using the customization facilities to create applications that are far removed from the domain of the base package. A customized implementation requires care in handling upgrades.

Customization projects fail for many reasons, including a poor understanding of the delta between what is available and what is required; inadequate knowledge of the base product, due to attempts to customize the product for situations beyond what would be normal use of the base product; and, many a time, due to performance issues arising out of heavy customization.

I have just one question: do we have to go through
the swamp again?

—From the movie "The Land Before Time X:
The Great Longneck Migration," 2003

Chapter 11

Migration

… an old system must ever have two advantages over a new one; it is established and it is understood.

—C.C. Colton,
English cleric, writer, and collector

From a management point of view, a migration project involves spending money to go from Point A to Point A. For example, one has had an Accounts Receivable system on the mainframe and now one will have an Account Receivable system running on an alternate operating system and database. What exactly has the business gained? This is important because many IT (information technology) projects that get funded are maintenance or migration projects, and such projects can be expensive.

Migration brings to mind the annual movement of birds from cooler locales to warmer lands, or salmon jumping upstream, or turtles rushing on shore — a natural, seasonal, programmed routine. If there are similar patterns to the migration in the software world, they are driven by major technological climactic changes, which happen once in a while. In the past few decades, examples of some of these changes include the move from mainframes to client/server, the Y2K migrations to packaged enterprise software, or the move to Web technologies.

It would be a fair statement that migration is about change, but not fundamental change. It is like old wine in new bottles.

181

Exactly the Same?

A manager or other decision maker considering embarking on an applications migration effort should remember one very important rule:

a realistic goal of the migration process is functional equivalents not 100% emulation

—From *Systems Migration*, Alan R. Simon

What Triggers a Migration?

Migration projects are triggered within IT departments due to a number of reasons, including:

- The existing application is creaking and has reached a natural limit, perhaps to the volume of data it can handle or the number of users it can support. This new requirement itself may be triggered by business growth scenarios, planned or unplanned.
- There is a need to move to more current technologies to provide features seen as essential from a competitive or customer expectation point of view.
- New standards or regulations have emerged within the company or the industry, requiring one to change.
- One is trying to bring something subcontracted outside into the company.
- One is trying to take something running inside to an outside vendor who wants to support it using a different technology.
- Mergers, which force one application to migrate to "another" technology.
- One is moving from an off-the-shelf (OTS) application to an in-house application.
- One is going from an in-house application to a customized OTS solution.

As most conventional business processes — finance, purchase, and manufacturing — were the earlier ones to get automated, they may just be at a stage in their life cycle where they should be retired. While doing so, it makes sense to move to the latest and the greatest. Even if the migration is painful, it keeps some of the troops motivated because they get to work on projects involving the latest technologies.

The Strategy of Migration

It is tempting to treat an opportunity for migration also as an opportunity to clean up the application: let us redesign the system, make it more powerful, more user friendly. It is like moving to a different house. Should one bring over all the old stuff, or get rid of it and start anew? Should one remodel the house one is moving into before moving in or do it later? While many may prefer to start anew, their options may be limited by either a lack of funds or the infeasibility of waiting for a remodeling project to be completed before moving in. Software migrations go through similar reasoning processes. While applications do not come across totally unchanged, trying to migrate and enhance an application at the same time increases the risk considerably.

The house-moving analogy can be carried a step further. Even if one recognizes that the old furniture seems to be out of place in the new house, it is prudent to live in the new place for some time, get used to it, and then make design calls suitable for the new house. After all, one is more than likely to discover certain things about the new house — light, shade, noise levels, movement of people in the house, lines of sight from neighbors' yards — that will affect one's design ideas and options. Despite recognizing this, many organizations tend to club migrations with enhancements. The argument in favor of doing that is driven by one's wish to "optimize" the opportunity. Another argument recognizes that the case for renovation gets weaker as one gets used to the (new) status quo. While one would like to get the most out of the move costs, one needs to avoid an undue emphasis on the short-term migration costs as compared to the total life-cycle costs. There may be advantages to such an approach as long as the scope of the work and the risks are properly evaluated.

The Use of Tools

In any migration project, the suggestion arises as to the use of migration tools. Migration tools do exist but provide limited degrees of automation. These could be tools for converting code in one language or environment to another (e.g., stored procedures or triggers). They are basically translation tools. Automated translation has not been an easy problem to solve, particularly for natural languages. Programming languages are more formal and bounded than natural languages; yet, the conversion tools may be unsatisfactory because, while syntactic conversion is feasible, the semantics do not come across well. Why do semantics not do well? The conversion may be too literal, or suboptimal or inelegant.

Gregory Rabassa, the noted translator of Spanish fiction, in his book entitled *If This Be Treason — Translation and Its Discontents, A Memoir,* speaks of his colleague Pete Weston:

> "Not satisfied with all the foreign tongues he had gathered in and learned well, Pete invented one of his own. As I think about it now I feel that it could be the basis for a test in translation. Why not make up your own language and then translate something from it into your native tongue, faithfully and making note of all difficulties you might come across? Then you could reverse the process and see if the new language is adequate for the translation of your native tongue."

Migration versus Porting

We can now see the difference between migration and porting. In migration, one moves away from what one is migrating, in most cases replacing the system being migrated. In porting, one creates a new version but the old version does not go away. An Accounts Receivable package migrated from VSAM to Oracle most probably would result in the retirement of the VSAM application and the existence in production of the Oracle version only. However, a CRM (customer relational management) package initially running on Sybase gets ported to Informix, or is supported on a different OS (operating system) or a different flavor of the OS, and yet support for all versions continues. Migration as a term should be used for one-off modifications done in IT (information technology) environments. Porting, correspondingly, is done by vendors who develop products and have to support multiple platforms. Although there are similarities in the work involved, the strategies that one can adopt and the options available are different.

Migration versus Reengineering

Is migration the same as reengineering? Possibly — the difference being one of the degree of change between source and destination. There are different expectations about the scope of work, the complexity involved, and, in a basic sense, project objectives. Many avoid the term "reengineering" because it evokes memories of the times when it was seen by many employees as a management consultant euphemism for laying-off employees, through the "re-engineering of business processes."

A migration invariably involves some change of technology, in one or all aspects of the system being migrated. An engineer, therefore, might want to call it reengineering. This can lead to the premise that a migration involves reengineering. However, from both a business and IT management point of view, the term "reengineering" should be restricted to changes in business processes. For example, extending customer support from a phone-based system to a Web-based self-service system would involve reengineering. There is a change in the business process of providing support. Moving an Accounts Receivable package from COBOL to Java may not be a reengineering, although there is substantial "engineering."

Upstream and Downstream

There must be some parameters, and limits also, to the feasibility of a migration. It appears intuitive to believe that similar things are easier to migrate. It should be easier to migrate an application running on one RDBMS (relational database management system) to another RDBMS than to migrate, for example, a non-relational database application to an RDBMS platform. In such cases, the technology is, perhaps, very similar, and the team has to watch out for implementation-level differences. This common basis also provides some framework to make the comparison. The difficulty in migration varies on how far apart the source and target technologies are.

It is easier to migrate from a less powerful technology or implementation to a more powerful implementation (Figure 11.1). Trying to go from a more powerful environment to a less powerful one is not only difficult, but it also may be infeasible. This is not very intuitive. If the target technology, for example, does not support the concept of "Roles," which is required and used by the source application, then it is not for the migration team to create an entire structure of roles in the target environment. If it did not come as part of the technology, some workarounds can be attempted; there may be a different and less elegant way of achieving the same result. But, often, that is not the case, or the workaround has adverse side effects and possibly subtly differing semantics.

Should the "more powerful" technology be called "upstream" or "downstream?" Recognizing the fact that it is easier to go from "less powerful" to "more powerful," and mapping it to common usage and perception that going downstream is easier than going upstream, the more powerful technology is actually downstream. So, in some migration projects, one is going downstream, and in others, one is struggling to go upstream. One should try to determine at the outset in which direction one is paddling.

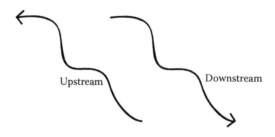

Figure 11.1   Migration paths.

How does one determine which of the technologies is "more powerful?" The first step is to prepare a list of features or aspects of the two technologies that will be used as a basis for comparison. In the case of two relational databases, these could be stored procedures, triggers, SQL support, error handling, etc. In any such comparison, there will be features that are in one, but not in the other. Between the two, pay attention to features that the source has which the target does not have, rather than the other way around, because one must ensure that all source features can be adequately handled in the destination. However, features that exist in the destination and not the source should not be totally ignored because these could provide avenues for reengineering and improvements.

Risks of Migration

If you have an existing system still serving you well, what is the risk associated with trying to migrate it? Many of these risks have little to do with technology. Just as in any project, there is risk that the business objectives may not be realized after the migration. Possibly another outcome could be that if the migration is not done properly, some functionality is lost.

The critical factors for success include:

- Sufficient knowledge of the source system at the appropriate level of detail; this cannot be assumed because it is "your" application, or because it has been around for a long time
- A clear awareness of the technical issues involved in the migration, particularly any impedance mismatches in technologies (the upstream–downstream issues)
- A map of the auxiliary processes, including data migration, support, training, communication impacted by and impacting the migration

- A list of third-party tools used in the source system, such as report writers, visual components, import–export tools that might be different at the destination
- A good plan for cutting over the migrated system
- A strategy for using the new system effectively — including changes to any business processes required
- Extensive training on the new system, because the users must overcome the years of familiarity with using the earlier system

Resistance to Migration

Migrations are often resisted internally, with great effectiveness. Some of the resistance is based on genuine doubts about being able to accomplish a successful migration, or doubts regarding the suitability of the "new" technology recommended. Appreciating this resistance is important.

The cost factor involved in a migration is quite important. Although the enhancements do play a role, essentially one is spending considerable resources to go from Point A to Point A. Is it really called for? Is it worth it? Is this the right time? These are some of the questions to answer before undertaking the job.

Migrations have two ends: (1) the source and (2) the target. In the case of legacy systems in particular, there is often a lack of sufficient knowledge of the source system, although it is successfully in operation. It is possible that the documentation is outdated, or else the original developers have since retired. Some might say that this is an argument in favor of migration. However, one can understand how such a situation increases the risk that what one gets will not be what one started with. In fact, in such situations, one may not even know what one has lost in the transition. This can also become a reason for the staff to resist the migration. Sometimes there may be resistance because they are afraid in revealing what they do not know about the systems they were operating.

It is also natural that there are legitimate concerns in the minds of staff members about their roles in the new systems (Figure 11.2). A migration

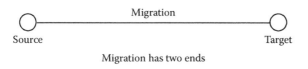

Migration has two ends

Figure 11.2 Resistance to migration.

involving the use of new technologies might threaten many jobs or the established way of working. However, every resistance encountered cannot be attributed to a "defensive attitude" on the part of those objecting. Sometimes, engineers have well-founded intuitive fears that they are not able to articulate well or do not take the trouble to do so. One should consult those who have been maintaining the system for years, and discuss whether the new solution will or will not work in one's business environment, encouraging a free and frank discussion.

Quite often, the new team of consultants brought in to deliver the migration takes an absolutely theoretical approach. They would say how the business processes should be, how supply chain should work, or how warranty management should be handled. This may be a result of interactions with senior managers who dream of a bright new world, still on paper. Such managers may not be aware of the many workarounds to the "official" way of working that actually gets things done. People lower in the hierarchy who are aware of this might protest too mildly as to be effective. Such people might even keep quiet, or may want to avoid attention to the workarounds for fear of getting into trouble. As a manager or migration analyst, one should not dismiss everything as "self-serving resistance" on part of the staff; for if one refuses to pay due attention to such issues, they might show up later in the migration project.

Scoping Migration Projects

Getting a proper inventory of the source system is key. While it is natural to focus on the application itself, one must keep in mind the auxiliary assets that are involved in its successful working. These might include load scripts, batch jobs, backup routines, clean-up routines, and the like.

It also is necessary to ensure identification of all the applications or systems with which the source is integrated. To give an example, if the source is using a certain commercial Report Writer to generate its reports, it needs to be verified that the Report Writer works with the target technologies. Also look at the versions supported. We know of one case where the migration team worked with a version of Oracle that was ahead of what was being supported in the customer's company. This was unfortunately discovered when they tried to roll the system into production. The company refused to upgrade the "corporate" database to a higher version because of its side effects, leading to the failure of the migration project. As often happens with legacy applications and the surrounding environments, one might also feel the need to replace these auxiliary tools and applications, as their vendors may not have kept up with the industry. This, naturally, increases the scope of the project.

Mistakes in inventory analysis are a major cause of migration failure, or scope expansion. Unidentified reports are discovered. The application may be providing data feeds to other applications. If the application is receiving data feeds from other applications or outside parties, then they also may need to change to provide the same or similar feeds to the target system. They need to check feasibility and budget for that within their projects.

One needs to decide how deep one should go into understanding the source system. What does one do when one discovers something that is wrong (known or unknown)?

There are at least two important threads: (1) functionality and (2) technology. If the technology is understood and a decent migration path established, a lot of functionality can take that path. For example, if one discovers that a lot of the business logic is in stored procedures and the stored procedures can be brought across to the target system with only minor changes, then one has a pathway to migrate the code without having to understand the functionality in detail. This may cut through a large swath of work.

In some sense it is advisable not to go too deep into the source because one can get lost in it. Categorize the source functionality as

- Can be migrated as is
- Can be migrated with some change in functionality, user experience, logic, etc.
- Cannot be migrated

For the latter suggest workarounds. There will always be a section of users who will be unhappy with "lost" functionality. Collecting usage statistics may be a good first step. Sometimes the functionality demanded may turn out to be very infrequently used. If the protest seems genuine, take it seriously. Users who have been using the system for years must be respected. When they say that the new system will not work if the "missing" functionality is not there, listen to them. They might not be able to articulate it well, or might be diffident in making their case — therefore it needs to be explored seriously.

Migration in Design

As discussed previously, most projects within IT departments are maintenance or migration projects. Application designers should assume that the application they are designing is a candidate for future migration. Good designers design systems to be flexible when it comes to functionality enhancements because such enhancement requests are well anticipated. Certain design choices today can help in a better migration tomorrow:

- Avoidance of the use of features in the underlying technology that are unique, or are major extensions to what can be generally expected in other implementations of that technology. Obviously, if the technology has been selected because these extended features are essential for the application, then the designer must make use of them.
- Incorporation of features related to making future data migrations easier, for example, an ODBC (open database connectivity) bridge or an object-relational mapping tool. Many migration projects get into trouble when it comes to data migration.
- General modular architectures that make the migration less monolithic and allow a phased migration.
- Use of standards (e.g., IETF [Internet Engineering Task Force]) instead of developing proprietary protocols that may make the migration effort considerably involved.

It is difficult to make a call on what the destination platforms will be for a future migration. However, certain design improvements can help that process and will be appreciated by those doing the migration many years later.

Migrating Data

Bringing data from the old to the new system can be either simple or very complex. Hence, the effort must be scoped properly. Even if the data model changes are minimal, there may be attributes and configuration parameters, such as RDBMS page size, number of database connections, access control granularity, or page locking, that need to be set differently in the target system. If the data models are substantially different, then the mapping effort can be considerable.

How much data should be brought across? The obvious answer is: all data that was being kept online in the source system because it could still be required in the target system.

What about archived data in the source system? One needs to decide if one wants to discard it, or also migrate it. There is little advantage in retaining it in the old format because one will not be able to access it once the "old" application has gone away. Migrating all the old data may not be feasible, or worth the effort. Sometimes it may make sense to walk away from old data in the new system while preserving the data (in some

neutral format such as ASCII comma-separated "text") on tapes or printouts for any future reference.

The Right Staff

Migration is detail-oriented work. Staying at a high level would be inadequate. At a high level, many technologies and platforms look very similar; for example, two cars are based on the same principles of internal combustion engines, or all relational databases support SQL (Structured Query Language). However, this kind of simplification could lead to underestimating the effort involved.

Before one recognizes the differences, one must acknowledge that differences do exist. There is a joke of a teacher advising one of her students — "Whenever you are in doubt, consult a dictionary." The student replied, "I am never in doubt." Likewise, we have seen engineers who have spent years working with just one RDBMS. They could never appreciate that another RDBMS might be handling things differently. Some of their pet features, such as Roles or Row level locking, may not be available in the destination system. We therefore suggest that a good migration mindset should consist of a healthy mix of doubt and skepticism, with a belief that hidden problems will surface.

While staffing a team, should one have more persons knowledgeable in the source technologies or the destination technologies? It should be the destination that is favored, yet it is also necessary that knowledge of both the source system (or application) and the technology is required (Figure 11.3). This is easily achieved by including a person who has worked on the source application, thereby bringing on board both the source technology and the domain knowledge.

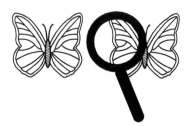

The ability to recognize differences at a fairly detailed
level is key to a successful migration project.

Figure 11.3 Spot differences early.

It Is Finished... or Is It?

It is extremely difficult to define the concept of "done-ness" for migration tasks. Meaningful testing usually cannot occur until complete programs have been built to the point of performing a complete function or activity that the users can verify is correct. Contrast this with the recommended development and testing methodology for new system development, which incorporates stub programming, unit testing, various levels of integration testing — all according to design specifications, *before* the users ever see the system. Therefore, the planning and management process must take into account these distinctions and account for them.

—From *Systems Migration*, Alan R. Simon

Summary

Statistically speaking, IT departments spend most of their time in either migration or maintenance work. Migration projects are triggered because the existing application has reached its natural limits, or there is a need to move from an in-house application to an off-the-shelf one, or vice versa. Such projects fail when the semantics of the destination system do not come across well, or third-party tools used in the source system (such as report writers, visual components, import–export tools, etc.) do not work in the migrated environment. Migration is different from porting and reengineering projects, although the objectives and approach may be similar. Staffing for these projects requires ensuring that skills for both source and target technologies are available within the migration team. Thus, getting a proper inventory of the source system is key to scoping a migration project. Bringing data from the old system to the new one can be complex — this effort is often underestimated.

Proper cut-over planning is necessary for a successful migration. Auxiliary processes such as those related to support, training, communication, as well as post-migration clean-up work should be part of the project plan for any migration project, whether it is retraining support personnel, the users, the sales teams, or others.

Quality in a product or service is not what the supplier puts in. It is what the customer gets out and is willing to pay for. A product is not quality because it is hard to make and costs a lot of money, as manufacturers typically believe. This is incompetence. Customers pay only for what is of use to them and gives them value. Nothing else constitutes quality.

—**Peter Drucker**

Chapter 12

Quality and Testing

It is quality rather than quantity that matters.

—Seneca, Epistles

The Definition of Quality

What is quality? How does one define quality? A layman might think that quality is about achieving one's best, going beyond what is expected. However, the accepted definition of quality concerns *meeting specifications*. Quality is the best that one can achieve as per specifications. From a business point of view, delivering beyond the specifications is a waste of resources. Such a definition, grounded on meeting specifications, has the advantage that it removes subjective definitions of quality. It enables implementation of practical processes to measure, verify, and ensure that the specifications are being met.

Is the idea that one must work only to specifications not restricting the development of good ideas as the process goes along? A developer can come up with a brilliant idea for a new feature — and so can a tester. The question now arises as to whether such ideas should be considered. The argument is not against using the idea, but rather about following the process: if one wants the brilliant idea to be included, one should change the specifications to include it. Once the specifications are finalized, the rest of the system — that is, the developers, tester, trainers, etc. — should be working to the specifications; otherwise, chaos can ensue.

195

Quality as Feedback

In systems terms, quality assurance is part of the feedback loop of the engineering system. The input to an engineering system is the requirements document. The output is the code. Quality assurance (QA) teams sample the output and provide feedback signals, in the form of defect reports, so that the output is brought closer to the requirements. This is an example of negative feedback. Carefully note that the term "negative feedback" is different from "negative criticism" and does not indicate a problem. It is called "negative" because it has a *damping effect* on the divergence between the output and the requirements. This damping effect is desirable. Engineering acts on this feedback and improves the code; and the output is again sampled, hopefully showing that it has moved closer to the requirements. How long this might continue depends on how many such iterations the project can afford, in terms of time and money, or on the application of a threshold of acceptable divergence.

Products and Processes

There is a well-known difference between quality assurance (QA) and quality control (QC) in the manufacturing world, perhaps more than in software. To put it simply, QA refers to the process and QC to the product. However, both are important. Quality products need quality processes. Good systems are needed to build good systems. However, many software organizations identify the QA department with *testing*, and have focused their attention on product (quality control) aspects more than the process aspects. Most of the quality-related costs are incurred in determining defects in the product to be shipped.

QA is not as actively engaged in many aspects of software development as it should be. They are often not invited to discussions about design and architecture. The fact is that the QA process, as it commonly exists, interfaces more with Engineering than with the customer. It therefore works off the same specifications as Engineering does. It is not seen as QA's role to challenge the requirements or specifications. As one might guess, this assumption of correctness of specifications has some risks, yet as a process it works. They are only following specifications.

The difference between QA and testing also lies in the attitude and approach of those in charge (Figure 12.1). QA is oriented toward error *prevention*. It should be employed throughout the software development life cycle, in managing and improving processes, making sure that documented standards and procedures are being followed. On the other hand,

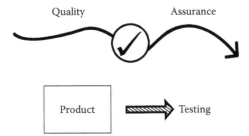

QA is throughout the life cycle, testing is after the product is ready

Figure 12.1 Quality assurance (QA) versus testing.

testing is oriented toward *detection*. Testing involves exercising the software under controlled conditions with an aim toward finding defects before a version is "accepted," or before the customers detect such defects. This stress on testing in the software industry is akin to treating a patient once a disease has manifested itself, rather than trying to prevent the initial infection.

> If programmers are responsible for thoroughly testing their code, the question naturally arises, "Are programmers and testers not duplicating each other's efforts?" Perhaps they do here and there but when programmers test code, they test it from the inside and move out. Testers start from the outside and move in.
>
> ... The combination of approaches works because programmers focus on code while testers focus on features. With the two working from opposite directions, the chances of finding unknown bugs are increased.
>
> —From *Writing Solid Code,* Steve Maguire

In any process, there are intermediate products that come before the final product releases. These intermediate products, such as requirements documents, data models, build documents, and infrastructure specifications, are artifacts with their own quality requirements. If the quality of the output is influenced by the quality of the input, then resources should be devoted to quality procedures related to the input, rather than concentrating on the output. The way organizations separate functions drives certain perceptions of responsibility within the organization. If there is a department called Sales, the responsibility for getting new orders is left to Sales — the rest of the organization does not consider selling its responsibility. When there is a QA department, quality is identified with that department. This should not mean that others ignore this aspect of quality in their work. The designer, architect, programmer, and technical writer all try to deliver quality output. Yet the formal seal of approval must come from QA. This skews the resource allocation toward the output.

Quality in Other Domains

Software development cannot be made very repetitive. Each problem, program, or application requires a unique solution. Although opportunities exist for the use of proven problem-solving algorithms, or re-use of code, the process cannot be made cookie-cutter style. This limits the extent to which automation can be introduced and to what it can achieve. Software development depends more on the quality of the team members than on the equipment and tools given to them — however sophisticated such tools may be. This reliance on human abilities leads to a variation in the quality of the output. On the other hand, the manufacturing of goods is based on repetitive processes: once the proper processes are in place, automation helps achieve consistency in production quality.

There is another reason why the software "production" process cannot be made uniform, especially with respect to quality. In software, the design and development are so intermingled, and iterative, that the process cannot assure quality. It is not "all design up front" and coding later. This means that the strategy often adopted in manufacturing — to make the design as good as possible, followed by a highly repetitive process — does not work in software. This is not to suggest that there is no healthy feedback between design, manufacturing, and field deployment in manufacturing. However, in software development, the phases are intermingled because the developer has several choices as to how he or she can code to a design. It is easy to implement the design differently, whether conscious or not. As discussed previously, both Engineering and QA work off the same specifications but the specifications that QA depends on could have been implemented in many ways by Engineering. This makes the QA task more difficult in practice. For example, if the specifications require that two users are not to be permitted to access a certain data store at the same time, such a feature could be implemented through the locking features provided by the database or through managing flags by the application. It would matter to an experienced tester in the way he could design tests.

There is another way in which a design affects QA. If the design changes frequently, it impacts the quality of the code because it creates the potential for patchy, retrofitted features, glued logic and code that strays from guidelines. QA should take into consideration while estimate testing cycle times that the application is being developed in a volatile design environment.

Quality under Constraints

Constraints aggravate matters. If the project is run in a resource-constrained and also a change-filled environment, as many projects are, the probability of defects is higher. Quality, therefore, is not related only to the design and the requirements, but also to the environment in which the work is done.

When the development and QA teams are working under deadlines, some of the approaches to handle the situation include:

- One can restrict the testing to key requirements (short cycle) rather than the full QA cycle. In short-cycle QA, the team may decide to fix only those bugs related to critical failures. It is a time-saving device that trades some risk for the time saved.
- Project managers may decide to avoid delaying the release by providing a software patch after the software release rather than addressing the known defect immediately.
- Bypass QA altogether using "production fixes." Development may advise the use of a "production fix," an ad-hoc hot-fix that is deployed in the production environment directly without much (or any) QA. This strategy is restricted to fixes that are "small" (e.g., changing the size of a field, or exposing a hidden field in a form) under the assumption that it can be applied in production without following the normal full QA cycle. This shortcut comes with some attached risk — recall the nonlinear effects of bugs and the tendency of systems to have side effects. If production fixes are to be added, it is best to follow a formal production fix process, so that the fixes are not left to the individuals doing the work. The fix should be documented to avoid failure of a subsequent release of the software.

QA Effort Sizing

Testing efforts depend not only on the size or complexity of the application, but also on the nature of the test cycle. The time and effort required depend on the number of tests utilized. It is important to keep in mind that a "good" code drop does not require less QA. In fact, the requirements are the same, regardless of the test results, because the bugs found are not corrected on-the-fly. Each time a bug is found, it needs to be documented in a bug-tracking tool, along with screen shots, as well as the inputs that caused it, etc. This takes time. Furthermore, a bug may manifest itself in many places in the software, all of which a tester needs to document. The quality of the coding and the adherence to standards during the requirements and specifications phase do have some effect on the speed of the process, but not as much as many development managers assume.

If one were to look for guiding principles with regard to estimating the QA efforts, they would be:

- *Nature of the application.* The testing effort largely depends on how the application will be used, rather than on the size and complexity of the application. For mission-critical applications such as medical or financial services, not only will there be a need to test the application thoroughly, but one also needs to test the application in more dimensions (refer to "Types of Testing" section), thus increasing both the duration of the effort and the size of the team.
- *Deployed environments.* The diversity of the environment has a direct impact on the testing effort. Distributed, multi-machine scenarios add to the complexity — and heterogeneous, multi-operating system environments complicate things even further. One must take special care when third-party applications or components are used in the system. The QA effort is not necessarily testing them, but merely verifying all their exposed interfaces. Developers may have neither the time nor the inclination to understand all the APIs (application programming interfaces) current, obsolete, or recommended. Documentation of these outside components may also be inadequate, leading to unexpected error conditions. Because the testing team is not likely to get much help regarding these components, they might avoid expending the effort required to debug or test some foreign code. Even when support is available, interacting with external parties adds to the lead time.
- *Acceptance audience.* The nature of the customer has an impact on the testing effort. Some users try to break the system intentionally. It could be a reflection of how quality conscious they are, although spending a lot of time during user acceptance, in testing obscure conditions, is often a waste of time. Sometimes, the same unexpected conditions are triggered by users who are not computer or software savvy, and enter "undesirable" inputs, showing that

the application was not "foolproof." One's QA team must be conscious of this fact. If the application is intended for such users, they should make an additional effort to test beyond the requirement or solution specification. In fact, code coverage-type tests are better suited for such environments. Between the two types, the computer savvy users are more forgiving when it comes to complaining about problems. Having a user educated about the complexity of the engineering involved in the product helps in adjusting his or her expectations.

■ *Development cycle phase*: The extent and type of testing also depends on the phase of the application.

  ■ New applications that are being tested for the first time will require more effort and more cycles of testing even if they are relatively simple.

  ■ Applications in corrective maintenance (user-reported defects are being fixed) require testing efforts that depend on the criticality and severity of the fixes being made. Because of the prior testing experience with the application at the time of its full release, estimating this effort can be easier. Regression testing should be accounted for in one's estimations.

  ■ When functional enhancements are being made in a product release cycle, additional time should be allocated for creating new test cases for the enhancements. The need for regression testing still continues.

  ■ Applications that are in adaptive maintenance (auxiliary development for supporting additional OS platforms and tools) need testers who are experts in the respective platforms.

Dealing with Poor Specifications

The approach that quality is about meeting specifications is not an issue by itself. The problem sometimes lies with the quality of the specifications. Specifications are, like models, abstractions of an often complex and messy reality. They are necessarily incomplete. This means that one can meet specifications yet fail in the real world. For example, an application's specification may say nothing about performance requirements or the support of multiple Web browsers.

QA often faces such situations. Should QA include such tests? QA may decide to ignore the issue of multiple browsers, or it may want to add such tests to the test suite. The right way to handle this is to ensure, through upstream processes, that such a requirement is added to the specifications. Such problems with specifications can be discovered early during the development of the test strategy. One common mistake is to not understand (and challenge) the specifications well enough before detailed test plans are prepared. A thorough review of the specification by QA is a valuable exercise for both QA and Engineering. This highlights the multiple levels of feedback that are typical of systems — there is the feedback about how well the specifications are being met, and then there is feedback about the specifications themselves. If this duality is recognized by managers, then the value of the QA process increases.

Specifications may be of poor quality for many other reasons: lack of details, or too much detail; poor expression; invalid assumption; and the like. However, one problem that can be expensive is incompleteness. Incompleteness emerges due to various situations that can often be prevented:

- The assumption often is that the entire ground has been covered but that may not be so. Each of these smaller specifications cover some ground and have their own specifications. For example, there may be a pop-up box that asks whether one wants to "save the screen." If one specifies the responses as "yes" and "no" only, it would be incomplete because "cancel" is a valid option that allows one to avoid both the yes and no options. Another example could be one of data management, where the "import data" module specifies only the requirements for importing data; the "export data" covers exporting data, etc. There may be a need for a nightly "refresh" process that does not fall under either the "import" or the "export" categories.

- While decomposition allows details to be specified in a manageable manner, it can prevent the larger picture from being addressed until it is too late. Addressing the larger picture is necessary because behavior at a higher level differs from the nature and behavior of its components. This is known as the *emergent property* of systems, and necessitates a (separate) specification at the high level, or each level against which QA should test. For example, if there are specifications for each screen of a multi-step order-taking process, there should be another specification for the entire order-taking process, and its associated behavior.

- Specifications can end up having a narrow focus, which is often based on the defined objectives or scope. A strong focus on the issue specified — the "defined objective" — leads to the oversight of other effects. This is similar to the situation where the doctor focuses on solving the "main" problem, say cancer, while anything else that happens is deemed a "side effect." However, these side effects could be more harmful than the focal issue; and even if they are not, they may disturb the larger system in unexpected ways. If one is writing the specifications, begin with a clear statement identifying the focus areas and state where side effects might emerge. For example, adding more validation on the screen may slow down response time. One should not assume that the user understands this "side effect."

■ Specifications may ignore the fact that what is being delivered is part of a larger system. How the product fits into the larger system is as important as its internal characteristics. This larger system includes aspects beyond *mere* functionality and features of the delivered product. It covers all aspects of the product — its ease of use, security, safety, maintenance, integration, training, auxiliary systems and processes, and upgrades. Without such coverage, products that "pass" QA might fail in other ways.

Good designers, when faced with multiple decomposition or design choices, take the cost of testing or verification as criteria for selecting the better design. This is common practice in manufacturing industries.

Test Plans and Cases

A test plan describes the scope, approach, and objectives of a software testing effort. It should be created carefully. A test plan not only helps the test team to think from requirements to final customer acceptance, but also helps non-QA groups understand the parameters that will outline the acceptance criteria of the product. A test plan consists of test cases. Each test case describes an input or event and the response expected based on the application working "correctly." It can help find problems in the requirements or design of an application because it requires thinking through the usage of the application.

Extreme Programming (XP) is a software development practice for projects based on the theory that developing test cases is useful for the entire software life cycle and not just the testing requirements that might change frequently, or are collectively indefinable at the start of the project. The approach is different, with test cases driving general development. Developers write unit and functional test cases before writing the actual application code. Customers help develop scenarios for acceptance testing while the source code is being written. Acceptance tests are continuously updated and run while development iterations are going on.

Types of Testing

Any application under development will have certain engineering areas or features that are more important than others. These factors are critical to the application's success and depend on the nature of the application as well as its specific implementation. For example, in a CRM (customer relationship management) application, the ease of user interaction is given more weight because the productivity of hundreds of users is key to the success of the application. In an E-commerce site, security might be more important, while in a bank reconciliation application, data integrity is crucial. The testing strategy for any application being developed is often determined by the relative importance of such factors.

After selecting the critical success factors, one should develop a testing strategy that places more importance and resources on these factors. To give an example, in the case of the bank reconciliation system, more time should be devoted to debugging and testing date-related modules, while less time should be devoted to the user interface screens. This may lead to the realization that the developers and the testers do not have adequate tools to create the required data, or that one may need a database administrator attached to this project to support the intense data management requirements.

It is rarely feasible to do all the kinds of testing that one would like to perform. As such, one should be careful in the type of testing selected. There should be a systematic process, backed by a comprehensive test plan. Random testing is inadequate. The testing process works best when done systematically. This also provides an assurance about the reliability of the results or conclusions being drawn. Simultaneously, it enables one to compare results from various test cycles, thereby determining whether the situation is improving, and to what extent.

Testing should always involve a premise, that is, testing for the correctness of a predetermined "something." There should be a hypothesis, based on behavior symptoms displayed by the software, that can be shown to be true or false, accepted or rejected. This approach is implicit in most test plans. For example, first, implicitly or explicitly, state a premise: "a date field should accept only valid date values." Then set up a hypothesis: "this date field accepts a Feb 30 date." Then prove or disprove that hypothesis by entering that date, and seeing whether or not it is rejected.

The various types of testing are discussed below.

Systems Testing

In any system, the behavior of lower-level components is not a sufficient predictor of system behavior; certain behaviors can emerge at a higher level. Such emergent behavior requires that quality be defined and assured at a system level. As James Madison said (and Robert Jervis quotes in his excellent book, *System Effects*): "had every Athenian citizen been a Socrates, every Athenian assembly would have been a mob." The wings, the engines, and the wheels may all be working fine independently and still the plane might not fly. Similarly, each of the screens may have passed QA; yet when the application is put together, the performance is far from satisfactory. Performance, therefore, is an emergent property of systems.

Systems testing validates the behavior of the system as a whole. An example of testing at this level is the beta test. It is an essential step that some organizations ignore, assuming that integration testing, which deals with integration between internal components, is sufficient in uncovering "system-level" problems.

Integration Testing

Integration testing is slightly different from systems testing. Integration testing deals with the relationships between the components of a system. If two modules, A and B, are tested together to ensure that the output of A is readable by B, it is an example of integration testing. Integration testing is essential whenever two modules are developed independently. Factors that determine the efforts required for integration testing include:

- Frequency of data exchange
- Number of integration points
- Quantity of data being transferred
- Whether it is unidirectional or bi-directional integration

Integration testing best captures any idiosyncratic behavior of a component, for example, one that does not check for (or sends) duplicate records and expects the receiving component to remove duplicates (de-dup). Integration testing has its own set of test cases, which are invariably of the black-box type. Even when individual modules have passed their own tests, internal problems can be discovered through integration testing.

Unit Testing

Unit testing deals with the internals of a component and conventionally refers to the testing done by the developer. Developers should be encouraged to test their code before submitting it for formal QA. The developer's closeness to the code, and his or her immersion in the coding process, permits a kind of corrective testing, which is different from post-facto testing.

If a test fails during developer testing, one should try and isolate the concerned part of the code. Faced with a long list of items to fix, developers have a tendency to make changes in many "suspect" areas of the code simultaneously. It is better to fix one problem at a time, re-test the fix for correctness, and then take up the next bug. If one changes code to fix multiple bugs and the re-testing shows that some bugs have not been fixed, it would be impossible to determine whether a particular fix is ineffective or a combination of some code change is, in fact, responsible. Similarly, while fixing a particular problem, a useful strategy would be to make only one code change at a time for a particular problem.

Black-Box and White-Box Testing

Black-box testing is based on the knowledge gathered from the requirements and functionality documentation. It is behavioral in nature. Black-box testing is concerned with only testing the specification; it cannot guarantee that all parts of the source code have been tested for faults. White-box testing, on the other hand, is based on the knowledge of an application's internals — the source code — and is thus structural in nature. Because white-box testing is concerned only with testing the software product, it cannot guarantee that the nonfunctional specification has been implemented.

It is not easy to classify testing as one kind or another. What may be considered black-box by one person may be considered white-box by another. To take an example, test-driving a car may be considered black-box testing by the quality control group that checks on the engine performance parameters. However, it might be considered white-box by the group that deals with the temperature, fuel injection, and valve and piston pressure within the engine block.

White-box testing is more expensive. It requires the product to be ready before the tests can be planned, and uses a more tedious and lengthy process to ascertain the right test cases and determine the correctness of the software. The "whiter" you get in testing, the more expensive it becomes. Thus, it is better to start the QA process with black-box tests. This can be done as soon as the requirements specification document is available. White-box planning can follow as software modules are developed and the respective black-box tests have been successful.

The ramifications of test failure are also different with black- and white-box testing. A black-box test failure may not require the repetition of all the white-box tests. The reverse, however, is not true. If software is changed to fix a failed white-box test, it may require the repetition of all the black-box tests.

To ensure completeness of test cases between black and white, it is a good idea to do some mutation testing. This is a method of determining if a set of test data or test cases is useful, by deliberately introducing various code changes ("mutants") and retesting with the original test data or cases to determine if the "mutants" can be detected. The idea behind mutation testing is simple: given an appropriate set of inputs, if a test set identifies the mutants generated by these inputs (i.e., if it is able to find these small errors), it will likely be good at finding real faults.

Regression Testing

In software, as in other systems, unintended consequences arise out of complex interactions between elements of the system. These unintended consequences can lead to misbehavior or failure of the product. For example, a new installation changes a configuration file that affects another application. An upgrade makes the historical data unreadable. Because unintended consequences do occur, regression testing is necessary even for systems that are highly modularized.

Many developers and testers do not understand the true nature of regression testing. It is a common mistake to test Version 1 of their software on Day 1's production data, and then test Version 2 with the production data from Day 2. This is not a true regressive test because between the two tests, both the software and the data have changed.

Let us illustrate regression testing with an example. Suppose one has completed a document, run spell-check on it, and corrected all the spelling mistakes. One now adds two more sentences to the document. Should one run the spell-checker again? Yes, of course: the two new sentences may have introduced spelling mistakes. So one runs spell-checker again. This is an example of regression testing.

There are a few issues with running the spell-checker on the document again. The "mistakes" in the earlier pass that had been flagged and ignored get pointed out again and must be explicitly ignored again. This is the reason why most regression testing is skipped. The problem lies with the fact that a mistake is in the eye of the beholder — what a spell-checker identifies as a mistake is actually an unrecognized word. The lack of recognition is based on the lack of inclusion in some baseline dictionary. Any dictionary is incomplete even with regard to commonly used words, and certainly for words and terms of local usage within a company or project. To avoid the flagging of such "mistakes," one can either keep adding exceptions to the dictionary, or adding clutter, or branch off local dictionaries, which may not be possible to do in all word processors.

On the topic of dictionary completeness, it should be noted that passing a spell-check does not mean that there are no errors. How many times have we typed the word "sue" instead of "use" in a sentence and got passing grades because both words are "in the dictionary?"

In the earlier example, because we have added only a few sentences, it is tempting to visually inspect the new sentences oneself. Would this be called regression testing? By one definition, it is not because the first test was done using the spell-checker, a kind of automated testing with embedded logic. By not using the automated testing, one risks missing an error condition as specified in the "test plan." Fortunately, spell-checkers do allow one to spell-check only the two new sentences. That would be acceptable for this example because the addition of two sentences is unlikely to have "side effects" in the rest of the document. However, in software, the addition of two statements is likely to have side effects, which complicate the scope of regression testing. Many a regression test is skipped or shortened because the tester or developer is very sure that "nothing else is affected."

Regression Problems

Very often, defects follow a set pattern. We can then use these to create anti-patterns, catalog them, and use them to guard against future defects. Some of these anti-patterns can be automated with tool support. Some integrated development environments (IDEs) used by programmers also have facilities to invoke such checks in the background while the developer creates code. These checks and patterns should be introduced as a step in the development and testing life cycles. They can be used as guidance for doing better reviews and become "watch points." Regression testing is another way of building watch points into the software development process.

Scope of Testing

How much should one test? The theoretical answer is that we should test everything; however, this is not feasible because the space of inputs, and corresponding possible logic conditions, is large enough. It is because of this that program correctness is considered in the NP-Complete class of problems. Furthermore, proving the existence of correct behavior in a piece of software is easier than proving the nonexistence of incorrect behavior. That is why we must rely on testing to get us to a state where we feel comfortable in releasing the software for use.

What should you test?

Critical to success

Functionally complex

Core components

Visible to customer

Has financial impact

Late additions

Figure 12.2   Prioritizing testing efforts.

Given that we cannot test everything, we have to use a combination of risk analysis, prior industry benchmarks, and one's own experience in determining what and how much testing would be adequate (Figure 12.2).

There are certain areas of the application and development scenarios that stand out as candidates for increased testing. More testing resources should be devoted to:

- *Features considered critical by the customer.* Every system or application has one or more critical functionalities. If these do not work, then it matters little if the others do — the system is a failure. The decision about what is critical must be made by the customer, not the developer or by the analyst.
- *Functionally complex modules.* There is an increased likelihood of bugs being present in applications or modules that are complex.
- *Core components.* Components that are heavily used or reused throughout the application are crucial. A bug here has widespread effects if it were to fail.
- *Features that are most visible to the customer* (even if they appear to be of cosmetic or of mere "nuisance" value). Users' first impressions are often difficult to change. These impressions are generally the result of interactions with, maybe, some trivial aspects of the application. Users assign a lot of importance to the user interfaces of the applications with which they interact. While it is understandable that one would like to focus on critical and severe bugs, it may not be advisable to prioritize these over those that are visible.
- Any feature likely to have a *financial impact*, however small.

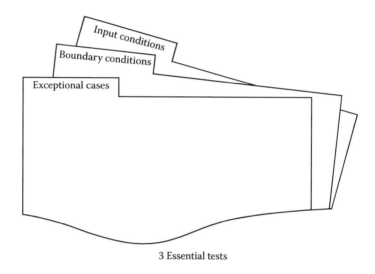

3 Essential tests

Figure 12.3 Never forget to test these.

■ *Late design additions.* Design changes brought in after the system has already been in development are more likely to have problems.

In all likelihood, problems will not appear uniformly throughout the source code. There will be areas where complex business logic is implemented — the probability of a defect occurring will naturally be higher. Defects repeat and often reflect individual developer's coding habits, and their blind spots. QA and Engineering personnel should work together to factor such occurrences into their test prioritization strategy.

In addition, there are three tests that are essential (Figure 12.3):

■ *Exceptional cases*: things in the requirement specifications that are not supposed to happen in the system — which most likely have been overlooked by the developer.
■ *Boundary conditions:* array limits, negative or null values, extremely large values (e.g., percentages value greater than 100).
■ *Input conditions*: wide range of inputs because one can never predict what users (or interfacing systems) will enter, knowingly or unknowingly.

Another aspect of testing is *periodicity.* Just as a person goes for regular medical checkups, one should also establish a process to examine the health of software periodically through diagnostic tests, even when the system looks and behaves properly and the customers are not complaining.

Automation in Testing

Automation implies that the speed of the processes will increase. In testing, however, increasing the speed of the process is only one of the benefits of automation. Automation dispenses with certain kinds of tests that can be executed unattended, thereby saving us some resources. Human beings are not reliable with repetitive tasks, especially when under pressure. After a few cycles, testers may tend to overlook bugs. A project would be a candidate for testing automation if one thinks that some aspects of testing (like smoke test or regression testing) are becoming tedious and time-consuming.

Automation also works well for things that one cannot test adequately using a manual approach. Load and stress testing are such examples. Many automation tools allow one to simulate load (e.g., thousands of concurrent user sessions), and measure system performance effectively. Other examples of automation tools are code and coverage analyzers, memory leak analyzers, software for managing and reporting bugs, source code and configuration management, file and database comparisons, and screen captures.

Automation introduces a change in testing styles. In manual testing, one is able to determine correctness of the software behavior on the basis of knowledgeable but subjective calls on screen outputs, pop-up messages, data files, functional transitions, and the like. In automated testing, the system does not have any subjective capabilities to determine such correctness. It works by rules or conditions. It is necessary to define what needs testing, along with the expected outputs. These definitions must be extremely detailed — sometimes to the level of defining exact coordinates as to where the output will show on the screen, etc. — so that the system can accurately determine the result.

When should automation be introduced into a QA life cycle? Automation may not be appropriate during early software builds when the test approach needs a thoughtful tester's approach to modify or tune the test plans. The QA team must have room for improvement at this stage before they can automate the process or tests selected.

Test Environments

Test environments are expensive, both to build and to maintain. In *product* companies, such an investment is more easily made because it can be amortized over the life of the product. In *project* environments, it is difficult to build the kind of test environments one would like, not only because there are so many different projects, but also because it appears that there would be one-time use of the environments. In such project environments, the investment is made in more general-purpose tools rather than in very specific environments.

The cost elements of the test environment include infrastructure elements — servers, licenses, etc., the creation and maintenance of test plans and test cases, and the creation and maintenance of test data.

The best environment to test the application is the one in which the software is going to be used by the customer. This may not always be possible, as the production environments are not fixed and final. Distributed applications, with multiple installs of the software at different locations, do not have identical configurations. Different versions of the same third-party hardware and software solutions may be deployed. It is practically impossible to recreate all possible hardware, software, data, and usage characteristics of the production environments in which the software will be used. The subsets that one selects for the in-house testing environments will be based on practical factors such as time, budget, and logistical feasibility. Sometimes, external testing and certification labs can be used for the other combinations, or else simulated environments can be created using ghosting techniques.

Because creating and maintaining test data are expensive, many departments try to use production data (scrubbed or not) as test data. This has its pros and cons. A successful run of the software using production data indicates that the software is likely to work in production. However, most production data, depending on where it is picked up, has had filters and gatekeepers upstream ensuring that "bad" data has not entered (e.g., one may have no records with an empty Account Number). However, bad data is necessary to test how one's software handles it.

Production data may have its own patterns across time. A sample taken "off season" is very likely different from one taken during "peak season." This could become important when it comes to issues of scalability and software performance. Also, this is one reason why good test data is created by hand, primarily using production data as a starting point.

Quality Improvements over Time

Applications that have been around for some time, and have been used frequently by many customers, are, possibly, cleaner because the defects observed in such applications have been pointed out to technical support and have already been fixed. It is not enough that the software has merely been around in the market. Unless many *active* customers have used the product, it is unlikely to have improved. One must recognize that product companies cannot, and do not, replicate all production environments.

"Install a patch for the update of the new version. If that doesn't work, install the new version of the update for the patch. If all else fails, install a patch for the new version of the update."

Figure 12.4 Quality improves.

This, and the emergent behavior of systems in general, leads to problems that can only be discovered in production. Products that sell well are often in better shape.

Sometimes, for commercial products sold in suites, improvement could be selective; that is, some of the modules are rarely exercised or implemented by customers (Figure 12.4). Therefore, one cannot assume that similar quality improvements have occurred across all modules of the suite. To give an example, many ERP (enterprise relationship planning) packages may have sold only their General Ledger or Accounting modules. The other modules — warehouse or CRM (customer relationship management) — may have had fewer implementations. This should not be taken as an argument against buying new software, or getting upgrades to existing software, that would have new (insufficiently field tested) features and enhancements. One should be aware that there might be a period of uncertainly, however small, every time something new is introduced in an existing application. Sometimes customers do not have a choice, as vendors insist that customers have the latest version of the product or apply the latest patch.

Bugs

It is a common misconception that most bugs in software are the result of programmer errors and bad coding practices. The programmers did write the buggy code and are responsible to that extent; however, the bugs may not have been introduced by their carelessness, lack of programming skills, or poor domain knowledge. In fact, in most projects, bugs are not "syntactic" language errors, as the obvious ones would have been removed by most compilers.

The definition of "bug" depends on perspective. For a customer, a requirement not met by the system is considered a bug. For a developer, a bug is something that does not match the specifications given to him. This sometimes leads to a "bug versus feature" dispute with the customer, especially during user acceptance.

Most bugs are, however, incorrect implementations of a desired end user need. The cause could be incomplete requirement specifications or incorrect interpretation by the developers due to a lack of detail. At times this ambiguity is due to the "obvious" being left unsaid. For example, the fact that each door and window in a house must have a latch is a fair expectation, reasonably well understood, and need not be explicitly stated to the builder. Such expectations on the part of the homeowner (the customer) may not match the assumptions of the builder. Often, projects fail due to the differences in what is assumed to be obvious "to any sensible person." The problem is that what might be obvious to a customer may not be so to the builder, however trivial it may be. This is a familiar problem related to getting good requirements. It is the problem of figuring out whether requirements are a push or pull process. As discussed previously, the QA interacts more with Engineering than with the customer. A change in requirements after the design is released can have serious consequences on code quality. A set of final requirements, if arrived at in two steps rather than one, is likely to generate more bugs. Some factors include:

- Depending on how the change request is handled, the code may have to be rewritten.
- New third-party software may have to be introduced, bringing its own complexity, to handle the changes.
- New developers, who would have missed the discussions up to that point, may have to be added to the team.

It is thus very important to spend some more time up-front on requirements. In development processes that specifically plan for iterative requirements gathering, the success of the process depends on ensuring that the factors mentioned above are in control.

Handling Change

Some changes in a given software environment can be more detrimental than others. Utmost care must therefore be taken while introducing partially tested third-party components into a system. Never assume that such changes will necessarily fit in one's own system just because they may have worked well in other environments.

It should also be kept in mind that, like a disease lying dormant for some time, some software problems may not show symptoms immediately. A seemingly mundane request by a customer to change a field type, especially that of an index, may affect the stability of the system in the long term. It may contradict a basic assumption in the system design made by the original architect or designers of such a system. Such changes should be introduced after a detailed impact analysis.

Inexperienced programmers can often introduce inadequacies into the system due to insufficient understanding of the system, tools, technologies and constructs, or pure human frailties (such as carelessness or tardiness). Various life-cycle models and programming practices have been created to overcome these inadequacies. Xtreme™ programming and Agile methodologies are two examples. Use them to improve developer proficiency and detect common patterns of mistakes.

Specification and Design Bugs

It has already been emphasized that software is designed to meet customer requirements. When something does not work, the question naturally arises if it is not working with respect to the design or the requirements.

The engineering definition of a bug is: something that does not work according to specification. If the specification itself is incomplete or inaccurate, then it is a different kind of problem, unlikely to be discovered by testing. Should we call incomplete specifications bugs? What does it mean when one hears the engineering team say, "No — it is not a coding problem. It is a design problem"? The question arises as to whether the requirement specifications were incomplete, or an incorrect design choice was made, or the designer overlooked something that should have been included. With some checks and balances, oversights are likely discovered during development or testing by comparing the delivery with the requirement specifications. It is only when the problem is with the specifications themselves that things become difficult.

Requirement specifications should be reasonably detailed, consistent, and useful to all members of the project team: managers, analysts, designers, developers, and testers. A good design maps these requirements to the software components being built. A good design document should provide the rationale for preferring a particular design, including a discussion of other options. The design review process should provide a high-level overview of how the required functionality was partitioned and assigned to subsystems or components. Many design review processes miss this. They concentrate on the design that has been "selected" rather than "preferred," thereby making the review process more of an announcement than a serious discussion of options.

When requirements are put together, they are often based on current needs. Even if they contain future plans, they are usually based on a *current* understanding of the future. This understanding can be flawed or inadequate. It is difficult to add design elements that have to take care of issues that are important but are not well articulated or understood, such as scalability or third-party tool integration. For example, while creating a Web-based system, the analyst may quantify the scalability need at a certain number of concurrent hits. The designer puts components in place to support this. The unexpected popularity of the site may cause this projection to be exceeded, resulting in frequent outages, much to the customer's dismay. Should the designer have accounted for this, even if it was not in the specifications made by the analyst, and should it be called a bug in the design or the specifications? This is being explained below.

A few years back, an explosion in its center wing tank destroyed a TWA jet. Since the dawn of the jet age, 14 fuel tank explosions have occurred on commercial aircraft, killing more than 530 passengers and crew. People consider it a grim monument to a faulty design. The industry recognizes the presence of flammable vapors, and minimizes the associated hazard by eliminating potential ignition sources. Clearly this is a conscious choice made to balance increased cost with customer safety rather than a design flaw. Just as with jet planes, in QA there can be no requirements for something that "should not be present in a system." So what *should* QA base its tests on? Should it test for all possible permutations and combinations of things that might result in a spark?

There are design expectations in any situation that remain implicit. Some have to do with actual designs as we understand them (every room should have a door or access to another room, and the door must open and close). Others are assumptions around some structural basics, for example, files are closed after opening them. It is the responsibility of the QA team to point out instances where they recognize that the design does not deliver on these implicit assumptions. But the QA team is not a team of designers, and they cannot be expected to go too deep into design issues.

Often, developers overlook things such as proper program structure, inline documentation, maintainability, and supportability (exception handling). All these impact the quality of the delivery. They are rarely included as a part of the QA scope.

To summarize, QA operates on requirements, while software is developed to the design.

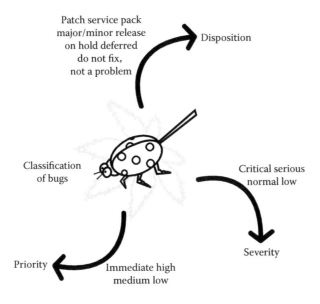

Figure 12.5   The classification of bugs.

Classification of Bugs

Severity indicates the impact of the bug or enhancement request on the customer's ability to function with the solution. Bugs can be classified according to the following (Figure 12.5):

- *Showstopper or Critical*: this typically implies data loss, data corruption, crashes, missing functionality, loss of functionality, or a usability problem that practically renders the solution useless for the customer until it is fixed. It is possible that many parts of the solution work, but enough is broken to prevent the solution from being useful to the customer or in preventing the customer from proceeding with the use of the system (refer to Chapter 1 Software Failure).
- *Serious* is similar to critical, except that an acceptable workaround exists for the bug, allowing the customer to continue to use the solution effectively. What is serious depends on the user. Sometimes seemingly low-impact problems may be assigned this severity; they may be individually small irritations but collectively exasperating. This often happens with error messages, look-and-feel, and usability. There may be "forest"-type concerns as opposed to specific "tree"-type concerns that a customer considers serious.

- *Normal* implies missing functionality, loss of functionality, or a usability problem that does not render the solution useless for the customer. They can continue to use the solution for all practical purposes even if an acceptable workaround does not exist for the particular bug or enhancement.
- *Low* typically implies missing functionality, loss of functionality, or a usability problem that has low impact on a customer's ability to use the solution (a fix would be welcome but very little is lost in the customer's ability to derive value from the solution).

Priority indicates the priority with which the bug or enhancement request will be taken up by the development team. Priority is assigned based on the *severity* of the bug or enhancement, other commitments of the development team, and available resources. There is often confusion between *severity* and *priority*. The difference is analogous to Important versus Urgent in a list of action items.

- *Immediate.* This is typically a priority assigned for Showstopper and Critical severity problems. This means a quick patch must be issued. All Immediate Priority problems must receive attention before those of any other type. It might also mean more resources are applied to the problem, typically because resources are busy with other Immediate Priority problems or more resources can do a better job of meeting customer need for a quick fix.
- *High.* This is typically assigned for Serious severity problems. High Priority problems receive attention as long as there are no immediate priority problems waiting for attention. Fixes should be made available at the next convenient patch or service pack (maintenance release).
- *Medium.* This is typically assigned for Normal severity problems. Medium Priority problems receive attention only if all Immediate and High Priority problems have appropriate attention and resources applied to them. Fixes must be made available in one of the next convenient service packs (maintenance releases) or minor or major releases. A Normal severity must not be assigned priority higher than Medium. Resource adjustment should not be required as the intent is to do the most with the resource allocated.
- *Low.* This is typically assigned for Low severity problems. Low Priority problems must get attention only if all other priority problems have appropriate attention and resources applied to them. Fixes must be made available in one of the next convenient service packs (maintenance releases) or minor or major releases. A Low severity problem should be assigned priority lower than Medium.

Resource adjustment should not be required as the intent is to do utmost with the resource allocated.

Disposition indicates the timing of the fix:

- *Patch.* This should be assigned to Immediate or High priority problems only. All immediate priority problems must be addressed in a patch prior to any High priority problems.
- *Service pack.* This should be assigned to High, Medium, and Low priority problems. Additional data associated with this disposition should be the major or minor release on which the service pack will be made available. All High priority problems must be addressed in a service pack prior to any Medium or Low priority problems, and Medium priority problems in a service pack prior to Low priority problems.
- *Minor release.* This should be assigned to High, Medium, and Low priority problems. Additional data associated with this disposition should be the targeted date, month, or quarter for the release.
- *Major release.* This should be assigned to Medium and Low priority problems.
- *On hold.* This should be assigned if there is a lack of clarity and agreement on severity or priority. Urgent action should be taken to change this disposition, especially if it is suspected that the severity could be Showstopper, Critical, or Serious, or the priority could be Immediate or High.
- *Deferred.* This should be assigned to Medium and Low priority problems only. This implies that there are no definite plans as of now to fix the problem. The disposition will be reviewed periodically and changed as appropriate.
- *No plans to fix.* This should be assigned to Medium and Low priority problems only, and more likely for Low priority. This implies that there is a definite plan to never fix the problem.
- *Not a problem.* This will typically be a reassignment of an earlier disposition that, a result of finding that something once considered to be a problem, is actually not a problem.

Understanding Bug Discovery

The "engineering code complete" stage is considered the point at which the development team has finished all coding (based on functional specs) and has handed over the code to QA after finishing their preliminary unit or developer testing.

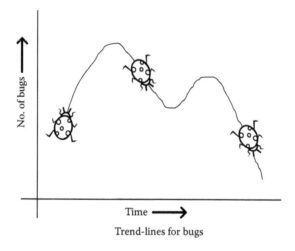

Trend-lines for bugs

Figure 12.6 Frequency of bugs.

The first round of QA typically generates a lot of bugs, some "real" and critical, and others that are not so serious. The discovery of bugs follows an upward trend initially, and then descends. This does mean that the software is ready to launch after the initial batch of bug detection. Figure 12.6 shows how the process generally works.

QA teams discover the most obvious problems in the beginning (first test cycle). These are typically related to form rather than content: empty fields, mandatory and nonmandatory checks, user-level validations, boundary conditions, improper messages, blank reports, etc. Once these bugs are fixed, QA starts to focus on the logical aspects of the product, using more detailed test cases with proper test data. During this phase of QA, one is testing not just the stability of the code, but also the behavior expected from the system. It is here that the next increase in bug detection occurs.

Most bugs require the attention of the original engineering team. At the time of the first code drop to QA, the Engineering manager could be under pressure to release some of the developers because they are done with their main task; the code has moved on to QA. However, to reallocate the engineering team at this time is premature. A substitute team may unintentionally add problems because they will not understand the entire code and its dependencies across the product. The original developers should be retained until one complete cycle of QA has been completed.

QA teams use a test tracking tool that records tests and classifies bugs. These tools allow development to focus on bugs classified as "High Priority." Even with proper guidelines, this classification may not be very reliable because there is some subjectivity in determining the seriousness of a bug. QA teams tend to take the software specifications literally, weighing all functionality equally. This can lead to differences in opinions as to how a bug is tagged.

The bug should be communicated and assigned to developers who can fix it. Often, the test tracking tool itself becomes the mode of communication. Engineers are expected to read the bug lists, or read notifications automatically generated from the tool. After the problem is resolved, the fixes should be retested. Any information relevant to regression testing should be conveyed from engineering to QA. Such information gets lost if not properly updated in test cases.

Release Management

A decision to release an application for general use is always fraught with risk because it is not always possible to test for (or remove) all software bugs. Naturally the question arises as to whether or not most of the bugs have been identified. Because this relates only to the QA group, it is considered QA's responsibility to decide when the software quality is sufficient. It is important to know that quality is only one of the parameters in the release equation. Other parameters, and often equally important, include externally communicated timelines, business goals, competitive pressures, or legal contracts. Consequently, the decision maker should be an individual or group that is aware of all such aspects.

Push and Pull: The Equation between Development and QA

The relationship between engineering and quality assurance (QA) is one of active tension and cooperation. The tension arises due to the "fault-finding" mode under which QA, by the very nature of its responsibilities, operates. The cooperation derives from the shared objective (which may often be hidden under the tensions) of improving the quality of the deliverable. It is crucial that organizations understand the push–pull relationship between the two.

Testing works in cycles; a test cycle consists of running through one set of predefined tests. This cycle must be taken to completion, if only to ensure that the quality of that code drop is well understood. Interrupted test cycles leave that status undefined. Without a reliable status, one cannot make a call about acceptability. The code drop could be so bad that it may not be worth the time and effort to complete the cycle. In that case, the cycle can be formally terminated. Such termination should also be

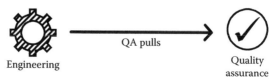

QA pulls

Engineering

Quality assurance

The relationship between engineering and QA

Figure 12.7   Engineering and quality assurance (QA) interact.

treated as cycle completion with a proper QA status given to it. Avoid terminating a cycle just because the development team made a new code drop.

The relationship between QA and developers is one of *pull* by QA (Figure 12.7). Understanding and implementing this equation will go a long way toward reducing the turbulence that ensues when the development team is continuously working on changes. Allowing Engineering to *push* the code, because they are ready, would lead to a volatility that leaves test cycles interrupted. That is, one circus has to leave town before the other can open.

The relationships among the various artifacts that make up software must be taken into account, and a well-defined order of play established, for the Development Release-to-QA process to work smoothly. Take as an example an application with four artifacts: (1) a database schema, (2) some batch jobs that run in the background (perhaps to clean the databases periodically), (3) the actual customer-facing application, and (4) a set of reports created outside the application using a different reporting tool that maps to the schema. The batch jobs, the application, and the reports do not have a common build, but work together as a system when released. They are separate artifacts for QA and Engineering. Now take a situation where the database schema changes; suppose a new field is added. That it affects the other pieces is well understood. However, the change has to propagate through the Development and QA teams in an agreed-upon play order. The order within Engineering could be, for example, that the Development DBA (database administrator) makes the change first, then the others make changes to the code in parallel to incorporate the new fields. There could be reasons why the other three cannot make the changes simultaneously. The report module may have to wait for the application to make the changes before it can import metadata from the application so as to put the schema changes into effect. If any one of the other three tries to make code drops before the other two are ready, the result is chaos. Although the pieces will be separately tested, unless QA has the luxury of multiple environments, its setup would be on the old schema. It might also be in the middle of test cycles for some of the other

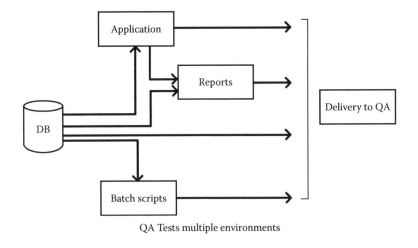

QA Tests multiple environments

Figure 12.8   Quality assurance (QA) consolidates across modules.

pieces. Going ahead with QA for only some of the pieces is not feasible. This is another reason why QA needs to *pull* the code, even if Engineering is ready to *push*. It can time the changes in its environment, ensure that all engineering deliverables are on the new version, and then start a new test cycle (Figure 12.8).

Any sort of simple dependency diagram, or a release plan, can capture this sequence of taking up modifications and releasing new versions.

Multiple Views of Quality

Software gets released when a certain quality, deemed sufficient, is achieved. Engineers and analysts may have a definition of acceptable quality that differs from what is used by *consumers* interacting with the system. Consumers are not limited to the primary end users for whom the software was developed. They include the organization's sales and marketing groups, implementation and installation sales support engineers, finance personnel, and perhaps even the external press who have their own ideas of what a system is expected to deliver.

An application is rarely deployed in isolation — it is part of a larger environment that includes various business processes. Not all consumers understand this complex environment. For example, data may be lost because of inadequate backup, or a report may generate inaccurate totals (when compared to actual physical inventory) because a data load did not happen properly at the backend. A user may very well tag these as quality issues. Unnecessary blame can easily be assigned to the software.

In the marketing world there is a saying that "perception is reality." The perception of quality regarding a deliverable may be completely different from what the QA reports show. The larger issue of quality, both actual and perceived, is something that should be actively brought into the development arena.

Quality Assurance (QA) and Testing Skills

As discussed previously, QA and testing are different. A good test engineer should have a perverse "test-to-break" attitude, a strong desire for quality, and an attention to detail. Tact and diplomacy are useful in maintaining a cooperative relationship with developers. Previous software development experience can be helpful, because it provides a deeper understanding of the development process and gives the tester an appreciation for the developer's point of view.

A QA person also needs the same qualities as a good tester. An ability to find problems as well as to see what is missing is important for inspections and reviews. Additionally, one must be able to understand the entire software development process and how it fits into the business aspects of the organization. Good communication skills and the ability to understand various sides of issues are important. Patience is necessary, especially in the early stages of implementing QA processes in an organization.

Summary: Quality Matters

Software development requires a sophisticated, general-purpose infrastructure that can adjust to and work with a varying mix of language, domain, complexity, and customer needs. It is an infrastructure that is weighted toward the quality of the people on the team rather than the equipment and tools. This dependency on human abilities leads to a variation in quality of the deliverable.

Quality software requires a good, healthy relationship between the Engineering and QA groups. The equation between Development and QA is one of push-and-pull; that is, it is a relationship full of active tension and cooperation. The tension obviously arises due to the "fault-finding" mode under which QA, by the very nature of its responsibilities, operates. Allowing Engineering to *push* the code because they are ready would lead to a volatility, which leaves test cycles uninterrupted. Realizing this can go a long way toward reducing the turbulence that ensues when the development team is continuously working on changes. One circus must leave town before the other can open its doors.

A proper understanding of where the risks lie, and where the problems are likely to originate, can help allocate scarce resources efficiently. Quality is also related to a culture that values and respects perfection in what it delivers. As a feedback system, it is invaluable in keeping the deliverable system in control.

The problem with communication ... is the *illusion* that it has been accomplished.

—George Bernard Shaw

Chapter 13

Communication

> The great thing about human language is that it prevents us from sticking to the matter at hand.

—Lewis Thomas

A computer program is an exercise in precise communication with the computer. Human communication is far more complex. It is often said that software developers are better at communicating with their computers than with their colleagues and customers. Yet, good communication, with everyone, is essential for successful functioning.

This chapter examines some of the communication aspects of software delivery: the different objectives of communication, avoiding miscommunication, the role of nonverbal communication in different stages of a software project, the unequal distribution of information within organizations and project teams, and related behaviors such as information hiding.

The Objectives of Communication

In any software development project, considerable information is exchanged. Communication is more than that. It works toward certain objectives such as understanding requirements, winning an argument, exerting influence, controlling a situation, or misleading someone else. If such objectives are not met, then communication has not occurred.

Take a look at one aspect that is important to software development: the objective of avoiding miscommunication. Miscommunication can be expensive. It can lead to rework and delays. In some instances, it can result in irreparable damage to the product delivered or a business relationship.

What compounds the problem is that, in many situations, one is not even aware that a miscommunication has occurred until its effects are seen at some later stage. A good communication plan or strategy, therefore, should include feedback or evaluation cycles. Communication is, at the minimum, a two-way street.

Communication Models

Communication and human discourse have been modeled for ages. All good models are abstractions and must be recognized as such.

One of the most influential communication models comes from Information and Communications Theory. It was designed in 1949 by Claude Shannon, an engineer for the Bell Telephone Company, to study the problem of transmitting messages efficiently. The terms and concepts related to this subject have specific engineering meanings that are different from their common English usage. A message is a set of signals for transmission, and no meaning is assumed. The objective is to ensure that a message transmits correctly and efficiently. Some of the definitions and findings resulting from this model are counter-intuitive. If understood properly, there are findings and points of interest that can map to many areas in software design and development.

Information is the measure of uncertainty in a system. There is more uncertainty if there are more choices in the messages that can be sent. When there is a lot of uncertainty, one needs more information to minimize the uncertainty. Another way of looking at it is that messages that are infrequent, which have a low probability of occurring, have more informational value. If a computer job runs every day correctly, and one gets a daily message saying that it ran properly, then a message that the job failed is a "surprising" message that carries more information because it is a less frequently occurring event. Report designers use this concept to design reports that highlight exceptions because such information gets more attention.

Noise is anything that significantly interferes with receiving the message. There are encoding and decoding techniques designed to overcome the effects of such noise — that is, recover the original message sent through a noisy channel with some calculable degree of certainty. For example, if one is trying to say something to another person across a noisy party room, shouting louder may not be as effective as changing "channels" and signaling by hand. Similarly, in a project, if a person is not responding to e-mails, then it would make sense to change channels and leave a voicemail rather than send another e-mail reminder.

We would encourage readers who are not familiar with Information and Communications Theory to read good books available on the subject.

The Problem of Miscommunication

Miscommunication can occur at many levels. On the sender's side, it could be due to errors in transmission or errors of content. When there are errors in transmission, the message is garbled. When there are errors of content, then *wrong* information is being sent. On the receiver's side, it could be due to misinterpretation.

Avoid Picking the Wrong Information

Quite often, the wrong information — an incorrect or outdated database schema, the wrong version of the specifications — gets sent. Such errors happen at boundary conditions. When someone asks for the *latest* version or the *approved* version or the *production* version of the code, one might pick up the wrong version. This is related to the possible states or messages that can exist: there may be many more versions of the code or document but only one *latest* version. The chances of picking up the wrong version are much greater than the chances of picking up the right one. Good organization or proper versioning tools aim to prevent such higher-probability mistakes from occurring.

Understanding the Sender's Responsibility

It is safe to assume that when one makes a request, one is transmitting on a noisy channel. Noise always exists in the form of distractions or inattention, or other such distorting factors. Whose responsibility is it to ensure that the message gets across, that is, decoded properly on the other side? It is the sender's responsibility. This must be made clear when communication plans for the project are being discussed. If one asks for the "project plans" and is sent a spreadsheet, while one was expecting a deck of slides, then one is solely responsible for not making the request clear that one expected the plans to be in a slide format, and not a spreadsheet.

Imprecise Requests

Being imprecise, as opposed to "precise," appears to refer to numbers or numerical entities. That is, however, not always the case. One can be imprecise when one says, "Let us meet at the entrance of Sears in York Mall," when there are many entrances to that particular Sears in that mall. (One might say that this is an example of incompleteness, not imprecision. We are not immune to ambiguity.) Database analysts are familiar with this problem when they try to define "unique" keys for tables that turn out to be not so unique after all in the real world.

Misunderstanding the Received Request

On the other hand, the information could be "correct" from the sender's point of view but it is being interpreted incorrectly at the receiving end. This is fairly common. The same e-mail sent to different members of the team gets understood differently. Receivers always read what they get within a cultural and personal context. A neutral-sounding statement can be interpreted as a criticism by a sensitive person. A person excessively sensitive to criticism can read "between the lines" even when there is no such intention. The history of the relationship between the sender and the receiver often has some bearing. It is safe to assume that people always read between the lines. If one has a piece of scrubbed, validated text that has been known to work for a particular situation, keep reusing it. If one has a good e-mail welcoming a new member of the team, the release of a new version or any other communication that is used regularly, keep it aside and reuse it.

The Rashomon Effect

The Rashomon effect is based on Akira Kurosawa's movie of that name about different "experiences" of the same traumatic incident. Brian Lawrence, in an article in *American Programmer*, draws attention to the so-called Rashomon effect in software requirements, and the difference between misunderstanding and ambiguity. "It's quite possible to have two or more perfectly legitimate interpretations of a single concept at the same time," he writes. The software requirements may not be just "misunderstood" — they are being perfectly understood but are being interpreted differently.

Inconsistency in Communication

Inconsistencies are to be expected. What is said in one document contradicts what is being said in another. Some of these contradictions may be obvious and identifiable. Others may not be so obvious. They may turn out to be contradictions only when things are viewed at different levels. For example, a law may be very consistent within a state but may become contradictory when applied across states. The design of a module may be consistent but contradictions appear when different modules are integrated into a larger system. This also happens in resource planning; resources are allocated at a project level and appear well balanced, but when all the projects are looked at at the department level, then contradictions arise and the overall set of plans becomes infeasible.

Inconsistencies can also emerge over time. Contradictions can emerge due to subsequent changes in the environment invalidating an otherwise perfectly valid situation.

All inconsistencies do not necessarily pose problems. Two applications may be exporting data in different formats. Unless these applications actually need to exchange data, the inconsistency need not pose any problem. Standards imposed on organizations often ignore this aspect of enduring inconsistency, forcing either or both those applications to spend time and energy in working out a common format because "consistency is always better."

Omission or Incompleteness

Omission or incompleteness is difficult to determine without a good baseline against which to compare it. How would one know whether something is missing unless one knows that it should have been there? Such baseline information comes from experience (or some template or process) underlying the work. Such a template would remind one, for example, that a project estimate should include the costs associated with data migration. Organizations that invest in such templates and processes improve communication and reduce mistakes.

Whether there is a transmission error or a mistake made in selecting the information to be sent, or a misinterpretation of the information received, they all result in a situation where miscommunication has occurred. If one knew that such a miscommunication has occurred, then there is, at least, an opportunity to correct it. In many situations, one is not even aware that a miscommunication had occurred until its effects are noticed at some later time. That is why feedback, sometimes in the form of playback, should always be part of the communication plan.

Information Dynamics

Setting Up Artificial Information Hierarchies

It is human nature to read between the lines about every aspect of communication and worry about its meaning in terms of one's inclusion and exclusion from groups, real or virtual. Managers must be sensitive to this. These aspects can cause more trouble than the content of the message. That is why some managers include all on the team, even if they are not directly concerned with the message. The message that they are communicating is that the receiver is still part of the team.

Selecting the Right Channel

People read meaning into the channels used. This is a cultural thing. Some channels are considered the right channel for certain messages and situations. A notice pinned on the notice board, a newsletter blast to all employees, or a letter addressed to "current resident" is considered an impersonal channel of communication. It may be impersonal although adequate for the purpose. Other types of communication may be handled by e-mail, leaving a note, or a detailed voice-mail. Some types of communication require personal meetings, whether they are formal or informal meetings. One would not like to lay off an employee or remove someone from a project through an e-mail or a voice-mail. A good manager always understands the importance of the channel selected for the communication.

Choosing the Set Carefully

People read meaning into with whom the information is shared. They wonder why a particular person is being copied. People look at copy lines in e-mails and distinguish, often incorrectly, between names on the "To:" and "Copy to:" lines, treating the former as "more important" than the others. Sometimes, the sender wants to signal that the "To:" line receivers should be paying more attention to this message than the "Copy to:" line attendees. Sometimes, the sender wants all the receivers to pay equal attention but puts only those who are supposed to take action on the message in the "To:" line. These protocols must be established implicitly or explicitly to smooth communications: whom will the "To:" line include, what does "copy to:" mean, and how the persons responsible for action will be identified in an e-mail sent to many.

Unequal Distribution of Information

Never assume that information, in any group, is distributed uniformly. That is as hypothetical as the assumption in economics of perfect markets on the presumption of perfect information. It is at times baffling to learn that several project team members do not know important aspects of the project, even up to the end. They sometimes do not know who the customer is, or what the key deadlines (release or go-live dates) are. Likewise, they may not be aware of important dependencies in the project. Priorities are not understood or recognized. Applying the Law of Requisite Variety (Chapter 2, Systems), the manager must ensure that each individual or sub-group (depending on how much variety the manager assigns to the team) understands certain key pieces of information.

Private Interests

The nondisclosure of information could be in some person's private interests. It could be hidden or made difficult to access. Information flow is closely related to the political dynamics in an organization or project.

Hierarchical Information Flows

Information is driven by having hierarchical structures in place. Most organizations have hierarchical structures that mimic military hierarchies, and more information flows up rather than comes down. The lack of information flowing down gets justified in many ways. However, it sometimes prevents those at lower levels from getting information that they could have used in making better decisions. Information flows should not map strictly to organizational hierarchies.

Need to Know

It becomes a problem when necessary information is not shared because of false assumptions about the "need to know," or false mapping of organizational hierarchies to information sharing hierarchies. The engineer in the other department may need this information more than the vice-president in one's department.

One objection to information sharing is that the information might be misused. If the real delivery dates in the client's order were told to the team, then the managers might lose their buffers. If financial information about profitability or revenues is shared, the employees on the team may make inappropriate demands. Such situations may very well occur. What is not clear is whether they can be avoided by withholding information.

Information Hiding

Even in these days of seemingly excess data and communication, team members can be impoverished in an information sense. We have come a long way since there were only a limited number of copies of a printed manual that "belonged" to someone who kept it locked. Many behavior patterns have, however, not changed. There is still a lot of information that is being kept hidden. Sometimes, it is no more than a reflection of the personality of the one withholding the information. For someone else, it could be a desire to become the "go-to" person for something. For others, it could be the need to "become indispensable," getting a sense of "job security" or "power" through such an arrangement. Managers must make conscious efforts to address such situations, as such behavior can be a drain on productivity and morale. The task of challenging such behavior becomes difficult when those demonstrating it are "indispensable prima donnas." But challenged they must be in the interests of the larger team.

The tactics employed for information hiding are several. They mostly work off the fact that there is a cost to information search. By making the cost of the search excessive or prohibitive, one can dissuade access to the information. Edward Tufte in his book, and also in his lectures, writes about how magicians hide information through distraction — they are waving something in their left hand drawing the audience's attention away from the sleight of hand occurring with the right hand. Similar distraction tactics are employed when one embeds important information in prolix e-mails, when "shared" files are updated without informing others, or when relevant topics are always "taken offline." In matrix organizations, the employee may share the information with only one of the lines of command; this often happens with vacations, where the employee informs the administrative manager but the project manager is caught by surprise.

Merely asking for more information to be documented is not the solution to the problem of non-information-sharing. A person wishing to hide information can still do so within voluminous documentation that is relatively useless, quickly out of date, or totally overwhelming (sometimes used in legal situations). The fact that the required information is not there may be discovered when it is too late. We discuss the issues with Documentation in Chapter 15.

Modes of Communication

Nonverbal Communication

It is said that nearly 80 percent of communication is nonverbal. Displeasure can be conveyed by silence, disinterest through the body language, or anger through tone, although the words may be polite and neutral. The difficulty is to how to deal with it. To take an example, if a specification is being discussed, the customer's body language should not matter much. Many technical persons assume that, after all, if there is a concern about any aspect of the specification, it will be pointed out directly. That is not always so. The point to note is that software development is as much a techno-political or techno-economic activity as any other, and not all messages are explicitly spelled out. It would be foolhardy not to pay attention to nonverbal communication. This is obviously most important in demos and walk-throughs.

Words versus Diagrams

Diagrams are better at representing the essence of systems and programs. Software is primarily logic and flow. Both can be well represented through diagrams. This makes diagrammatic representation highly suitable for software. However, a good description of a system in words still has considerable value. What can be better expressed in words than in diagrams? Although diagrams up-level, isolate, and draw out the essentials very effectively, there is a certain clarifying power in well-chosen words. Analysis, prethinking, and details need words. A design that finally gets selected is actually one of various other design options and threads of thought that the designer created, but rejected. These discussions and thoughts can be better addressed in a written document.

Communication Tools

The Map Is Not the Territory

It is not surprising that many professions have tried to evolve a vocabulary and set of conventions to communicate effectively. Engineering drawings, E-R (entity-relationship) diagrams, flowcharts, and other methods of representation provide tools for communication. Such solutions try to address, invariably, representation of content. Many of these representational techniques are pictorial or diagrammatic. The content can, at times, be incorrect: one can draw a flowchart that has the wrong logic or does not take care of many conditions. The technique or tool may not be sufficient to reflect the various angles and viewpoints required for proper understanding. We have to keep reminding ourselves of the military dictum: the map is not the territory.

A Good Worker Needs Many Tools

It is a well-known fact that a good worker always carries many tools in his or her toolchest. But in corporate environments, there is always an attempt to reduce the variety in tools. In the name of "standardization," "integration," or "re-use," there are fewer tools available from which to choose. There is often one modeling tool, or one slide creation software, that becomes the "standard." Practitioners may end up having insufficient variety in these tools to handle the variety in the situation they are trying to control. These tools may improve with time but that does not compensate fully for the lack of variety now.

These tools and representational frameworks are languages that we use for thinking. As James Martin and Carma McClure say in their book entitled *Diagramming Techniques for Analysts and Programmers*,

> "…what we are capable of thinking depends on the language we use for thinking. When mankind used only Roman numerals, ordinary people could not multiply or divide. That capability spread when Arabic numbers became widely used."

One should carefully select the tools that one uses on a project.

Channels

Communication in projects employs many channels: phone, e-mail, spreadsheets, slide presentations, corridors, documents, meetings, and many others. Content is generated and retained all over the place. Even if all communication had "perfect content," it should be no surprise that this multiplicity of channels could lead to miscommunication. This section examines some of these very familiar channels.

Slides and Diagrams

We must address the issue of PowerPoint and related slide tools. Power-Point has become the *de facto* corporate vehicle for sharing information. Fortunately, the rampant use of PowerPoint remains the prerogative and domain of managers and "manager types." (In fact, some managers are called PowerPoint types). Software developers have not embraced this tool and remain skeptical. Tufte has a good pamphlet criticizing Power-Point for its low information content and poor use of real estate. Power-Point slides seem to contain cryptic bullet points drawn from the age of the telegraph, all the way to long sentences cut and pasted into the slide from some other document. Designers are sometimes forced to shoehorn detailed technical diagrams into slides, thereby reducing them to unreadable "chartjunk."

E-Mail

E-mail is ubiquitous. We have drawn attention to the fact that information about a project is spread across many channels. E-mail is one of the most-used channels. The information in e-mails can be called semi-formal. It consists of notifications, tactical issue handling, and technical discussions. Attachments may be formal documents or forms. An e-mail thread is like a call-response unit in music, although it may go on and on and is less pleasing to the ear.

We now examine a few issues related to e-mail. An important one concerns what to do with the e-mails. There is a lack of rigor in e-mail threads, which makes it unsafe to delete all but the latest e-mail on a topic, although the send-reply threads within the e-mail may have captured the entire life cycle of the e-mail. If they must be retained, a good option would be to retain them in folders at a high level of granularity: Project A or Project A-QA. Trying to organize them with any more granularity is not worth the effort.

Why are so many people copied on every e-mail? This is a coupling problem. It is a partitioning problem. It is also a push-pull problem. There are many who are convinced that all those who are likely to be impacted now or later, by any piece of information contained in that e-mail, should be included in the distribution. All project members are coupled together all the time. It is easier to send to an entire distribution list than to partition a list each time. It is also driven by the need to deflect possible complaints and excuses from others that they "were not informed." People may be added to the copy line just to draw attention to one's achievements up the chain. The net result, however, is e-mail clutter of gigantic proportions.

Some people use copying e-mail as an implicit escalation, a preemptive move. For example, it implies that "your boss is seeing this request; you better respond to it." Doing it all the time, and for trivial or routine actions, dulls the effectiveness of the tactic. There is also no assurance that the manager is paying attention to it anyway.

Copying e-mail has changed the information dynamics within organizations. We would recommend that organizations or teams operate according to well-defined policies made known to all employees or team members. Here is one that we proposed:

- *Sender only policy*. The senders keep the e-mail permanently. Receivers delete them more frequently. If the receiver needs an e-mail that he or she has deleted, he or she asks the sender to resend it.

■ *Receiver retains.* This is the policy that most organizations are operating. This is the reason why people save or archive messages in their in-boxes, and rarely save or archive their Sent folders. This may also be driven by the thinking that the sender "knows" what he has sent but that he is less familiar with what he receives.

■ *Both retain.* Less coordination is required. As disk space and local search become cheaper, this may be a non-issue.

Subject lines in e-mails are difficult to populate effectively. The fact that it is called a "subject" line does not always help. If one is attaching minutes of a meeting, should one say "Attaching Minutes" (SenderAction and Object), or "Review Minutes" (ReceiverAction and Object), or just "Minutes" (Object only). SenderAction is easier because the sender knows what he is doing, and it avoids complexity when there are multiple ReceiverActions required. If one is conveying status, a simple sender-based statement may be sufficient — for example, "Approval received for Release 3 requirements."

Replying to e-mails rather than responding separately maintains a thread. That is obvious and is useful to the sender who expects a reply. Responding to an e-mail separately carries the risk of not being recognized as the response expected. This can happen when there is a subtle change in the sub-e-mail channel used. As an example, when someone asks for a presentation, instead of attaching it, one opens the presentation and uses the facility in the presentation tool to forward it as an attachment. This changes the subject line. If the requestor was expecting a reply to his or her e-mail, he or she may mistake this as a different presentation for a different thread, and not the one for which he or she was waiting.

Any communication that becomes too routine tends to get ignored. Vary the frequency and content of the communication so that the receiver gets interested enough to open the e-mail. Everyone is getting overwhelmed by the volume of e-mail, and cutting through the clutter is also the sender's responsibility.

Action Items

Action items are another popular artifact of the managing process. People are taking action items away from meetings. Managers are maintaining action item lists. They are obviously useful — if handled correctly.

Action items are just that. They must have some action associated with an item. As such, they are best written as "verb and object" pairs:

"Raise Purchase Order," "Release Test Plan," "Get Approval for Change Control 21."

What should be their granularity? Because action items must be assigned to individuals (or teams) and tracked separately, they must be sufficiently granular to be understood by the receiver. Our recommendation is that an action item list should be quite granular and specific. For example, "Tim to forward John's e-mail to Mary" is a unit of work that can be verified in the next meeting. This is not a high-level document mapping to a software life cycle. It is lower and more detailed than the Project Plan. To the extent possible, all action items should map to some entry in the Project Plan. (Tim's forwarding the e-mail to Mary is part of the "finalize design specifications" activity in the Project Plan.)

Action item lists should be as uncluttered as possible. The list should be limited to the item, the person taking the action, the date that is expected, and some remarks. The item should, because of its very nature, be action oriented. The name of the person in the "Person" column is the person doing the task, who may or may not be the person "responsible" for the task. Managers may, in the end, be responsible — having their names in the columns does not serve much purpose, unless they will do the task themselves. The date is often specified at a degree of granularity that is not appropriate. Use flexible terms such as "Next Week," "ASAP," "On receipt of approval," whichever might be most suitable. They will be taken more seriously. Often, "Remarks" columns double as minutes of meetings and become longer and longer until the entire column is just ignored. It is not necessary to record every remark made about the action item in this column. Keep it short so that people read it.

Does one need an action item list when one has a Project Plan (in MS-Project or some other PERT based tool)? Yes, one does. They serve slightly different purposes. A good, easy-to-read action item list is key to day-to-day monitoring and management of projects.

Demos

Software seems to be working well until it goes into demos. Something always seems to go wrong. This may be one of the many errors popping up at an inopportune time, although many suspect that arranging a demo is itself a cause for triggering misbehavior. We do not subscribe to such superstitious ideas although we would like to draw attention to Bill Joy's observation that the word "demonstrate" has embedded in its etymology the same roots as the word "monster." So maybe there is something to it after all.

One is often forced to demonstrate an application that is not fully ready. The point to keep in mind is that impressions matter, as marketing folks know well. If the product is in bad shape, do not try to arrange a demo. Users will nod their agreement that they understand that it is a work in progress, yet get apprehensive that the software is "in bad shape." This can have adverse side effects on the projects. Just as there is a point at which an application is ready for release, there also is a point at which an application is ready for demo — and not before.

Demos must be done in very controlled environments. Some points to be aware of include:

- Understand clearly what the demonstration is set up for. Is it to show that progress is being made, or is it part of the requirements validation process? Modulate discussions accordingly.
- Test what you are demonstrating a few times and stick to the script. A demo does not always show all the features in the application. Decide on what you are going to show and show only that. It is tempting to get carried away and click at something that you think "should work" but have not tested yourself.
- Control the demo environment strictly. Set up the environment early. Do not change demo machines at the last minute. Keep proven user IDs for the demo. Select parameters (date ranges, customer IDs, etc.) for reports and queries that you know will return good data.
- Take detailed notes. If it is a demo to an important audience, have other team members in the room take notes, as it is very difficult to do the demo, handle questions, and take notes at the same time. The note-taker and the person doing the demo should pay close attention to nonverbal reactions to what is being shown.
- Do set the expectations of what will be seen and what will not be shown before the demo. If the reports are not being shown, say explicitly that the reports are not yet ready and will not be shown in that day's demo. Let the users not find that out after going through the entire session expecting reports to be shown at the end. If there are known bugs that the developers are working on, let them know about it when you come to that portion of the demo.
- Provide basic information about the environment you are demonstrating. Are you showing the Development, QA, UAT, or the production versions? Which database is being accessed? What placeholders are in place? For example, messages on screens, logos, etc. might be placeholders, and the live system would have different content. Explain where the differences are between the demo

and what will be rolled into production. For example, in production, the log-in procedures may be different, they may be coming in through some other URLs, and firewalls may see the screens a little differently.

■ These days, many demos are done over Web conferences and the nonverbal feedback gets attenuated. In such environments, you have to watch out for the possibility that what you are seeing full-screen may get slightly truncated because of all the administration paraphernalia on the viewer's screen. At a minimum, slow the pace of the presentation and avoid very fast cursor movements.

Demos are very essential steps in any software development. They provide good validation from the users and can help catch serious errors in direction up-front.

Other Aspects of Communications

Most internal communications are done through e-mail, and e-mail communications were discussed in a previous section. However, there are other interesting aspects of communication.

Informal Communication

Every company, project, or social organization has powerful channels of informal communication. Formal communication rarely reveals the entire or accurate picture. People discuss their fears and anxieties, gossip about colleagues and managers, and share information about projects and problems. Ignoring this ground reality would be a mistake. Environments can be created where the value systems discourage the negative aspects of some of these behaviors.

It is safe to assume that a lot of information will leak out in any organization (Figure 13.1).

Communicating across Fault Lines

Communications across what one can call *fault lines* should be different from internal communications. When one is communicating across departments or with subcontractors and vendors, the communication may have to be more formal and has some implicit legal aspects. It is essential to identify and restrict such formal communication to a few persons on the project, perhaps the managers or the leads. However, work-related com-

Informal communication matters

Figure 13.1 Water cooler conversations.

munication between team members cannot always go through these channels and needs to be more direct. The team members must be made aware of policies toward such communications, their retention policies, and how they should exercise judgment when it comes to sensitive issues related to technical problems, schedules, finances, and scope of deliverables.

Escalation

A good escalation process is needed in any project. Proper and timely escalation of problems is essential. Timely escalation allows others in the hierarchy to remain informed and gives them an opportunity to intervene as necessary.

Although the advantages of timely escalation are well recognized, it is often the case that developers and managers do not escalate issues when they should. These could be issues related to one's own deliverables or someone else's for which one is waiting. This happens for a number of reasons, including:

- They are hoping that the problem will go away or get resolved "very soon" and, therefore, do not think they should escalate "at this time."
- An escalation is often seen as a form of complaint. If one has put in a request to get something done and it is getting delayed, one might hesitate to escalate as it would seem like a complaint against the other person. This is a common cause for delays in projects. One should always escalate in a timely although professional manner.

E-mail allows one to escalate diplomatically by copying the manager on the e-mail thread. This may not be sufficient, however, because managers may not have the time to go through entire e-mail threads to discover that something is not being delivered on time. Formal escalation is advisable. The person escalating should inform the parties concerned that the matter is being escalated. This keeps the escalation professional and helps maintain relationships.

Another reason why timely escalation is advisable when delays are encountered is because the other person may be delaying for he or she need his or her manager's authorization to re-prioritize their work. An escalation helps clear some logjams at the other party's end.

Automatic escalation exists as part of certain automated processes. This is common in call center or technical support situations. One might recall that such automatic escalation has a term identifying it — algedonics — as discussed in Chapter 2 on Systems.

Communication Techniques

This section examines three ideas that the authors of this book have found useful and effective.

PGP

Edward Tufte says, "When presenting complicated material, follow PGP (particular/general/particular)." This is a valuable organizing method. When one wants to convey a point in a paragraph, one can structure it so that one begins with a particular example ("Toyota sold more than X electric cars last year"), then makes a general point ("Electrical cars are becoming commercially successful lines for car manufacturers,"), and then ends with a particular again ("Even Honda and other manufacturers have come out with models such as Y and Z.").

Tagmemics

Tagmemics is a theory considered by some to be a fringe linguistic theory. We do not go into those details here. Of interest to us is one of its extended concepts: the suggestion that an event or an object can be seen as a static unit, a dynamic unit, or a field. This can be considered an ordering principle for one's thinking, useful in communicating better. As a static unit, the event or object must be considered on its own. For example, this is the online help module for this application. As a dynamic unit, this online help module is part of a changing series of online help content — the current version is release 3.1. As a field, it stands in relation to other content in the application and other ways of getting help: the online help must change if the application content changes. We need to mention that the user has others ways of getting help, for example, through the user manual or by calling a helpdesk number. If one was describing the online help module, these three angles — static, dynamic, and field — can be a useful way of organizing what one wants to say about online help.

McKinsey's MECE

Ethan Rasiel, in his book entitled *The McKinsey Way*, describes the problem-solving process called MECE, which is an acronym for Mutually Exclusive Collectively Exhaustive. Every issue that one wants to address should be separate and distinct. The set of all such distinct issues should cover all that needs to be covered. This is a good communication approach, as well as a good problem-solving approach, when one is trying to get a number of points across, whether it is in a presentation or in a requirements document.

MECE

MECE structures your thinking with maximum clarity (hence minimum confusion) and maximum completeness. MECE starts at the top level of your solution—the list of issues making up the problem you have to solve. When you think you have determined the issues, take a hard look at them. Is each one a separate and distinct issue? If so then your list is *mutually exclusive*. Does every aspect of the problem come under one (and only one) of these issues – that is, have you thought of everything? If so, then your issues are *collectively exhaustive*.

—From Ethan M. Rasiel, *The McKinsey Way*

The Tree Structure

The tree structure is a familiar organizing mechanism. It has some nodes at higher levels, branching out as one goes deeper or lower. If one organizes one's thoughts or presentation as a tree, one struggles with familiar issues. Does a new point (issue) deserves its own branch? If variations of that point are required in two or more places, does one put them in two places? Issues of horizontal and vertical continue to exist. For example, if one has to file status reports for many projects, should one have a separate folder entitled "Status Reports" containing status reports for each project, or have sub-folders under each project's folder called "status reports?"

One resolution mechanism that we have found useful is to think in terms of a "delete" function. For example, if the status reports are kept within project folders, then when the node folder — "Project A" — is deleted (it could actually be archived; delete is being used in a logical sense), all information including the status reports is likely deleted or archived. If that is what is required, then status reports belong within project folders.

How to Get the Message across Efficiently

There are two important aspects of sharing information:

1. Keep the format simple.
2. Repeat the message as often as necessary.

Keeping the format simple is not so easy. One must work along two vectors: (1) form and (2) content. This is a design problem. Paul Rand, the noted designer, says, "Design is relationships. Design is a relationship between form and content." Whether you are conveying schedule information, technical information, budget information, or any other kind of information, there is content and then there is form. The same content has different degrees of effectiveness when presented or worded differently. There is a lot that software designers can learn from graphic designers and advertising experts who know how to get their message across efficiently.

Content

The Minimal Set

What is the minimal set of documentation that one needs to build a software system? Let us apply the house-on-fire paradigm. One has just 30 seconds to pick up one document and run out of the building. One would naturally like to pick the document that will allow one to recreate the system best. Will one choose the Requirements document, the Design document, the Test Plans, or some other artifact? Many would say the Design document because a well-written Design document should allow one to go back to Requirements, and also go forward in rebuilding the system.

The question now arises as to what a project team needs to know. They need to know at least two pieces of information all the time: (1) schedules and (2) priorities. Schedules must be at two levels: (1) near term and (2) the larger picture. Priorities can be at various degrees of granularity. There are priorities within lists of features. There are priorities within test plans. Good communication requires the manager to convey priorities clearly to the team.

Status

The status of a project is often monitored by a green/yellow/red status. Many assume that it is obvious to both the project manager and the others what the status stands for. It turns out that the "project status" can have several different interpretations.

Green Status

What does "green" mean? It is a positive color and can be expected to denote positive, fertile outcomes:

- Green as Good. A green status means that the project is meeting management's plans and expectations.
- Green as Go. This is the traffic model. Everything in the project is moving, hopefully in the right direction.

Red Status

Red is the color for danger. There is some warning implied in the status going red:

- Red as Stop means things have come to a stop.

The differences between these interpretations are discussed below when we write about status as a predictor and status as a snapshot.

Yellow Status

Yellow is the proverbial "middle ground." It is practically defined by what it is not — green or red. It does not raise an alarm; it gives fair warning and keeps everyone informed that one is not yet out of the woods.

Snapshot or Predictor

What does the status represent? Is the status a predictor or a snapshot?

Status as Snapshot

As a snapshot, the status reflects events of the past reporting period. It is a call being made at the end of a time-bound period. It says that based on the developments during that time period, the project status is Green. Fluctuations within that time period are ignored. If a vendor called on Monday and said the shipment would be late and then called on Tuesday and said it would be on time, the status at the end of the week should not change. This also implies that the status is affected more by unresolved issues at the end of the time period. In short or fast-moving projects, because situations change frequently, the snapshot interpretation is less valuable.

Status as Predictor

Is the status a predictor? If so, a Green project status says that nothing happened during the week that could affect the remainder of the project. The status is invariably forward looking based on a backward look. The status does not reflect events of the past week that have no impact on the future of the project.

Status as "Call to Action"

We recommend that status colors be changed on a "Call to Action" basis. Many events happen in a project that can keep status colors in a state of flux. There is a risk of excessive and meaningless thrashing. A status change should be a call for action. It should be triggered only if action is required. If one takes a project from Green to Yellow, one is asking management to intervene at a certain level — escalates an issue with the management of another department, gives one more money or more time, etc. This requires that if one does not need some action, then do not change the status, even if things have shifted within the project.

To avoid arbitrary change of colors or calls to action, it must be supported by a set of neutral trigger conditions defined at an appropriate level of detail. For example, Yellow be defined with respect to both Green and Red. If we are going over the planned spend at this stage in the product by below 10 percent, change the status to Yellow. If it is more than 10 percent, change it to Red.

Status as Information

There is a natural reluctance on the part of many project managers to ask for help, or escalate a problem. The manager may appear in poor light. Occasionally, it is based on an optimism that things will be brought back under control soon. Some managers prefer to bring the status to Yellow at the earliest possible time, because some issues will always crop up.

In some environments, one does not like to be the messenger of bad news. In other environments, formal notification of bad news is frowned upon, while informal notification is acceptable. The official documents only show the good stuff. In such environments, formal status reports are often unreflective of ground reality.

For the receiver of a status report, status flags are often used as a partitioning mechanism. The receiver might concentrate his or her attention on projects in "Red." Without some historical analysis of the reliability of such flags in one's particular environment, this is a risky and unreliable approach. It must be accepted that managers vary in their ability or inclination to set flags properly.

The Three Popular Vectors

The vectors most commonly selected for status reporting are money, time, and scope. In software development projects, these vectors do serve useful purposes, yet may be inadequate indicators of project status, mainly because they ignore the nature of the project. They also ignore the fact that the vectors of interest may be different at different points in the life cycle of the project.

Another reason given for selecting these three is that they are good candidates for comparisons between projects. Money takes numerical values, which allows meaningful aggregation between departments and divisions in the reporting chain. Time could also be considered numerical, but adding a two-week delay on one project, with a five-week delay on another, is rather meaningless. Scope gets squeezed into some percentage that is again meaningless, even within a project, much less across projects. A 10 percent increase in scope identifies the scale of the problem — it is not 50 percent — but the number should be taken no more seriously than that. Furthermore, the effects of a change in scope may already be reflected in changes to money and time — making all three Red can be confusing.

If one's project is being monitored using only these vectors, one must treat them as a minimal set that is necessary but not sufficient. Use them for reporting to external agencies as required, but do not depend on them alone for active project management. Do supplement them with more meaningful vectors and metrics.

Granularity

Ashby's law of requisite variety (Chapter 2, Systems) governs status settings. If one is tracking five things, then one needs five indicators. If one has four vendors, each of them may be on time or running late on delivery. If different approvals are required, some may have been obtained, while others are in the pipeline. Trying to club all this lower-level information and assign status at a higher level can be done through some kind of a weighting algorithm, but this must be explicitly recognized.

Summary

Software development is basically a process of communication between customers, developers, and machines. Good communication is essential for successful software development where miscommunication can lead to rework and delays. Communication models from communications theory aim to ensure that a message is transmitted correctly and efficiently. Some of the ideas regarding noisy environments can be applied to software development, where, to take one example, there is often inconsistency and incompleteness in requirements. When it comes to software requirements, the Rashomon effect, wherein the requirements are being interpreted differently by each, can cause problems. As for the distribution of information within a team, it can be assumed to be unequal. Sometimes this problem of unequal distribution is caused because the management hierarchies are confused with information hierarchies — essential information is not given to the persons who actually need them but rather to those in the chain of command because they have the requisite authority to get it. Information hiding can be an issue in software projects and should be tackled head-on. If there is one take-away message, it is that one needs good communication to build good software.

The reality is more excellent than the report.

—Ralph Waldo Emerson

Chapter 14

Reports

There are no facts, only interpretations.

—Friedrich Nietzsche

For the business user, reports are the most critical outputs of the system. For designers and developers, reports are rarely the most important aspect to deliver. It is essential to recognize that reports have high visibility within an organization. Management judges applications on the quality of the reports generated, sometimes ignoring the complex back-end logic and processing built into the system. The priority given to reports in systems development needs to increase.

Reports also reveal something else. Various aspects of the management styles that exist within an organization can be judged by the reports that managers use in managing the business; the reports that get used, as well as those that get ignored, can reveal what management considers important in running the organization.

The History of Reporting

The term "report" has within its Latin roots the word *portare*, which means "carrying." Reports "carry" information. They carry information from one occasion, situation, or location to another. Like vessels and pipes that store and transport fluids, reports come in all shapes and sizes. They convey different things to different people. A good report is one that conveys what it has to convey — efficiently and effectively. The beauty of the vessel cannot override the objective of delivering the right content, although good report design plays an important role in how that content is received and absorbed. Reports should be like windows that let the outside view in — the viewer wants to see the view, not the window.

In the 1960s, systems called EDP (electronic data processing) were used to record and process data electronically. Data has been processed in organizations for centuries — it was the electronic nature of the processing that was emphasized. Subsequently, management information systems (MIS) were created to generate a limited set of predefined reports. In those days, processing costs were expensive, and, consequently, access to computing facilities was restricted. Reporting methodologies and requirements adjusted to those constrained environments. Because most of the processing was batch mode and involved considerable lead-times, it made more sense to avoid asking for or delivering fine-grained sets of data. Formatting facilities were basic, especially where line printers were used. Some may recall the big bold job number or username drawn out of smaller ASCII characters on the front page of a report that helped one pick out one's own printouts. Reports were bulky data extracts generated on a scheduled basis, supplying information in a batch mode. It worked well for getting access to historical data, and many managers made good use of it.

Later, when *decision support systems* (DSS) were introduced, reporting became more interactive, needing more resources and powerful engines to deliver them. As the power of computing moved to desktops and users became familiar with powerful desktop tools, their expectations of the reporting they were getting from stovepipe applications changed. The reality was, however, that the desktop tools were often more powerful than the reporting tools on centralized servers. In the area of reporting, considerable legacy thinking remained — the mindset did not change, but the graphics did. With the Web driving much of the current experience, another sea of change in expectations and possibilities in reporting is already becoming apparent.

One of the problems with the legacy reporting mindset is that these information systems produced mountains of paper, most of it ignored. (A common techniques for pruning distribution lists for batch reports was to stop sending them for a few cycles and see who asks for that report). Heaps of reports were generated, just because it was possible to do so. This encouraged people to create *executive information systems*. They were supposed to streamline processes, giving the executives exactly, and only what they wanted. Decades later, armed with a host of specialized systems such as CRM (customer relationship management), ERP (enterprise resource planning), SCM (supply chain management), SFA (sales force automation), BPM (business process management), etc., the truth remains that a set of good, meaningful reports that can help run a business, is still difficult to find.

Where does the fault lie? It lies in our attitude that once the data is in, getting it out will hardly be a problem. It is still oriented toward providing the ideal way of getting the data in, and in efficiently processing and storing it. This leads to lower priorities for reports during the design phase. In fact, recognizing the extent to which applications are judged by their reports, project managers and designers should bring reports early into the design process.

Reporting Hierarchy

No single report can capture the dynamics of a business. It is a set of reports that can do so. What the contents of the set should be varies by the application but we recommend a general approach for defining the set based on Abraham Maslow's Hierarchy of Needs, something that is very familiar to students of management.

Maslow created his famous Hierarchy of Needs pyramid around 1943, saying that human beings are largely motivated by unsatisfied needs, and that certain basic needs must be satisfied before higher ones can be met (Figure 14.1). According to his theory, the most basic need is related to physiological survival — air, water, light, sleep, etc. Once such needs are satisfied, they no longer motivate. Then comes the need for safety and security. In the context of work, this could include physical safety (say protective clothing, and secure office environments); protection against unemployment, loss of income; etc. The next level is some degree of need for social grouping, love, and belonging. These could translate to working with and adjusting to colleagues, teamwork, and communication. These are followed by the need for the respect of our peers, and for self-respect. These *esteem* needs are about being given due recognition for a job well done. A promotion or reward might satisfy something like this.

Maslow referred to these four levels of needs as *deficit needs*. If one does not have enough of something, he or she feels the need for it.

The top level of the pyramid is a bit different. It has to do with growth motivation (in contrast to deficit needs), or self-actualization. Self-actualization is about how people think of themselves. This is often measured by nonquantifiable things such as the extent of success or challenge at work.

For any business, cash represents the bottom of the pyramid. Just as food, shelter, and water are needed to meet our most basic needs for

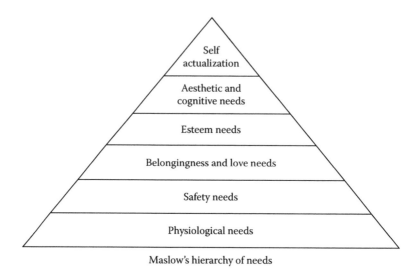

Maslow's hierarchy of needs

Figure 14.1 Maslow's pyramid maps to reporting needs.

survival, in Maslow's pyramid cash is the ultimate survival tool for a business. Healthy organizations soon reach the second level, that is, profit, followed by the higher levels of creativity (adjusting the business model as market dictates), growth, and proceed to the highest level, independence.

When a business owner has met all these needs, the company will typically find itself in a healthy position. However, problems start to occur when an organization or business unit focuses on a higher need, such as growth or independence, without first focusing on more basic needs, such as cash and profit.

Because reports are used to get the pulse of the business, it is essential that they also reflect Maslow's Hierarchy. Management reporting should be structured like a pyramid, with summary reports at the top going to a few executives, while detailed operational transaction reporting goes way down. In addition, there should be reports that cater to the needs expressed in this hierarchy at various levels. Using this model to analyze the report portfolio is a good design tool. Maslow's theories also apply to human beings, and a lot of reporting about business deals with goods, monetary transactions, and the like. One should also consider the proper use of a powerful model like this when designing the reporting for an organization.

What Is a Good Report?

It may be easier to define the characteristics of a bad report; put simply, such reports:

- Waste managers' time
- Result in considerable post-processing
- Can lead to wrong conclusions
- Are just ignored

Good reports help detect, analyze, and solve problems, presumably before they occur. Good report design involves the collection, and also the presentation of information. That is, it must be goal oriented and must address various aspects of the problem life cycle: one report to solve the low inventory problem, and a very different one to get a handle on the cash flow problem. A problem-solving approach to report design is necessary for both the report designer and the manager.

A report must provide answers to a reader's real-world situation and be designed to support the questions of the actual problem-solving environment. What information does he or she need to know, and when? Report designers need to take a page out of the documentation folks who have realized that putting softcopies of end-user manuals within the application is not a replacement for providing context-sensitive online help. This context sensitivity is what should be built into good reports.

A good report must be crafted with care. It should be designed with all the care that is given to other application artifacts, such as UIs (user interfaces) and databases. It is quite common to see that expert advice is taken for UIs while report design is left to the analysts or engineers, who are rarely specialists in this field. Last but not the least of the problems is that the development community has probably never tried to manage a business using any reports, much less the reports created by them.

The Need for Good Report Design

Report design is, like so much else, an exercise in communications. Even if one recognizes that an effective report is one that is appropriate to its purpose and audience, designing it would not be easy. Any decision maker in an organization has a mental model of the real-world problem. He or she views his factory or store in a certain way, sees flows of goods and cash in a particular manner, etc. The report must fit into the reader's mental model for it to take hold. It must also present only the information integral to the user's communication needs. This is the bigger problem. Dealing with mental models, managing outbound communications — are these not something more suitable to marketing types than engineers? Because of this gap and the different mental models out there, it is better that the user whiteboard some report designs rather than leave it to the engineers to take the initiative and deliver "the reports that can come out of the system."

Reports, like many other things, can be misused and misinterpreted. If some managers are looking for data to support untenable positions, then poorly designed reports play into their hands because smudgy data can be interpreted in many different ways. Other decision makers may use the report to find data to support their initial hunch, rather than analyzing the data and drawing a strongly supported conclusion. A report should therefore be designed in a way that it leads to unambiguous conclusions.

Avoiding the Last Mile of Reporting Problem

There are very few cases where data presented by reports is used without any post-processing. It is fairly common to see data being exported from a report to a spreadsheet so that some more processing can be done on it. In fact, many well-known software packages have touted the "Export to Excel" button on their GUI (graphical user interface) as a great usability feature. Should this be considered a failure of a report editor? Why can this last mile of data processing also not be handled? The fact that post-processing of a report delivered at great cost is still required only shows that report design still has some way to go.

Surveys show that managers are extremely frustrated at having to spend, on average, 500 to 750 hours per year (one third to one half of their year's work) searching for relevant information on the Internet.

Types of Reports

Reports can be of many kinds. Two of them are (1) informational reports and (2) analytical reports. The former focuses on presenting relevant facts clearly and concisely; while the latter focuses on the analysis and interpretation of data, to make recommendations.

Many designers do not recognize that reports come in various forms, including snapshot, trend analysis, transaction reports, comparison reports, statutory reports, summary reports, drill-down reports, analytical reports, and consolidated reports, to name a few. They do not make a conscious effort to select the report type most appropriate for the context of use.

Kinds of Reports

Offline reports. Such reports are usually used when the data is large or the report logic is complex. Offline means that the report is based on a snapshot of the database and is not executed on the live database. Typically, the database may be a replica of the live database but on a different machine. Because these reports are complex and take a significant amount of time to render, it is believed that executing them will affect the performance of the overall server and may slow the ongoing online transactions. Such reports are common with Online Transaction Processing (OLTP) systems and data warehousing engines.

Scheduled reports. It may often be the case that organizations may not have the luxury of separate machines or IT staff to spare for report generation. In this case, it is best to make use of a report scheduler that can generate the report at a specific time (or periodicity) — usually chosen when online user interactions with the application are minimal — and e-mail it to a predefined set of people. This technique is an optimal approach to send information to a number of people who would instead have generated the report one at a time, putting load on computing resources. A side benefit is that people can look at the report at their convenience (e-mail).

Online reports. As the name indicates, these reports are generated on a live database (while other users are using the system), and will have the most up-to-date information. End users like this concept but should be made aware that online computations come at some expense — performance. One way to make sure that users do not inadvertently try and generate a report that will be a CPU-hog is to restrict the number of records or pages that would need to be fetched from the database. One can achieve this either by validating the filters used by the user or by writing database queries appropriately so that they return only the first "x" rows. Remember, however, that there would be little one could do if the report logic is itself complex.

Static reports. Instead of e-mailing reports (there may be security or privacy concerns), one can also save scheduled reports in a shared common area where people can access it. Reports can be rendered in various formats — pdf, html, or excel, as the environment demands. They also can be archived for future recall. In fact, organizations have been known to do post-processing on archived reports to perform trend or statistical analyses. This form of reporting can reduce the up-front license costs of using the OTS or third-party reporting software for the customer because the generated reports can be displayed on an intranet. Granularity of access for each report can also be controlled more effectively, irrespective of the application itself.

Dynamic or real-time reports — portals, dashboards. Is this an oxymoron? Reports are based on historic data — then what does a real-time report have? They have been broadly classified as "reports" because their objective is to report on the status of the organization at that instant of time. These are not really hardcopy type reports. Instead, they are GUI oriented with dials, moving histograms, and changing numbers similar to the digital dashboard of automobiles. Such dashboards communicate a lot of information in a succinct way — with colors and numbers — that will give the general health of the organization at a quick glance. Dashboards can take a development life of their own and should not be clubbed in the same category as reports.

Graphs, drawings, and figures are a universal means of communication. Report creators prefer text and numbers in their report, using pictures as a complement. However, they should aim to express the information with pictures and use explanatory text as a complement. This is a change in approach that requires some care. The aim is to stimulate the brain — not strain the eyes.

Report Design

While designing a report, the following factors should be considered:

- Who will use the report (i.e., the intended audience)?
- How many people in the organization will need access to the report?
- Where is the output needed (i.e., screen, database, hard copy)?
- What is the purpose of the report (i.e., information or analysis)?
- What is the performance expected while generating the report?
- How frequently will the report be needed (i.e., the information refresh rate)?
- Is there any special condition or regulation under which the report is produced, stored, or distributed?

The purpose for writing a report should be very clear before beginning to write it. There can be major differences between the structure and contents of two reports on the same topic, just by virtue of the message they are trying to convey. For example, a spreadsheet containing the sales data of organizations' products in various regions over two quarters is a decent way of showing multivariant data. The same, represented graphically, can be used to obtain guidance and trends by region or product. Within the same data, anomalies in the revenues earned at various times of the week, month, or quarter could be good to review, prepare for the future, or even persuade sales managers in the organization to take countermeasures.

This brings us to a very important aspect of a report — that of style. As one goes higher in the organizational chart, the need for day-to-day operational data is replaced by the necessity for "business" information, that is, parameters that directly affect revenues. A CEO may not want to look at the working hours or time-offs of his 4000 shop floor employees in various shifts. Instead, he would like to know the productivity of his individual manufacturing units by shifts. Thus, it is important for the report creator to fully understand the style and pitch that would work best for different audiences, while keeping the idea and the logic of the report pretty much the same. Today's business intelligence (BI) tools allow this kind of drill-down or rollup capability. Recall from Chapter 2 on Systems that the variety in the reporting decreases as one goes up the hierarchy.

A good report should communicate the required information to the intended audience in a relatively short period of time. As a report writer, one may feel better to report as much as possible or believe that more information likely produces a better understanding. However, this is not the case — unnecessary information or too much detail creates clutter and hinders understanding.

The *title* should indicate the contents in a clear and precise expression. It helps to understand the contents. Priority can be decided by the title.

The 80/20 Rule: For any report use, 80 percent of the message one wants to communicate should appear within the first 20 percent of the space. Readers should be able to gauge the essence of the contents and, in a short time, determine if they want to scroll down into the details of the entire report. It should almost always be the case that one should start the report with the conclusion. This is how headlines in newspapers work; they give away the main story but make the headline attractive enough to get the reader to learn more. If one wants to draw attention to more than one conclusion within the same report, present them in the order of their importance.

Simplicity in thought, and communication, is very important in report design — less is more often works. Most business depends on some basic fundamentals in a dynamic environment. Because a report conceptually needs to map to portions of it, it should be no more complex than necessary. Unnecessary ratios, performance indices, ratings, and global economic indicators may be impressive but should be used only if required.

Reports need to *make a point*. They present data that supports an argument or helps establish a point of view. It need not always be the mere presentation of information in the database on a screen or paper, in the text or graphics, with indicators on areas of importance to which the reader should pay attention. For example, in a trend report, shown as a graph or in a tabular form, red or green arrows pointing upward or downward can show gradients along with the numbers.

Reports, for the most part, should be *self-explanatory*. There should not be confusion about the usage of terms in it. For example, if a report lists "the number of employees," it should be clear whether this number also includes part-time employees or contractors. Footnotes come in handy when such clarity is needed.

One of the design decisions that should be taken is the split between reports and queries — which of the information requirements of the user should be formalized as reports and which should be left to queries? Note that reports can be run on-demand; that does not make them queries. By the same token, queries can be scheduled; that does not make them reports. There is a section on queries later in this chapter. One of the key factors in helping to decide is based on what we have already said — that reports must be problem-solving tools. They are not data retrieval mechanisms. Retrieved data dumped on the screen or paper does not constitute a report. If one knows the problem that the user is tackling, knows how the system can generate information to help solve it, and knows how to represent and organize that information in a way that supports that problem-solving process, then one has a report.

Quality

It is important to proofread reports. Developers tend to submit code for creating a report without a full check of the output to confirm that it is doing what it is intended to do.

Apply the following report proofreading checklist:

- Does the report match the original intent for which it was created?
- Is it comprehensive enough for its audience?
- Is all the included information relevant? Remember that less is more as long as the data is the same.
- Is the style clear and concise, and is the layout quickly readable?
- Are the conclusions based on a true interpretation, and are the analyses of the data presented later on in the same report?
- Are your recommendations reasonable?
- Very important: have the spelling and grammar been checked?

Doing QA (quality assurance) on reports presents its own set of challenges, which differ from those for testing the main body of the application. Most of the problems deal with data. The hurdles include:

- The lack of sensible and sufficient data.
- The inability to verify that the report is generating the correct results. Because reports can use complex logic to arrive at their content, it may not be possible to have a second path to generate the same results without writing complex SQL or small programs.
- In the case of parameter-driven reports, the number of permutations and combinations that the user can input is enormous. Without understanding some business context, one does not know how to assign priorities to the test cases for reports.

Queries

The industry has been presenting users with query tools to get to the data that they have spent money in storing. The hope has always been that the end users will, given the right tool and attitude, create their own queries, run their own reports, and eliminate a useless load from IT.

Most application vendors provide an interface through which database queries can be written. Vendors often add a layer on top of the interface to hide the details of the database schema, cross table joins, and query language syntax. While these masking layers might be adequate or inadequate, sophisticated (natural language interfaces) or not, the problem lies deeper.

Any software application, simple or complex, has a *data model* underlying it. A data model aims to identify the attributes of data elements and organize the relationships between them, both logically and physically. It should be based on business rules surrounding the data. Writing meaningful queries requires a very good understanding of the model. Apart from the formal normalization rules that should be followed in defining a data model, it is important to keep simplicity in mind. Avoid using cryptic field names and labels for data elements. Furthermore, one should understand the business definitions of the concepts underlying the model. If there is any confusion over definitions such as the "number of employees" example above, it will be difficult to write queries that fetch the correct result. For example, if a manager wants to determine how many widgets were sold on a particular day, one must not only agree on the definition of a sale, but also on the definition of daily sale (i.e., should one subtract returns of widgets bought earlier, should one include those ordered earlier but paid for the day before, etc.). If the definition in the manager's mental model of the real world — "a sale is when such and such an event happens" — does not match the designer's model, the query tool cannot solve this problem. Even if the definitions were aligned, the actual task of getting values may involve complex processing that requires proficiency in the query preparation — both syntactic and semantic. To expect managers, who may not be able to distinguish between the various types of indexes or an outer join from an inner join, to handle all kinds of queries, especially when many an experienced developer has sometimes gone wrong, is unreasonable. Thus, the adoption of such interfaces has been limited to simple ad hoc queries.

This difficulty, compounded with the general tendency of users that they do not have time to "create" reports, often makes report generation a continued "IT" activity.

In some cases, product manufacturers and their vendors have themselves used query interfaces for their convenience. Instead of creating new reports, which may be cumbersome to do, they have written complex database queries through these interfaces that end users can run. These should not be considered replacements for reports.

Queries versus Reports

Queries and reports are different; but because they appear similar, reports are often treated as query outputs and little else. From the software person's point of view, they are data retrieval mechanisms. If one has the query correctly formulated, one has a report. As explained previously, a report should be goal oriented, formally organized, and more than a query output on paper or the screen.

Needless to say, reports, as well as most information shown on the screen, are the result of queries being fired on the database. Is the difference then in the degree of formality? Is it that a report brings with it elements of style, format, color, pagination, etc. that are missing in a database query?

Reports are much more than formatted query dumps and must be approached that way. The objective of the report is not to get the data out of the database (data orientation), but to present useful information to the report reader (user orientation). The operative word is "useful." The report creator is expected to go beyond any data model limitations that the application may be perceived to have. A complex set of queries may have to be written, intermediate data stores may have to be created, or new business logic may have to be introduced in the application if the user needs to see some data that is otherwise not being captured or computed. A considerable amount of post-processing — such as statistical analysis, risk and sensitivity analysis, and multi-dimensional scaling — may be needed on the query data. Useful also implies that the user's need has been well understood and an appropriate report type chosen. The report designer must recommend when a trend analysis report is better suited as compared to a snapshot report. To summarize, the focus should be on movement of information from a screen to the user, rather than on moving data from a database to a screen.

Why a Printout Is Still Preferred to Seeing Data on Screen

It is a well-recognized fact that there is a vast difference between the way people read screen (softcopy) text and printed (hardcopy) material. The difference between the two media arises due to human biology (human eyes react better in passive light reflected off paper than in light emitted from a computer monitor), and also due to the relative degrees of freedom between the two. Screens can display only a small percentage of the content, usually as much as a single printed page can carry. Users tend to be a little impatient with screens (computer applications) — the dynamism of the medium allowing them to scan for "more" information than is immediately available (hyperlinks). In contrast, hardcopies, by their restrictive nature, help focus on the subject at hand. Further, printouts of reports are preferred so that the reader can carry it around, fold or lay individual pages over each other for more clarity, annotate them, and, habitually for some, disfigure them.

It is important to take the above factors into consideration while designing reports. On-screen reports should have a Web-acceptable font, pleasing colors, navigational tools to traverse through a report, and possibly well-defined headers and footers on each page to give a sense of independence. On the other hand, when the same report is printed, the report tool should automatically readjust the margins, headers, color (preferably grayscale), and fonts. For example, dark backgrounds, which look good on slides, rarely print well.

Off-the-Shelf (OTS) Reports

Many of the reports that managers see today are not built from scratch but come from OTS products or customized versions of OTS products implemented within the organization. OTS reports can sometimes present their own set of issues.

Most OTS products have a suite of built-in reports that are available to end users. These out-of-the-box reports are usually generic and come with a set of predefined "filters" through which users can narrow down the information presented to them. These are analogous to the concept of parameterized queries in databases and, as a concept, probably originated from there.

While implementing an OTS product, there is a general tendency to downplay the effort needed to provide the correct set of reports. The discussion with end users typically results in a line item in the implementation contract that reads "12–15 reports will be provided." Sometimes, more qualified statements such as "Reports for departmental heads and executive management," or "seven snapshot reports, four drill-down reports, and up to four statistical analysis reports" are added. However, both of these are inadequate descriptions.

Reports have high visibility in an organization, and are often the whetstone on which a new system is judged that the acceptance of the system often hinges on this. If the report requirements are not properly understood in the beginning of the project, and later it becomes apparent that changes to data model or complex graphical representations must be introduced, the entire project timeline can lie in jeopardy. Unless the OTS product is being used as a replacement for an existing application (in which case the reporting needs are better known), it is important to get detailed inputs on reports. These inputs include the organization, access control needs, textual or graphical nature, information to be presented, and usage patterns.

Reports are also a quick way of obtaining insight into what an OTS product provides and supports. If one wants to make sure that the OTS product will meet one's requirements, it is advisable to use reports as one of the starting points. It is possible that the required information may be available in the data model but not included in the standard reports. It is also likely that the information or concept may not be handled by the product at all. Reports can reveal these aspects and raise doubts (questions of OTS product suitability in the organization) fairly quickly.

Like all other customization, one will need to draw a line somewhere. Building a report customization editor within one's OTS product may be interesting from a customer point of view, but it is not very practical. Most customers have a resistance to learning a new language, although it may be fairly simple. They will, instead, ask one to create more reports (or customize existing ones) "since the tool already exists and you are experts in making it happen." It may be better to provide an interface to a standard report writer (the most common one in the target market segment) that the customer can use to create and deploy reports to their liking. One must be careful of the hidden costs of such report writers and deployment environments because the customer must bear the burden of their respective licenses.

Report: Other Aspects

Report Performance

Report performance is a key factor in the impressions that users form about an application. Most users do understand the complexity vector — that there are certain types of reports that need to scan and analyze more and will take longer. They are also aware that reports that need to process a lot of data will take longer. It is therefore good to, at the outset, classify reports into *simple*, *medium*, and *complex* reports. When the reports are released, the expectations of performance can be adjusted easily and tuning efforts devoted appropriately.

Performance can be an issue when using OTS reports where, many a time, the queries are generated by the system and cannot be hand-tuned. As discussed in Chapter 9 on OTS products, one is buying someone else's design and they may not be doing something the way one would have done it. Do not promise performance with third-party reports without benchmarking them for one's environment.

Security of Reports

Reports are produced, distributed, and stored. They have to be designed and kept appropriately. One is for reasons of economy. The other is for reasons of security. An old report can still convey a lot of valuable information because many things do not change frequently. For example, an employee report from four months ago will get one the names of most of the current employees.

Most businesses do not have formal filing and distribution tracking mechanisms as in the intelligence or military organizations. It can safely be assumed, therefore, that one does not know where the data now lies and who has access to it.

Sometimes reports have strict security filters. An employee can see or not see certain fields or data. They may or may not access certain reports. These kinds of restrictions require one to build and install special gate-keeper layers. Do not assume that database-level controls are adequate to manage such security.

Summary

Reports are critical outputs from any application. Applications, however, continue to give more importance to processing and storing data than to the delivery of reports. Good report design is difficult. It requires one to select the type of report appropriate for the business need, understand the mental models of the user, and manage outbound communications. This is not easy. A good report should be able to communicate the required information to the intended audience in a relatively short period of time. Because reports are used to get the pulse of the business, the set of reports that come out of an application should reflect Maslow's Hierarchy — with reports that map to the needs as expressed in this hierarchy at various levels.

Queries come into a more natural category of data retrieval. They need to be treated as different from reports. Attempts to give self-querying facilities to managers have failed because generating a good query requires a deep understanding of the data models underlying the application.

All the details of the life and the quirks and the friendships can be laid out for us, but the mystery of the writing will remain. No amount of documentation, however fascinating, can take us there.

—**V.S. Naipaul,**
Nobel Laureate

Chapter 15

Documentation

I am not sure if this is a bug or a documentation error...

—From a message board

That documentation is a critical component of any product or service is unquestionable. From a jet aircraft to a small tube of toothpaste, one comes across all kinds of documentation. We may not read it when we become conversant with the brand or its usage, but we definitely need it when we start something new. We all occasionally read the "nutritional facts" or the ingredients list on a food item that we have been using for many years — especially when a new report comes out from a national medical association. A mundane thing such as a blender will come with pages of text about its sleek design, the lifelong guarantee on it blades, the various options and power settings, the definite do's and the absolute don'ts, and almost always a couple of pages of troubleshooting guidance. Some manufacturers will also include a recipe book in the instruction manual, showing as to how the grinder plays an essential role in making a sumptuous meal. Of course, we also have the clichéd VCR programming difficulties.

Types of Documentation

Then why is software documentation considered in a different light? We never hear of any other kind of documentation as often as we hear

273

"software documentation is, in practice, poor, incomplete and inconsistent." To answer this, let us look at the various categories of most product documentation:

- *Illuminative*: intra- or inter-development team, engineering design, production, QA, management reporting
- *Instructional*: functionality guides, user manuals, administration guides
- *Reference*: troubleshooting guides, cheat sheets
- *Informational*: promotional product announcements, competitive landscape, cross-industry relationships

Illuminative Documentation

Illuminative documents in different industries use different styles and go to different levels of detail based on their perceived needs and criticality. In software, we have industry benchmarks, SEI guidelines, and intra-organization standards. Dijkstra mentioned the "Separation of Concerns" in 1974, which had direct applications to documentation. Newer paradigms like Extreme Programming, Agile methodologies, and even the not very popular concept of Literate Programming by Knuth are all efforts to make documentation more formal and consistent. How diligently these norms and recommendations are followed varies from place to place. Because these are meant for internal consumption, they are always given a backseat compared to the other kinds of documents that are inherently more customer facing.

Such illuminative documents assist in communication between the business domain experts and the software experts within an organization. They cover details about all the aspects of the software life cycle in terms of specific roles and responsibilities of the various groups involved. They are very important from a software maintainability perspective. It is one stage of the life cycle (software deployment, or maintenance, or sustenance) where developers spend most of their time and resources. One needs to understand code blocks (especially in OOPS approach), what worked and what did not work (in migration projects), and why things were done in a particular way.

Instructional Documents

Instructional documentation, in contrast, has no industry norms and standards that define it. The content and "size" of the documentation has changed significantly over the years, and is typically in direct proportion

to the price of the software. In fact, the term "shelfware" arose as it was known to be used to bulk up software delivery packages. As software was expensive but not really physical, packages were made glossy and large with bulky user manuals to make the customer feel good about spending all the money. Even in the mainframe days, senior managers kept a row of manuals on their office shelves — it looked impressive. The more clever ones removed the plastic covers from them and dog-eared some pages randomly.

But why are these documents not considered useful? Is this a phenomenon in the software industry alone? Like most other things, one buys software on the basis of its features and specifications, not on the basis of the completeness of its documentation. Have you ever rejected a car because its user guide was not colorful or a self-assembly furniture unit because the instructions on it could make sense only to an expert carpenter?

Software is a bit different. The user has a lot of freedom in interacting with it. Unlike hardware devices that have a few buttons or dials that can be moved, software is like an open playing field (Figure 15.1). A simple input screen or form opens up all kinds of options for a user. A field for "Name" is open to accepting numbers, characters, pictures, special characters — whatever can possibly be entered using the keyboard and mouse. The software should not only be able to take care of pointing out the errors, but the documentation is also expected to be precise and say exactly what can and cannot be entered. On the contrary, one will not find too many users manuals for DVD players that say one should not put a tortilla or pita bread in the CD drawer. It is "obvious" there.

Reference Documentation

Not all documentation generated during the creation of an application can be considered reference documentation. The term is being used here with respect to the end user. Such documents could be troubleshooting guides, cheat sheets, or assembly guides. It is a standard practice to give some kind of reference documentation along with a release.

The problem with reference documentation, as with most documentation, is the difficulty in striking a balance between overwhelming detail and practical guidance, between having to cover the many exception conditions and the normal scenarios.

One way of improving the reference documentation is to watch for the stick-it notes that users stick to their monitors while using applications or notes they have written that they keep referring to while using the screens. These may contain codes and descriptions, short cuts, errors and how to handle them, phone numbers to contact, field entry tips (do not

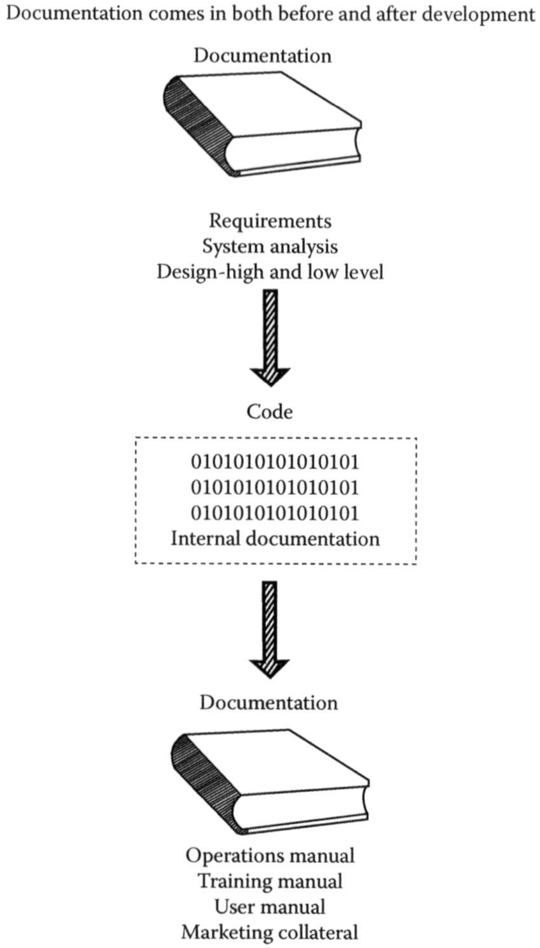

Documentation comes in both before and after development

Documentation

Requirements
System analysis
Design-high and low level

Code

0101010101010101
0101010101010101
0101010101010101
Internal documentation

Documentation

Operations manual
Training manual
User manual
Marketing collateral

Figure 15.1   Documentation is spread.

use capitals) and others. Picking up such information requires field usage but it lets you improve the reference documentation by distilling them to a core practical set. Details can be presented as backup material.

Informational Documentation

All documentation contains information. This category refers to documentation that covers more of the background information. It could be made available in the form of marketing literature, product announcements, white papers. Technical persons sometimes tend to dismiss such "marketing," which in turn leads to material being published that appears glossy, shallow and weak, which merely reinforces the original impressions. Good design of informational documentation is important. Designers and managers must devote the necessary time to interact with those who prepare such documentation so that the right information is conveyed with proper emphasis where it needs to be.

Generating informational documentation is a two-step communication problem — from technical to the marketing persons within the company and from them to the outside world. Done early on in the development process, it can be a useful process, if only to see how internal and external perceptions of something can be so different. At times the discussions can lead to some design improvements in the application itself.

A workhorse of the software industry has been the white paper. They are used as a marketing tool. It is an attempt to inform while subtly, and not so subtly, positioning ones product. The sponsored nature of the document engenders skepticism. A lot of information gathering has, of course, moved to the Web. This allows a powerful opportunity to keep the information up to date at minimal costs. Unfortunately, not every company uses this opportunity properly — information provided may be shallow or out of date, more style than substance.

Problems with Documentation

There are some problems in our approach to documentation in the software industry, including:

- Just as in other products that we use, software usage is also largely repetitive. Most users do not need to refer to documentation after the initial learning phase. This is why formal classroom training is considered a better option by some software vendors. It is certainly good, but users change over a period of time. That is why "train the trainer" is preferred. More importantly, however, it is only in software that one will find that two software products created by different vendors in the same business domain (e.g., CRM [customer relationship management] or ERP [enterprise resource planning]), solving similar problems, will likely be very different in usage. A cursory glance at the user interface will not tell enough to be able to start using the system. Unlike DVD players, cell phones, or blenders from different manufacturers, the learning curve for software is much slower. This strongly reinforces the continued need for documentation.
- In the early days of computing, we expected developers also to be able to do end-user documentation. Programmers have not

necessarily been the best when it comes to writing documents, especially for end users. This has changed over the years, and technical writers and subject matter experts are used most often these days.

■ Documentation is usually organized linearly. This is not how most people use software. Because you can jump from one screen to another or click on any of the multitude of icons on a screen, users expect hardcopy documentation to follow the same stream.

■ Online help and online documentation are preferred over printed user manuals. Not only does it make the accessibility to the document much easier (not having to walk to get a physical paper manual), but it also makes the help context-sensitive and thus faster (rather than having to open a paper manual to the "right" page). Here we have faltered in two of the most basic requirements: (1) that software documentation is written with the end user in mind, and (2) that it is supposed to be illustrative.

■ Software documentation should be more illustrative; it should have examples of usage in it. Just writing that a field called "Base Sale Value" in a user input form needs to be filled in with "a numeric figure corresponding to the base sales value of a product" is not enough. A short example to say what a base sales value is, its relationship to the price of a product, and how it can be used in the sales process is easier to comprehend. It is this business usage of the application that is often lacking in user documentation that emerges from technical teams.

■ Good documentation takes time. To be able to put screen shots in a manual or online help requires that the developers have the screens ready. If documentation should follow development, there is a chance that there will be a time crunch (not too many releases are delayed due to inadequate documentation) and the quality will suffer. So documentation writers usually create documents on the basis of design or solution specification documents, and put place-holder screens. This is also risky because the specifications documents may not be up to date.

■ Software documentation also must be more complete with regard to context and, in cross-references, across the entire software documentation. Just by saying that a "Vendor Type" field is mandatory for a sales order to be entered in the system is not complete. Not only should one specify what type of input it needs, but one should also provide all possible values that are acceptable, with a reasonable explanation for each.

■ Documentation is a "pull" activity. Many times it is observed that technical writers create documents on the basis of their understanding. It is left to developers and managers to advise or clarify things to the documentation staff in case of a disparity. From a practical standpoint, however, it may be better to assign the responsibility of document "correctness" to the writers; that is, they should have to reconfirm doubts with developers in case of ambiguity.

Summary

Documentation is a necessary component of any product or service. It is necessary for business continuity, especially because staff turnover can be quite high in many software development environments. There are various types of documentation. Selecting the appropriate documentation to provision the user is important.

It went many years,
But at last came a knock,
And I thought of the door
With no lock to lock.

—Robert Frost, "The Lockless Door"

Chapter 16

Security

The ultimate security is your understanding of reality.

—H. Stanley Judd

Application designers and managers have traditionally paid more attention to functionality and performance of the application rather than to security. There is a need for designers and developers to increase their awareness and knowledge of security-related issues. The fact is that security is a vast and complex domain, and one can get lost in details of algorithms and technologies. Therefore, this chapter examines some aspects of security that require greater priority.

A good security system must address four aspects of security:

1. The *business* aspects of security: its strategic value, the concept of risk, security costs, and its trade-offs.
2. The *technical* aspects of security: its design, verification, and limitations. This, in itself, is a large and specialized subject and we shall touch on a few areas only.
3. The *human* factors: critical to the success of security systems.
4. The *process or procedural* aspects: those aspects that help bridge the technical and human aspects, giving organizations some assurance that, if processes are followed, a certain state of security can be achieved.

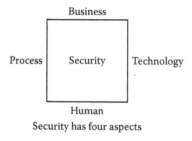

Security has four aspects

Figure 16.1 Important aspects of security.

It must be explicitly understood that when referring to security, we are talking about a "system." Security is not a static, one-time point solution that can be achieved and forgotten. The security problem requires a systems approach to solve it. As in any system, there will be interrelationships between the various entities (Figure 16.1). There should be processes for feedback, regulation, and control. In its stable or equilibrium state, the system is secure while being functional. To achieve this state, the system must be able to respond, often in complicated ways, to various shocks that threaten this equilibrium. Any system requires time to respond (known in systems science as the relaxation time) to bring the system back to its stable state. If another shock occurs before this relaxation time has elapsed, the system moves to a new state of disequilibrium and would need a new relaxation time to recover. The system also could go into a state of oscillation.

There is another facet of the security problem that should be recognized. The systems behavior can often be nonlinear — a small mistake can lead to massive damage. It should be the designer's objective to bring such behavior into linear zones, so that small mistakes have small impacts, and large mistakes have larger impacts.

Risk and *threat* are two commonly used terms when one talks about security-related issues. Innumerable threats exist with arbitrary probabilities of occurrence. They can leave different (harmful) impacts on the assets that will be protected. There are so many possible natural threats — earthquakes, hurricanes, floods, etc. — that it is not physically possible to respond to every threat. A threat becomes a risk when its possibility of occurrence crosses a reasonable threshold. If it is summer, then the probability of occurrence of hurricanes in the Atlantic rises and may very well constitute a risk that needs to be addressed for some coastal communities. This differentiation assumes importance because security is all about protection against risks.

This chapter examines the increasing importance of security related to information systems, and discusses the four elements of a good security system outlined above — business, technical, human, and process.

The Demand for Security

The security environment is changing rapidly. Information is now recognized as a commodity of (increasing) value by management, customers, and also by criminals. This increase in value arises due to developments on both the supply and demand sides of the information equation. On the supply side, more information is being created and converted to digitized assets. This leads to increased inventories to protect. Not only is there more to protect, but also there are assets in digital form and thus easily transferable: stealing a disk of medical records is easier than carting away shelves of files. On the demand side, information has become more valuable because, here also, most of the transactions involving people and business are electronic in nature. Using stolen information electronically is less expensive and provides a degree of anonymity (as the famous New Yorker cartoon said, "On the Internet nobody knows you are a dog"). Another advantage is that it allows one to work at an attractive distance — one does not have to walk up to a bank counter with a stolen check. We are thus in a situation where on one side there is more to protect, and on the other, any failure to do so can cause immense harm.

For corporations, the need to protect their information has always existed. The threats have morphed over time. Traditional threats, such as those related to industrial espionage or competitive intelligence gathering, were handled by restricting access to information, and by keeping data in databases deep within the IT (information technology) infrastructure. However, with the increase in networking, large volumes of data exist in documents and Web pages, scattered in geographically diverse places. This larger exposure has altered the security environment. For many large corporations, internal threats have become a major factor. It is not just the rogue employees whom one has to worry about, but also careless behavior on the part of regular employees — lost CDs and laptops being an example. In fact, one is often not clear who is "internal" and who is "external" as systems integrate across business partners. To have everybody connected, without having well-thought-out security frameworks and policies, is dangerous.

Consumer expectations about privacy and responsibility also have changed. Consumers are aware that companies are tracking and retaining a lot of personal information. They expect corporations to protect this information with a higher degree of reliability and responsibility.

Individuals also have to take personal responsibility for the information with which they deal. This is not something new. People have always managed their bank account numbers, drivers' license numbers, social security numbers, phone numbers, names, and addresses in environments where transactions were much less electronic in nature. This set of information has since expanded to include the account names and passwords for various Web-based accounts — banks, brokerages, E-commerce sites, e-mail accounts, and other Internet transactions. Personal information that existed earlier as physical objects, such as letters and photographs, are now digital — people use e-mail instead of letters, and retain digital photos instead of prints and negatives. Physical access is needed to steal physical assets. Electronic access is needed to steal digital assets. These digital assets are often located on vulnerable home machines, carelessly left connected to the Internet. Most users do not understand the security aspects of this changing environment; except for what little information about incidents they happen to obtain from the popular press. Although an active "personal security tools" industry has emerged, somewhat similar to the electronic home security business, many of the issues remain unsolved, expensive, and difficult to implement.

Security Crosses Conventional Application Boundaries

Most businesses have not been organized with a view to security needs. They might have been organized as functional departments or projects or by products, or a matrix version of all these. Whatever the organization is, certain boundaries get established, such as "my department," "your department," "my project," "your project". While thinking of security, one must cast a wider net, looking beyond the product, project, or department of which one is part. Depending on the culture within the organization, this may not be easy to achieve. This is one of the reasons why security exists as a centralized function — for example, Department of Homeland Security. The assumption is that going up one level will make working across organizational boundaries easier.

For the application, its responsibility ends with the successful processing of a required transaction, or the output of some required information. Once outside the application, the information might scatter in known and unknown locations (Figure 16.2). It resides with other departments, supply chain partners, ex-employees, contractors, and regulatory agencies, to name a few. It resides in various formats — e-mails, printouts and documentation, and other devices and media. It may even exist in databases that are outside one's control. Tracking any of these, even at one

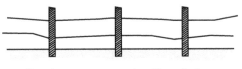

Security crosses conventional boundaries

Figure 16.2   Vulnerabilities may exist elsewhere.

degree of separation, is practically impossible — or otherwise prohibitively expensive.

While scattered information adds to the complexity of the situation, such scattering is likely a subset of the total information; for example, the data that resides with your dealer is most probably only the dealer's data and not the entire corporation's data. Military and intelligence agencies operate on a similar "need-to-know" principle: if an agent is captured, he or she cannot compromise the entire operation. At the same time, one must recognize that even subsets can reveal sufficient structural information concerning the larger set, for example, by looking at the dealer's data, one can figure out what information is being captured in the central databases. Although incomplete, this could be of some value to interested parties.

How does the size of the organization, or the scale of the operations, affect security needs? Larger perimeters are more difficult to protect. They need more resources to protect everything and are likely to give rise to situations where certain portions are not as well protected as the others due to resource limitations. Attackers know this well and actively look for less protected points of entry. This leads to the familiar comment that the chain is only as strong as its weakest link. So how does one find the weakest link?

The Weaker Links

Gregory Bateson (1904–1980) was an important social scientist of the twentieth century and one of the founders of cybernetics. He comments on this problem in his book entitled *Mind and Nature*:

> "Under tension, a chain will break at its weakest link. That much is predictable. What is difficult is to identify the weakest link before it breaks. The generic we can know, but the specific eludes us. Some chains are designed to break at a certain tension and at a certain link. But a good chain is homogeneous, and no prediction is possible. And because we cannot know which

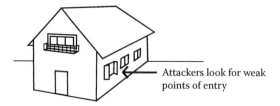

Figure 16.3 The door is not always the primary target.

> link is weakest, we cannot know precisely how much tension
> will be needed to break the chain."

This can work in favor of security professionals. In a good chain, finding
the weakest link requires considerable energy and professionalism.

Security professionals devote considerable effort to trying to determine
the weakest link (Figure 16.3). They begin with logical analysis and use
various tools, such as penetration tests, to identify the specific within the
general. Some candidates in software, where vulnerabilities are more likely
to exist, include:

- Applications (in-house or off-the-shelf). Applications constitute one
  of the bigger security vulnerabilities. They are often black boxes,
  with little visibility on the outside, for what goes on within the
  application.
- Major changes to the technology or architecture of existing applications. Whenever such a change is put in production, it is likely
  that something has been missed or misunderstood.
- New or upgrades to existing hardware infrastructure.
- Legacy applications that have come out of their protected silos,
  through enterprise integration or Web access, but cannot support
  latest security requirements in a structural manner.
- Physically removed infrastructure elements, such as remote offices,
  vendors, or partners.
- Employees and contractors — existing or new. The extreme case
  is to treat employees as if they are outsiders when it comes to
  security; relaxing these requirements is an exception. When it
  comes to knowing about vulnerabilities, one's knowledge of the
  history of the application is also quite helpful. Employees who
  have been around for some time should be included in security
  analysis. They carry valuable information not always available
  through formal documentation.

Security Is Linked to Value and Ownership

Security is linked to value. People and organizations protect and secure what is of value to them. One protects one's house because one owns it. One does not spend money trying to protect the neighbor's house. The concept of value is closely linked to ownership, which, in turn, is related to property rights. This does not mean that one can protect only what one owns directly — one can invest in protecting certain aspects of the neighborhood because it indirectly affects one's own house security, quality of life, and real estate values. Why is it important to determine the owner? It is important because this person or entity that gets value from keeping the asset secure ends up bearing the costs associated with the security. These costs can be nontrivial.

Because most organizations have limited security budgets, resources must be allocated among competing security needs. Before one starts funding the most obvious areas — such as data — one must understand the larger space that constitutes one's security problem domain. One needs to understand that data, per se, has no intrinsic value. It is the "use" to which this data can be put that gives it a value (Figure 16.4). Stealing a person's social security number makes sense only if it can be used to get something else of value — more information, or physical goods, or any service. This differentiation between the data, and how it attains value only when used, provides one with an opportunity to intervene at a different place in the larger system. It allows one to work with a model that is more sophisticated. A loss at one point in the chain can be compensated by actions elsewhere. Instead of trying to physically recover a lost credit card, it can be disabled in the credit card system, and

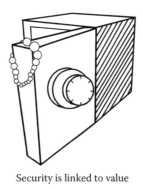

Security is linked to value

Figure 16.4 People protect what is valuable.

transactions prevented; customer fears of loss are assuaged through "no-loss" or limited-liability guarantees. While one can debate whether this can be considered a security solution, from a business point of view it does address the security problem, or at least its impact on the customer. Such approaches demonstrate the fact that a security system has many elements — business, technical, process, and human behavior — and one can choose to invest differently among the various elements, depending on one's needs and the situation.

Identifying the Correct Entities to Protect

An entity at risk should be well recognized by those responsible for handling the risk. In the case of national security, the armed forces are very clear that their objective is to protect the nation's boundaries and its key infrastructure assets. However, in the world of information systems, when one speaks of information security, there may be some ambiguity regarding what should be protected. It seems satisfying to think that something called "information" is being protected but this is too generic a term. In fact, there are a number of things that come under this generic umbrella: data, applications, services, infrastructure, to name a few. Recognizing the entity to be protected is very important to obviate the risk of protecting the wrong entity.

Take the case of services. Although the application is "working properly," there could be threats to the continuity or the quality of the services provided to the customers. One form is also a "denial of service." The actual denial of service can be achieved in many ways, one being through consuming all available resources on some portion of the infrastructure, so that genuine customers have nothing left to be serviced. In other scenarios, business operations may be badly affected if the internal systems are attacked. If e-mail systems are down, or CRM (customer relationship management) applications used by the helpdesk are prevented from being available, then operations are affected in ways that cause considerable harm. Here, the objective is disruption — not the stealing of information.

Attackers, it is possible, are not after disruption or theft of information assets, but wish to affect the company's reputation or brand through security incidents that get widely (and adversely) reported in the public media. Do not jump to the conclusion that data is the most important thing that security must address. It may very well be so in the majority of cases but priorities can differ.

Security needs to be balanced
with business needs

Figure 16.5 The right business perspective.

The Business Perspective

Security, first and foremost, must be put in the right business perspective (Figure 16.5). As an application designer, one needs to look at what security is trying to achieve and why a particular entity is being secured. While ensuring that one's solution is part of a larger security strategy, one's options are driven by the costs, returns, and trade-offs of making an application very secure.

Priority Varies with Industries

The importance given to security varies with industries. In the case of the entertainment industry — music, movies, games — the entire company or industry recognizes its value because, in such industries, the information assets are the main source of revenue. Some other sectors such as financial services, Internet banking, or credit cards, which depend heavily on electronic transactions, are very clear of their need to protect their systems and data. In such industries, security gets everybody's priority.

In other industries, they may not be so. Manufacturing industries may provide security for goods, plant, and premises, but not for information assets. Similarly, some small and medium-sized businesses may be complacent; because they are small or out of the mainstream, they may assume that they do not face such risks. Sometimes such customers do not want to invest in security at all. However, analysts and designers may need to make a business case for them also, especially if they sense potential risks in the system.

How much should one invest in security improvement and for what returns? For some businesses it may be possible to recoup some of the investment to get a marketing or competitive advantage by drawing attention to its security investments. Designers must advise customers that increased security, while essential, can affect some other business metric such as performance or throughput, as can be seen in the case of increased security for air travel. A healthy balance may emerge through trial and error as customers appreciate the need for security and accept some "inconvenience" while businesses start embedding security as part of their normal deliverables and learn to absorb the associated costs.

Security Needs to Protect the Right Thing

While everyone agrees that it is imperative to protect things that are important, sometimes organizations end up protecting the wrong thing. There could be a number of reasons why such mistakes occur, the most critical being a faulty prioritization process. It is good to have guidelines that bring some objectivity into the prioritization process, because every department considers its applications and data to be of critical importance (Figure 16.6).

One should avoid getting caught in a circular argument about prioritization: "we give priority to things that are important, things with higher priority are important." Sometimes applications are classified based on different needs that have little to do with security. An application might be classified as a "Class A" or "Tier 1" application from a support or downtime point of view. Such classifications may not be relevant from a security point of view. Most applications classified as high or strategic are likely the ones that the company would like to allocate security resources

Security needs to protect the right thing

Figure 16.6 Protect the important things first.

because they are considered important to the company. However, there could be a "less important" application that poses a greater vulnerability, for example, an accounting package whose downtime may not be critical may still require higher prioritization when it comes to security.

Prioritization is a techno-political process and must be recognized as such, particularly if there is contention for security funds. The prioritized list that emerges may reflect the political landscape better than the risk landscape.

One prioritization method that analysts could use is a Risk and ROI (return on investment) model. One can classify the risks and use them to set priorities. Events that can put the company out of business are obviously more important than those that will interrupt operations for a day (e.g., the loss of e-mail files of an employee). Some kind of financial impact analysis can also be done, although it is difficult to quantify intangibles such as loss of customer confidence when such events occur.

While it is difficult to determine what assets should be protected, at times companies do not even know, with any degree of accuracy, what assets they actually have. A server or software may not be on the accounting books or in the documentation but yet be present physically. If it is there, it is part of the security system.

There is another reason why the wrong thing may get protected. What is seen as important by an organization is not necessarily what the bad guys want. This is a point-of-view problem. For example, information about business plans and political dynamics in the executive suites may be more valuable for a competitor than the current order book. For an investigating agency, a compromising e-mail may be of more value than the salaries of executives. If one is going to protect what is of value, one must first know what is meant by value, and be clear about whose value one is talking.

Not every asset has value forever. Along with identifying "what" should be protected, one must specify "how long" it must be protected. Management needs to revisit the security needs and allocations on a regular, perhaps annual, basis. This is similar to individuals who continue to pay insurance premiums to get coverage for household items that are not worth being covered anymore as they have become old, and replacement costs would be lower. Sometimes this duration is driven by legal considerations — the company has to keep the records secure for a certain period of time.

Sometimes entities fall outside the security net because one does not recognize how they are interconnected. An E-commerce application may depend on the e-mail server to send order information for processing. The E-commerce system may be protected while the e-mail server may not be, because this dependency is not realized. This is another reason why security must be viewed from a systems perspective. Diligent efforts restricted to only some portion of a larger system may leave other doors open.

What Are the Options Outside of Technology?

Technology is not the only way to protect against risks. Insurance is a popular form of managing risks in other industries. The insurance related to information security, however, is a relatively nascent area and the options may be limited.

Not every risk must be resolved through investments. A business may be prepared to bear the costs associated with the risks if and when they materialize. It may be a valid choice for some small and medium businesses. In a similar manner, some companies may not have a full-fledged security initiative, but choose to increase the security of some of the existing processes. For example, a company may start encrypting backups and treat it merely as an enhancement to the back-up process.

In certain environments, it makes sense to display some aspects of the available security. A visible security apparatus can discourage aggressors. Signs put up by home security agencies, or, for example, car alarms, act as a deterrent. They exploit the fact that the intruder has a limited window of opportunity in which to work, and would prefer to invest his time and opportunity elsewhere, where there is no such deterrent. Many Web sites have started putting on security logos. Sometimes, the logo reassures the customer more than it deters the attacker.

Understanding Security Costs Is Important

Businesses are still trying to understand the costs of security. It is clear that it is not a one-time cost. Security costs extend throughout the life cycle of the application and could be substantial. Even if the application is not functionally enhanced and left untouched, it may require security maintenance because new threats, new information, and changes to implementation environments can make a "secure" application insecure.

We are at a stage where security costs are often underestimated. As more experience is gained, these estimates will definitely improve. Because these costs can increase the overall cost of the project and infrastructure, there may be a temptation to ignore them, leaving security to be taken care of by someone else. Bid evaluation procedures should be modified to explicitly bring out security-related costs.

Existing projects may not have included security-related development costs in the initial estimates. This might surprise some customers who assume that applications are built to be secure. The analogy can be home security systems that do not come with the house, as opposed to door locks and window latches. Costs to retrofit security frameworks eat into the funding for new applications, leading to uncertainty and frustration in IT departments.

If insecure environments can negate the secure applications and secure applications can become insecure over time, is this a losing battle? As software architects, we have to guide and convince our customers that it is not foolish to spend money on application security. It is clear that security will be an ongoing battle with recurring costs, and businesses need to plan for it. As long as there is a need to fight the battle, and we are on a war metaphor, business must pay for a standing army.

What Is the Vendor's Role in Security?

Another aspect of security should be well understood by architects and designers: some security features must come from the vendors themselves, and be embedded in the product or tools. Airbags must be designed and built-in by the car manufacturer. Software applications become more secure because the underlying layers provide certain security features or models. Bolting solutions on top of applications or tools that do not recognize or support security concepts may turn out to be very expensive, infeasible, and provide a false sense of security. Recognizing what responsibility belongs to the vendor and what belongs to the customer is therefore important.

Offshore Security

As companies continue to expand offshore, one cannot assume that secure environments can be created easily in all countries. Security is a combination of business, technology, process, and human factors. To this must be added cultural factors. Some countries, because of their past social systems, may already be obsessed about security. Others may have always kept things open and might find it difficult to implement certain formal procedures because the employees may become uncomfortable with procedures that go against their social codes.

In some countries, legal recourse may also be limited if a breach occurs. Laws that exist on paper may be difficult to implement, due to slow-moving court systems or inadequate investigation skills with the local law enforcement agencies, especially when these are related to computer crimes.

The Technical Perspective

Software comprises many layers. As a developer, one cannot guarantee that the application one has developed is secure, based on testing alone. One will have to trust the other layers. This trust can be based on detailed testing, or on assurance from the vendor. Any statement about security, therefore, must be a conditional statement. Furthermore, when a number of applications or tools work together, the security models being implemented may themselves not be aligned. A user may have certain privileges in one portion of the stack, say the report writer, which is different from what he or she has at the database level.

Modularity

Object-oriented programming methodologies allow for modular code and better reuse. Reuse raises issues of trust. If the code is in small blocks, then it is easier to determine its correctness. If it is found to be secure, its reuse, either as it is or after encapsulation, will likely be secure.

Modularity is a natural way of handling complexity (Figure 16.7). Breaking a piece of work into more manageable units allows one to get better coverage although it also increases the number of pieces to be managed. The reason why modularity allows improved manageability of each unit is because of what Gerald Weinberg calls the Square Law of Computation: "Experience shows that *unless some simplifications are*

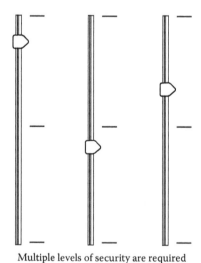

Multiple levels of security are required

Figure 16.7 The security equalizer.

made, the amount of computation involved increases at least as fast as the square of the number of equations." The bigger the unit, the more difficult it will be to manage it. Modularity helps security. It is easier to verify smaller modules than monolithic large modules, which may be so complex that security verification is difficult.

Physical versus Logical

Mention should be made about physical versus logical protection also. As is well known, when users delete data, whether it is in a file or a database, or an e-mail folder, it is a logical deletion. For the application, that piece of information is deleted. Yet the data may exist physically for some period of time, within some data store, until it is physically overwritten. This must be taken into account by application designers and operations support.

Applications make copies. Documents sent as attachments in e-mails invariably make a copy. The e-mail application or the receiving person manages this copy outside the application. Copies may exist with other applications as temporary files or "caches." Their life cycles are often not taken into account by developers while designing security. Protecting merely the master is not enough when so many other copies exist.

Encryption

Intruders use one of three means to compromise the security of a computing system: (1) interruption, (2) interception, or (3) interjection (Figure 16.8). This is a generalization of intrusion detection suggested by Pfleeger. The first compromises the availability of information, the second compromises the secrecy aspect, and the third compromises the integrity aspect.

One way to prevent unauthorized access to a system is by encrypting the data that flows through it. Encryption transforms data into a form that is unintelligible.

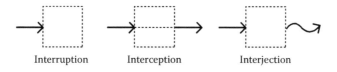

Interruption   Interception   Interjection

Figure 16.8 Intruders use these means.

From a theoretical computer science perspective, encryption belongs to the NP-Complete class of problems, which basically means that one can potentially decrypt a string in "polynomial-time" by guessing an answer. If one tried to use the brute-force guessing logic (trying all permutations of guesses), it would probably take hundreds of years on the fastest machines available today. But then, the corollary is also true, that we may break it in the first few attempts if we used a combination of guesses and a "smart" algorithm based on pruning options in a Breadth First or Depth First approach. Although this means that there is no guarantee to security through encryption, it does add a certain confidence level and comfort feeling within us.

Encryption is a vast topic and we would not like to enter into the technical details. Still, it keeps rearing its head in business environments where a demand is often made that "all sensitive data be encrypted." This meets with understandable resistance because many technologies cannot handle it well, especially on-the-fly. There is also a price to pay in terms of performance and computing resources.

Simon Singh has given a very good history of Encryption and Cryptography in *The Code Book*. He mentions that before encryption, there was steganography, where it was enough to hide the message itself. The process used was cumbersome and not very effective. "To convey his instructions securely, Histaiaeus shaved the head of his messenger, wrote the message on his scalp, and then waited for the hair to regrow. This was clearly a period of history that tolerated a certain lack of urgency."

Access Control

This deals with checking access privilege (needed or not), allowing just enough privilege to data to accomplish a task (need to know basis), and verifying if the action performed on the data is limited and permissible. In fact, access control algorithms can be made sufficiently intelligent to learn the access patterns of various users, and go beyond the static parameters. Whenever any activity outside the norm occurs, access can be granted but the activity can be logged for future verification.

Granularity of access needs to follow the "least privilege" principle — give the minimum set of privileges needed to fulfill a task, and no more. For example, access to a function or area in a screen should be completely denied to someone who does not need it. In other cases, access can be restricted to certain records or areas of the database, or to partial data within the record if that is all that is needed. For an application to implement the correct granularity, the underlying technologies need to support this. Security aspects, then, become the criteria in selecting tools and technologies.

Limiting Disclosure

Information disclosed should also be minimal (Figure 16.9). For example, if a user ID or password is incorrect, it is better to say "invalid username or password" instead of "user not found" or "incorrect password," indicating more specifics. One's vacation auto-responder e-mail or one's voice-mail need not give details of one's vacation. If access is required for emergency situations, it could be arranged through an "air gap," in the form of directions to contact another person, who can then provide further details, presumably after evaluating the request.

There are ways of neutralizing sensitive data. Aggregation is one way of disclosing information *about* secure data: a hospital may share data on diseases through statistical measures. It may reveal detailed data without actual names and identities being disclosed. The danger is that sometimes a lot more information gets revealed inadvertently. For example, if there are only two stores of a certain type in a zip code, and the "sale" totals

"The boss is worried about information security,
so he sends his messages one alphabet letter
at a time in random sequence.'

Figure 16.9   Limiting disclosure.

at the zip code level are published, then each store can figure out the sales of the other by subtracting their own sales from the totals.

Production Environments Can Create Problems

On the implementation side, the application developer may have little control over the production environments in which the application will run. Making assumptions about the environment, and the level of security it could provide, is rather risky. As environments change, the parties (organization IT, software and hardware vendors) involved in putting the change in the production environment may not understand its impact on these applications. If they do not communicate the changes properly or in time, either security holes are created or the application misbehaves due to tightened security.

Patch and Upgrade Management Are Critical

Getting the latest patches to the OS (operating system) and databases is critical. There is more automation on this front in PC-based systems, where every user has encountered notices for automatic updates for their desktop applications, than there is in larger IT based enterprise systems. Patch and upgrade management is a serious and time-consuming task.

The installation of a patch is a change. Changes can introduce problems. It is not safe to assume that every patch or upgrade has improved or maintained security. Adequate testing on both the functionality and security fronts is required — otherwise, a confirmation from the vendor on similar lines.

Information systems can be viewed as simulators. We are familiar with spreadsheets, business applications and computer games though we may not view them as simulators. If we do, though, many behavioral or lifecycle aspects of such systems become understandable, especially the issue of why updates and revisions are required and, in some sense, unavoidable. John D. Barrow in his recent book on infinities "The Infinite Book" touches on the subject of simulators:

Suppose the simulators or at least the first generations of them while having very advanced knowledge of the laws of nature, still have incomplete knowledge of those laws. ...But what will happen to the simulated realities set in virtual motion by simulators with only a partial knowledge of the laws of nature needed to sustain them over long periods of time. Eventually, these realities would cease to compute. They would fall victim of the incompetence of their creators. Errors would accumulate. Prediction would break down. Their world would become irrational. They would be heading for the virtual analogue of death in a biological organism when errors accumulate to a lethal level. The only escape for them is if the creators intervene to patch up the problems one by one as they arise. ...fill gaps in its logic that its creators had not noticed.

This is the logic behind patch management. It will not be possible to get everything right before releasing something. As long as the issue of partial knowledge is recognized, it can be addressed through processes such as patch management and upgrades, as the software industry does.

Multiple Levels of Security

Many enterprises depend predominantly on network-based security to prevent intruders from entering the system. Unless there are second and third levels of defense, a security breach would allow a free run down the plains. One of these levels of defense should include protection or recovery from outer breaches. As in the case of the Hurricane Katrina disaster, the defense depended primarily on the levees — not breaching. The systems and processes to handle a situation if a breach happened turned out to be inadequate.

Learning from the Human Security System

The human body is provided with a unique security system, which is alert and active around the clock. An in-depth study of this system — its ability to detect an intruder, take steps to neutralize it, and at the same time, sound an alert in the body — has no parallel. We now try to examine some basics to learn how it can affect and improve the software security system.

The human immune system continuously defends our bodies by identifying, immobilizing, and destroying infectious bacteria, fungi, parasites, and viruses. Some of these infectious agents use new disguises and evolve new strategies for attack over time. It is a dynamic confrontation similar to the ones computer systems face with attackers and threats.

The body uses multiple levels of defense within its immune system. The organs of the immune system are made of lymphoid tissues that are positioned throughout the body. The lymphatic vessels and lymphatic nodes are the parts of a special circulatory system. The first line of defense involves several kinds of physical and chemical barriers. Sweat, tears, saliva, and mucus are chemical barriers, while the skin and other membrane-lined body passages are physical barriers. The second line of defense is the inflammatory response — swelling, redness, warmth, and pain in the area of an infection are common. This is basically due to an increased blood flow that takes the white blood cells to the infected area. The third line of defense is the immune response. At this stage, the immune system is fully active in recognizing, attacking, destroying, and "remembering" each kind of pathogen or foreign substance that enters the body. This recognition usually happens through identifying unique proteins that appear on the invaders' outside surfaces. This stage also involves the production of antibodies and specialized cells that bind to and inactivate foreign substances. The variety of antibodies is very large, with different antibodies destined for different purposes.

The above discussion gives useful ideas for software security systems, which we now examine:

- Not all destruction needs to be immediate. Some antibodies just coat the foreign invaders with proteins that tag them for the circulating scavenger (white) cells, which will then engulf and destroy the intruder. Applications, likewise, can have built-in generic virus-check capability that tags abnormal activity for a more detailed analysis and action by other, more powerful virus detection programs running in the background.

- During the infection annihilation process, the body also may develop a fever. This is usually not because of the virus and the toxins attacking the body cells. It is an unusual response of the body intended to make the internal environment less hospitable to these invaders. This is another important lesson for computer security; if we cannot destroy the intruder immediately, we can retard the spread of a virus by creating an environment where the virus cannot multiply swiftly.

■ The immune system detectors work locally to determine the presence of an infection. No central coordination takes place, which means there is no single point of failure. Computer security and applications could be built in a similar fashion to ensure that security violations, threats, and intrusions can be detected by each component of the system.

■ The challenge with computer security is to determine the difference between normal activity and potentially harmful activity in the system. It is said that the human immune system weighs the danger of an invader, based on the latter's origin, seriousness, and frequency, rather than the relatively simple equation of distinguishing between self (the body) or non-self (a foreign object), as previously thought. Furthermore, it is able to tell the difference between tissue undergoing natural cell death, inflammation due to muscular injury, or really an intruder attack. Similarly, primitive intrusion detection systems that simply determine threats by recognizing incoming malicious code are not as effective as systems that are able to assess risk by gathering information from a variety of sources through software agents that monitor activities, understanding "normal" behavior so that it can classify anything that looks different as "suspect." This is where behavior-based recognition can be more effective than signature-based detection. Behavior-based detection is common, for example, in law enforcement, retail establishments, or in casinos.

■ Our body retains the ability to recognize the organism that infected it for many years thereafter, yet it does not constantly assume a defensive posture unless there is another threat.

■ After an attack on the body, the body uses its healing processes to return to normal. These are active and powerful processes that are important to threat management. If there is no recovery after battle, then battles can be very damaging even if "won." We do not have effective parallels in computer applications. Computer security could likewise develop systems that "heal" themselves and can recover autonomously from an attack.

■ There is little variation in computers and operating systems. Most are extremely similar in architecture and hence easier and more effective to target. On the other hand, natural systems use a strategy of immense variety and diversity to ensure that there is survival at some level, perhaps at the species level, if not the individual. The extensive diversity also presents thousands of differing potential targets. Following proven architectures always makes the attackers' job easier.

A Counter-Intuitive Approach from Field Sports

An interesting lesson that information security can learn from sports is to know what exactly to defend and how to act when an attacker has entered a secure perimeter. In soccer or field hockey, for example, if the ball is lost to the other team, the quickest way to recover is to simply run straight back toward one's own goal. Defenders have the singular objective to protect the ball from crossing their goal line. They need to assemble and create a cordon around that area. The defensive danger zone is recognized as the area in front of the goal. In that zone, defense players are coached to clear the ball quickly, to kick the ball hard and far — this is not the place to dribble. Similarly, if there is a breach in one's software system, focus on protecting the key assets before trying to repair the breach.

The Human Perspective

Human factors are critical to security. They impact security in at least two ways — once during development and the other during operations.

Software development lies in the domain of individuals. The programmer is supposed to be conscientious in his or her coding practices. To a large extent, writing "secure code" has not been their highest priority. It cannot be assumed that developers know how to write secure code to begin with. This is no different from the fact that developers cannot be presumed to know how to deliver systems tuned for performance. Most coding is done to meet functionality, by which is meant business functionality, while security and performance do not get delivered automatically.

Recognizing this situation, an organization should evolve security coding guidelines for developers to follow. These coding guidelines should include technology-specific suggestions because vulnerabilities differ between technologies. Guidelines should cover all aspects of the development life cycle. It should include the use of tools such as software configuration and source code management (SCM) so that access to the code can be controlled and traced. One should also introduce peer reviews of code and documents to determine potential security vulnerabilities.

People can introduce security flaws in systems — sometimes unknowingly, and at other times with malicious intent. People have been known to join organizations just to find the security systems used. Breaches in banks have occurred with the connivance of staff members.

Most IT organizations now believe that an overwhelming majority of their developers use their computers irresponsibly and do not follow instructions of their IT staff. They download open source modules or "objects" from unsafe places, install unauthorized software, and are almost borderline casual in sharing "company confidential" programs to others over e-mail. Some of these actions may open doors to security threats that are not well understood.

Not all security attacks are through technical or electronic means. Social engineering attacks are driven by a keen understanding of human behavior patterns. Some of these techniques garner passwords, access information, or personal data for misuse from unsuspecting customers and employees.

Employee Separation

When there is a separation (resignation or layoff), there may not be a clear understanding of the knowledge employees carry with them — which may include valuable details about vulnerabilities of the system. Sometimes these layoffs are also handled in a physically compressed time period with little handover or debriefing. Security guards standing to collect laptops, or network access being switched off, help in only some aspects of security. One problem that exists despite sufficient information being there about avoiding it is that many an application or object remains under the "ownership" of employee user IDs. Automatically deleting or inactivating such user IDs can have a cascading effect, which is often difficult to predict. Such organizations may not deactivate user IDs very quickly. It is seen as not being an issue because the ex-employee's network access is turned off. Avoid allowing production jobs to be owned by individual user IDs. Developers should build cleanup mechanisms in an application to handle user ID changes without affecting any data loss.

Specialization

Responding to security threats has become a special skill. The problem with specialization, however, is that one can get into a mode of transference of responsibility. Security is left to the "security organization" responsible for security, and one can only hope that they are doing a fine job. Appropriate response, however, lies somewhere between mass mobilization and total specialization. Security awareness in the public (nonofficial security) domain has always been encouraged ("Loose lips sink ships" posters during World War II) and many companies have regular security-related education programs or initiatives.

Processes and Procedures

This section examines some of the processes and procedures needed to support technical approaches to security.

Data Classification

One common approach to the classification of data and resources is to label them as Public, Confidential, Secure, Top Secret, or some such impressive term. Access control and distribution policies are then defined for each type. While the policies relating to the handling of a particular classification may be well thought out, the problem that is often faced is how to select the correct classification in the first place. Except for trivial or obvious cases, users remain confused about how to classify data. This tends to make them over cautious and classify data more stringently than the situation demands. This affects information flow to both internal and external parties, the latter being denied information, which they could safely have accessed. Or they could classify it lower to avoid the hassles of getting various permissions.

Sometimes, specific data attributes and fields, or combination of fields, are classified as sensitive. The existence of such fields in any table or database gets the entire table or database classified as sensitive. The actions triggered by such classification may be onerous — say, "encrypt everything" — something difficult to implement for various reasons.

Incorrect classification can have unexpected side effects related to social behavior. Certain categories of classification become a sign of importance of the content itself — if a memo were important, it would be "Top Secret," and so on. What was meant to be a directive for distribution is taken up as a signal of its priority. The reverse logic is then applied and people automatically assume that memos for public distribution contain "less important" information. Sometimes, the cost of maintaining the classification apparatus with all its arbitrariness and impreciseness is not worth the security it provides.

Exceptions

There is a struggle between having a sound and stringent security policy on paper, which cannot be implemented, or having a more realistic policy. The policy remains on paper for legal coverage reasons. Anything infeasible or too bothersome is then handled through an exception mechanism that reviews and grants exceptions to the security requirements on a case-by-case basis. Large applications may operate for long periods of time under exceptions that keep getting renewed. This may be a clever way of solving a tricky problem: operating under an exception satisfies adherence to the security policy because exceptions are part of the security policy. This is a practical way of operating as long as all parties understand that getting an exception has not made the risk go away.

The exception mechanism does make the risks identifiable and traceable. It forces one to think through the issue and allows others to look at the risks.

Responding to Attacks

Appropriate communication is key to responding to a breach. Psychological aspects of human and organizational behavior have always been part of conventional security. In the information security field, there is need to understand their implication better, to avoid overreacting. Martial arts in their various forms are based on the philosophy of self-defense. Most people, when attacked, demonstrate an emotional reaction that is either a paralyzing panic or else an undisciplined, blinding rage. Years of serious training in martial arts are required to take out the emotional charge.

Quite often, IT departments assign too much authority to one person playing a certain role, who could ultimately turn out to be compromised or incompetent. He or she could shut down the entire system. Some organizations have concepts of dual control, especially for supervisory functions where the password is split between two managers. Both of them must be entered for the system to go into supervisor mode. This is somewhat similar to checks that must be signed by two officers of the company for amounts larger than some threshold amount.

Adherence

How does one get people to adhere to controls? People use something when they are convinced of the need to follow the processes. This conviction may be the result of a painful experience. Adherence is helped by adequate displays of seriousness by management about such issues. Repeated clear communications are essential. The problem sometimes lies not with a reluctance to follow procedure, but with the difficulty of interpreting what may be incomplete, impractical, or contradictory orders or standards.

Contradictory Orders

Many organizations have disjointed or conflicting security policies and procedures. This section looks at how the U.S. Navy handles contradictory orders. Note the information flows between the person issuing or receiving the original order and the person issuing or receiving the contradictory order. Also note how execution is kept separate, and given higher priority, from the task of informing all parties concerned.

According to Navy Regulations At 0815:

If an officer contradicts the orders issued to another by a superior, the officer who issues the contradictory orders must immediately report that fact, preferably, in writing, to the superior whose orders have been contravened.

If an officer receives a contradictory order, he or she must immediately exhibit his or her orders, unless otherwise instructed, and represent the facts in writing to the officer who has given the last order. If that officer insists upon the execution of his or her order, it must be obeyed and the circumstances should be reported to the office issuing the original order.

—From *The Naval Officer's Guide*

Summary

It is time to pay more attention to the security aspects of deliverables, making it perhaps as important as functionality and performance. A good security system covers business, technical, human, and process factors related to the systems being implemented. While recognizing the argument about the "weaker link," the problem still exists as to how to identify the weaker links.

Cost is involved in making applications and environments secure. This cost must be borne by those for whom security has utmost value. It is quite important to ensure that the right entities are being protected, remembering that what is important to you may not be important to the criminal. Security costs must be balanced with business needs.

Human factors continue to present vulnerabilities for software in production. Software development and support is a very person-oriented enterprise, and the culture within software companies and IT departments has not given due importance to security.

Chapter 17

Conclusion

We hope this book helps the reader reflect on many issues that concern the building of a functional, reliable system. Some of these issues are about the creative aspects of software, and others are about the managerial aspects of its creation. Both are important for successful delivery.

It is the nature of software development that there is no single process that will work all the time. Software development is a creative process and, as in writing a book or creating a song, the creative process that lies at the core of what is created is often difficult to explain and has many subjective elements to it. And although the core may not be tractable, a lot of activities around it are. Creative acts require organization, discipline, processes for trials and revisions, management of logistics and physical delivery, as well as marketing of the delivered creations. As software organizations have been building good and commercially successful software for years now, some of these management processes are better understood today.

We have proposed a simple framework for software design, development, and its management called SEE (Solution-Engineering-Execution). As clarified throughout the book, this is not yet another process or methodology that will ensure good software. It is an organizing influence for the way one approaches the problems in the field. Solution in SEE refers to the thinking behind the solution. What are the various solution choices? Why are we choosing this particular solution among them? There is often a jump into *engineering* without spending enough effort on the *solution* aspect. Engineering in SEE covers activities such as architecture, design, technology selection, management approach, plans, and controls.

This is an extended definition of *engineering*. It includes expected technical aspects of development along with its management aspects. Both are important. For example, a lack of good communication within a team can cause many, if not more problems in software delivery than perhaps some technical aspect of a selected programming language. *Execution* in SEE covers all aspects of delivery. It goes beyond building the deliverable, to cover its release, implementation, marketing, enhancements, support, staffing, financials, and others. Execution deals with all non-engineering activities from conception to delivery. (We place the engineering management-related activities within the *engineering* layer of SEE.)

Many books list what is required to be done to achieve some goal. The problem is that the sum total of all that is said to be required to be done turns out to be more suitable for an ideal world rather than the constrained real-world environment in which one operates. As authors we have tried to avoid falling too often into that ideal world advisory trap.

SEE also offers an opportunity to solve problems by looking at the larger picture. If a problem cannot be solved technically, it could perhaps be solved as a combination of technical and business solutions. For example, many projects fail because the requirements are not properly specified. Instead of trying to ensure perfect requirements, which we are not sure is possible for any nontrivial situation, alternate approaches could be put in place that will ensure reasonably reliable and functional systems. Such an approach would require a combination of technical and managerial methods. For example, the product roadmap could be better understood, which would help recognize where the anticipated changes are likely to come; the architecture could be made (more) flexible based on that; change control systems can be put in place that minimize the cost of changes, considering the nature of the relationships and the environments in which the work is being done. Our SEE approach is an organizing influence that will help one approach the problem of poor or changing requirements as a systemic problem that requires a solution spread across engineering and management.

One point we would like to touch on is that one should have fun in what one is doing. As organizations grow larger, as business pressures dominate, software creation becomes a job just like any other. Our unscientific survey shows that there are many in the software industry who are not having fun creating software. Perhaps it is part of the growing-up process. If so, our prescription is to try to bring the fun back. It is a necessary component of the creative act and SEE and other suggestions notwithstanding, there is no substitute for it. Wait, you say, you are confusing the creative spark with the managerial drudgery of converting the creative spark to reality. No, we are not getting confused. The nature of building software is such that at both the idea and the execution levels, one needs to be creative.

In this book we have drawn, primarily, from three areas: (1) systems science, (2) software engineering, and (3) project management. As we are building systems, some knowledge and understanding of systems science concepts is essential for the designer and the architect as well as for the manager and the customer. Software engineering is the application of engineering principles to the design and production of software — its relevance is more obvious, although its use is not as widespread as it should be. Project (and general) management ideas are essential for any delivery in project, product, or consulting businesses.

Certain problems recur across domains, times, and technologies. These are small and large issues that often cause confusion in communications, lack a satisfactory understanding or solution, and need some ground definitions to make things work smoothly. In fact, over the years, these problem areas have not changed very much. They continue to be estimation, requirements, technology selection, build versus buy, change control management, staffing, and some aspects of release management. At a more fundamental level, software creation is very people intensive, depends on a core set of individuals, is substantially manual, and is difficult to specify with the engineering rigor seen in other industries. We have touched on most of these long-standing problem areas, offering what we hope are some practical guidelines to improve the situation for some of these.

Many of the problems arise due to definitional issues. Two companies rarely mean the same thing when they refer to the "design documents." Sometimes common terms such as "configuration" and "customization," or "migration" and "porting," may not have acceptable definitions across groups. This is not to say that efforts have not been made by the standards committees to standardize definitions. However, the net situation is that a lot of communication problems arise due to differing definitions and consequent expectations. We have therefore spent some effort in probing how certain terms are used or understood in the industry.

If there is one suggestion we would like to give designers and architects in this conclusion chapter it would be to pay attention to non-software domains. Good systems design draws on a large body of topics and experience. There are problems that professionals encounter again and again in different guises in areas far away from software, fields such as aviation or medicine or civil engineering or the military. Many of these problems — how to secure one's assets, communicate properly, specify what one wants done, track changes, store records — have had good practical solutions in these other domains. However, many designers do not pay sufficient attention to the lessons that can be learned from non-software fields.

For designers and architects, there are other "soft" aspects that they need to understand and implement. A point that should be remembered is that complex systems, similar to large and successful companies, are built around "proven" value systems and processes. Certain things are done a certain way in good companies because that is the right thing to do even if it costs a little more or takes a little longer. It is not all altruism: the right thing to do may lower long-term costs and increase return on investment. One must adhere to such value systems if one is convinced that it is the right thing to do as a professional.

As with any book, this one is just one view of the software world based on our thinking, reading, and experience in software systems design, development, and implementation. We hope to contribute to the larger body of knowledge in the software and systems domain through this book and the SEE approach to building software.

In a wide-ranging book such as this, there is a limit to the depth to which one can take each topic. There is a wide body of literature on systems development and we have not covered basic material. Some experience in the software field is assumed on the part of our readers. We hope we have provided some fresh approaches and creative thinking to familiar issues, with some stress on the cross-domain and cross-functional aspects of the topics we discuss.

Through the hustle and bustle of daily work commitments, try to step back and "understand" that experience. Write down why something worked and others did not. Add to your personal repository of good solutions. Build your library of good design concepts and management techniques. And, at all times, look at other systems, beyond software.

Wish you all success in building better software.

Bibliography

Agency for Healthcare Research and Quality, *Hospital Quality Indicators: Inpatient Quality Indicators Overview*, AHRQ Quality Indicators, Agency for Healthcare Research and Quality, Rockville, MD, February 2006.

Alexander, C., Ishikawa, S., Silverstein, M., Jacobson, M., Fiksdahl-King, I., and Angel, S., *A Pattern Language — Towns, Buildings, Construction*, Oxford University Press, New York, 1977.

Anderson, T., *The Way of Go*, Free Press, New York, 2004.

Ash, Robert B., *Information Theory*, Dover Publications, New York, 1990.

Ashby, William R., *Design for a Brain*, 2nd ed., Chapman & Hall, London, 1966.

Ashby, William R., *Introduction to Cybernetics*, Chapman & Hall, London, London, 1956.

Ashby, William R., Principles of the Self-Organizing Dynamic System, *Journal of General Psychology*, 37, 125–128, 1947.

Beer, S., *Cybernetics and Management*, 2nd ed., English University Press, London, 1967.

Barrow, J.D., *The Infinite Book*, Pantheon Books, New York, 2005.

Bass, L., Clements, P., Kazman, R., *Software Architecture in Practice*. Addison Wesley Longman, Inc., Reading, MA, 1998.

Bateson, G., *Mind and Nature: A Necessary Unity*, E.P. Dutton, New York, 1979.

Beer, S., *Brain of the Firm,* Penguin Press, London, 1972.

Behuniak, John A., Ahmad, I.A., and Courtright, A.M., *Production Software That Works*, Digital Press (now part of Elsevier, New York), 1992.

Benington, H.D., Production of Large Computer Programs, *Annals of the History of Computing*, October 1983, pp. 350–361.

Benington, H.D., Production of Large Computer Programs, *Proceedings of the Ninth International Conference on Software Engineering*, Computer Society Press, 1987.

Bernstein, P.L., *Against the Gods — The Remarkable Story of Risk*, John Wiley & Sons, New York, 1996.

Boehm, B.W., *Software Engineering Economics*, Prentice Hall, Englewood Cliffs, NJ, 1981, chap. 33.

Boehm, B., Clark, B., Horowitz, E., Westland, C., Madachy, R., Selby, R., Cost Models for Future Software Life-Cycle Processes: COCOMO 2.0, *Annals of Software Engineering Special Volume on Software Process and Product Measurement*, Arthur, J.D. and Henry, S.M., Eds., J.C. Baltzer AG, Eds., Science Publishers, Amsterdam, 1, 45–60, 1995.

Booch, G., *Object-Oriented Analysis and Design with Applications*, 2nd ed., Benjamin-Cummings Publishing, Redwood City, CA, 1993.

Booch, G., Jacobson, I., Rumbaugh, J., *The Unified Modeling Language Reference Manual*, Addison-Wesley, Reading, MA, 1999.

Bright, J. and Schoeman, M., Eds., *A Guide to Practical Technological Forecasting*, Prentice Hall, Englewood Cliffs, NJ, 1973.

Buschmann, F., Meunier, R., Rohnert, H., Sommerlad, P., Stal, M., *Pattern-Oriented Software Architecture — A System of Patterns*, Wiley and Sons, New York, NY, 1996.

Cerruzi, P.E., *A History of Modern Computing*, MIT Press, Cambridge, MA, 1998.

Churchman, C.W., *The Design of Inquiring Systems: Basic Concepts of Systems and Organizations*, Basic Books, New York, 1971.

Churchman, C.W., *The Systems Approach and Its Enemies,* Basic Books, New York, 1979.

Cox, W.M., Mass Customization, Federal Reserve Bank of Dallas Expand Your Insight, September 1, http://www.dallasfed.org/eyi/tech/9909custom.html, 1999.

Date, C.J. *An Introduction to Database Systems*, Addison-Wesley Publication, Reading, MA, 1995.

DeMarco, T., On Systems Architecture, *Proceedings of the 1995 Monterey Workshop on Specification-Based Software Architectures*, U.S. Naval Postgraduate School, Monterey, CA, September 1995.

DeRemer, F. and Kron, H., Programming-in-the-Large versus Programming-in-the-Small, *IEEE Transactions on Software Engineering,* 2, 321–327, June 1976.

Dijkstra, E.W., *A Discipline of Programming*, Prentice Hall, Englewood Cliffs, NJ, 1976.

Dörner, D., *The Logic of Failure,* Addison-Wesley, Reading MA, 1997.

Drucker, P.F., *The Frontiers of Management*, Heinemann, London, 1986.

Drucker, P.F., The Shape of Things to Come, *Leader to Leader*, 1996, pp. 12–18.

Dyson, E., *Release 2.0*, Broadway Books, New York, 1997.

Fine, C.H., StClair, R., Lafrance, J.C., and Hillebrand, D.G., *Meeting the Challenge U.S. Industry Faces the 21st Century the U.S. Automobile Manufacturing Industry*, U.S. Department of Commerce, Office of Technology Policy, December 1996.

Forrester, J.W., *Industrial Dynamics,* new edition, Productivity Press, Portland, OR, 1961.

Forrester, J.W., *Urban Dynamics,* MIT Press, Cambridge, MA, 1969.

Forrester, J.W., *World Dynamics,* revised edition, Wright-Allen Press, Cambridge, MA, 1973.

Friedman, George, *America's Secret War,* Doubleday, New York, 2004.

Gallager, Robert G., *Information Theory and Reliable Communication*, John Wiley & Sons, New York, 2001.

Gamma, E., Helm, R., Johnson, R., and Vlissides, J., *Design Patterns: Elements of Reusable Object Oriented Software*, Addison-Wesley, Reading, MA, 1994.

Garlan, D. and Shaw, M., *An Introduction to Software Architecture*, Advances in Software Engineering and Knowledge Engineering, Volume 2. World Scientific Press, New York, 1993.

Grove, Andrew S., *High Output Management*, Vintage Books, New York, 1995.

Hayakawa, S.I., *Language in Thought and Action*, 2nd ed., Harcourt, Brace & World, Inc., New York, 1963.

Jacobson, I., Booch, G., and Rumbaugh, J., *The Unified Software Development Process*, 1st ed., Addison-Wesley Professional, Reading, MA, 1999.

Jervis, Robert, *System Effects — Complexity in Political and Social Life*, Princeton University Press, Princeton, NJ, 1997.

Kapor, Mitch, A Software Design Manifesto, *Dr. Dobbs Journal,* 172, 62–68, 1991.

Kececioglu, Dimitri, *Reliability Engineering Handbook*, Prentice Hall, Englewood Cliffs, NJ, Vol. 1, 1991.

Keegan, John, *A History of Warfare*, Vintage Books, New York, 1993.

Keegan, John, *Intelligence in War*, Alfred A. Knopf, New York, 2003.

Kepner, C.H. and Tregoe, B.B., *The Rational Manager*, McGraw-Hill, New York, 1965.

Knuth, Donald E., *Literate Programming*, Center for the Study of Language and Information, Stanford, CA, 1992.

Kroeger, Michael and Rand, Paul, Graphic Designer, www.mkgraphic.com, 2002.

Kruchten, P., *Architectural Blueprints* — The "4+1" View Model of Software Architecture, *IEEE Software,* 12(6), 42–50, 1995.

Kruchten, P., *The Rational Unified Process — An Introduction*, 2nd ed., Addison-Wesley-Longman, Reading, MA, 2000.

Latham, Edward C., *The Poetry of Robert Frost*, Henry Holt and Company, New York, 1969.

Lawrence, Brian, Unresolved Ambiguity, *American Programmer,* April 1996, Vol. 9(5).

Lazar, J., Jones, A., and Shneiderman, B., Workplace User Frustration with Computers: An Exploratory Investigation of the Causes and Severity, *Behaviour & Information Technology,* 25(3), 239–251, 2004.

Lewis, J.P., Large Limits to Software Estimation, *ACM Software Engineering Notes,* 26(4), 54–59, 2001.

Mack, William P. and Paulsen, Thomas D., *The Naval Officer's Guide*, Naval Institute Press, Annapolis, MD, 1983.

Maguire, Steve, *Writing Solid Code*, Microsoft Press, Redmond, WA, 1993.

Martin, James and McClure, Carma, *Diagramming Techniques for Analysts and Programmers*, Prentice Hall, Englewood Cliffs, NJ, 1985.

Maslow, Abraham H., *Motivation and Personality*, 2nd ed., Harper & Row, New York, 1970.

McLuhan, Marshall, *Understanding Media: The Extensions of Man*, McGraw-Hill, New York, 1964.

McLuhan, M., Fiore, Q., and Agel, J., *The Medium Is the Massage,* Bantam Books, Random House, New York, 1967.

Mitchell, Henry, *On Gardening,* Houghton Mifflin, Boston, MA, 1998.

Moore, Geoffrey A., *Crossing the Chasm,* Harper Business, New York, 1991.

Moubray, J., *Reliability-Centered Maintenance,* Butterworth-Heinemann Ltd., Oxford, 1991.

Nowlan, F. Stanley and Heap, Howard, *Reliability-Centered Maintenance,* Dolby Access Press, San Francisco, 1978.

Nowlan, F. Stanley and Heap, Howard, *Reliability-Centered Maintenance,* Department of Defense, Washington, D.C., 1978. Report Number AD-A066579.

O'Connor, J. and McDermott, I., *The Art of Systems Thinking,* Thorsons, London, 1997.

Ohmae, K., *The Mind of the Strategist,* McGraw-Hill, New York, 1982.

Pacioli, L., *Summa de arithmetica, geometrica, proportioni et proportionalita,* 1494.

Paulisch, F., Software Architecture and Reuse — An Inherent Conflict?, *Proceedings of the 3rd International Conference on Software Reuse,* Rio de Janeiro, Brazil, November 1–4, 1994. IEEE Computer Society Press, 1994.

Perry, D.E. and Wolf, A.L., Foundation for the Study of Software Architecture, *ACM SIGSOFT Software Engineering Notes,* 17(4), 40–52, 1992.

Perry, D.E. and Wolf, A.L., Foundations for the Study of Software Architectures, *SIGSOFT Software Engineering Notes,* 17(4), 40–52, October 1992.

Peters, Tom, *Professional Service Firm 50,* Knopf, New York, 2000.

Petroski, Henry, *Invention by Design,* Harvard University Press, London, 1996

Pfleeger, Charles and Shari Pfleeger, *Security in Computing,* 3rd ed., Prentice Hall, Englewood Cliffs, NJ, 2003.

Pierce, John R., *An Introduction to Information Theory,* Dover Publications, New York, 1980

Prieto-Diaz, Ruben and Neighbors, James, Module Interconnection Languages, *Journal of Systems and Software,* 6(4), 307–334, 1986.

Pugh, E.S., Ed., *Organization Theory, Selected Readings,* Pelican Books, Harmondsworth, 1971.

Rabassa, Gregory, *If This Be Treason: Translation and Its Dyscontents, A Memoir,* New Directions Press, 2005.

Rasiel, Ethan M., *The McKinsey Way,* McGraw-Hill, New York, 1998.

Robertson, James and Robertson, Suzanne, *Complete Systems Analysis,* Dorset House Publishing, New York, 1994.

Royce, W.W., Managing the Development of Large Software Systems: Concepts and Techniques, *Proc. Weston,* August 1970.

Royce, W.W., Managing the Development of Large Software Systems: Concepts and Techniques, *Proc. ICSE 9,* Computer Society Press, 1987.

Rubin, H., ESTIMACS, *IEEE,* 132, 23–34, 1983.

Saraswat, Prakash, *A Historical Perspective on the Philosophical Foundations of Information Systems,* Bentley College, November 1998, http://www.bauer.uh.edu/parks/fis/saraswat3.htm.

Simon, Alan R., *Systems Migration A Complete Reference,* Van Nostrand Reinhold, New York, 1992.

Singh, Simon, *The Code Book: The Science of Secrecy from Ancient Egypt to Quantum Cryptography*, Anchor Publications, London, Spring 1998.

Symons, *Software Sizing and Estimating – Mark II FPA*, John Wiley & Sons, United Kingdom, 1991.

The Unambiguous UML Consortium page: www.cs.york.ac.uk/puml/.

Toffler, Alvin and Toffler, Heidi, *From War and Anti-War — Survival at the Dawn of the 21st Century,* Little Brown & Company, Boston, 1993.

Tufte, Edward, *The Visual Display of Quantitative Information*, Graphics Press, Cheshire, CT, 1983.

Tufte, Edward, *The Cognitive Style of PowerPoint*, Graphics Press, Cheshire, CT, 2003.

Umpleby, S.A. and Dent, E.B., *The Origins and Purposes of Several Traditions in Systems Theory and Cybernetics,* Taylor & Francis, London, Vol. 30, No. 2, February 1, 1999.

U.S. Food and Drug Administration, *General Principles of Software Validation,* Final Guidance for Industry and FDA Staff, Center for Devices and Radiological Health, 2002.

Veryard, Richard, *Information Modelling*, Prentice Hall, New York, 1992.

Volk, Tyler, *Metapatterns*, Columbia University Press, New York, 1995.

Washington Post, Statistics on Losses Due to Software Bugs in 2001, *Washington Post*, May 17, 2002.

Weibull: Prof. Dr. E. Borghers, Prof. Dr. P. Wessa, *Statistics - Econometrics — Forecasting*, Office for Research Development and Education, http://www.xycoon.com.

Weinberg, Gerald M., *An Introduction to General Systems Thinking,* John Wiley & Sons, New York, 1975.

Wikipedia contributors, "Luca Pacioli," Wikipedia, *The Free Encyclopedia*, http://en.wikipedia.org/w/index.php?title=Luca_Pacioli&oldid=102877310.

Winograd, Terry, *Bringing Design to Software,* Addison-Wesley, Reading, MA, 1996.

Woods, Tiger, *How I Play Golf*, Warner Books, 2001.

Yourdon, E. and Coad, P., *Object-Oriented Analysis*, 2nd ed., Prentice Hall, Englewood Cliffs, NJ, 1991.

Zachman, John A., A Framework for Information Systems Architecture, *IBM Systems Journal,* 26(3), 276–292, 1987.

Appendix A

Discussion of Terms

Since 1852, English speakers have been able to consult *Roget's Thesaurus*, a reference book of synonyms, antonyms, and equivalent words. Writers use this reference to select words with the right weight and shade of meaning, thereby improving their writing considerably. Scientific terms and expressions in professional usage appear far better defined and precise than normal English words: a glossary of terms is considered sufficient. This appendix discusses terms that systems professionals often use, and also confuse. The idea is not to arrive at a particular definition, but rather to explore ideas underlying multiple definitions or interpretations.

Logical versus Physical

Practically everything has a physical basis. The most complex programs, and the smallest signals in the brain, run on physical devices. In discussing systems, the difference between logical and physical is often between high level and low level, between modeling and implementation (Figure A.1). In most situations, the difference is obvious or fairly clear. For

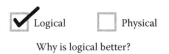

Why is logical better?

Figure A.1   Logical versus physical.

example, Shakespeare's plays are logical entities, which can have multiple physical existences — as books, on the stage, as audio tapes, etc. There would be no confusion between the logical and the physical in such cases.

People usually relate to everything logically — using names. Data and information on computers are referred to logically, through a file name, and not the sectors on a disk. Naming introduces a logical concept to things that are physical.

Logical entities can also be grouped differently from the physical reality underneath. For example, an automobile dealership application screen may contain the customer's name, the VIN (vehicle identification number), the vehicle miles, problem details, and an initial estimate for a repair job. The physical organization of the same could be in four different database tables or flat files, cross-referenced by the customer ID and the part ID. These tables, in turn, may themselves be viewed as logical entities that group certain kinds of information together going all the way to the physical bits stored on the disk.

In some cases, the mapping is not specific. One's bank statement is just a logical view of the money that one has in one's name in the bank. It is not mapped to any particular bundle of notes, which the bank has physical possession of in its vaults.

Another example is your LAN (local area network). The logical view is a bus that runs through the entire network, and various devices (computers, printers) are connected to it. However, the physical topology is very different; it is a star, where each of these devices on the network connects to a central hub or router.

Thus, logical is a way of compressing information, an abstraction for human beings to comprehend better, instead of getting into details.

In many systems, we use a logical representation to describe the *role* of an entity, whereas the physical nature describes its actual *appearance*. A traffic signal at each intersection has a red light, which is logical, indicating a physical stop for all vehicles. The light by itself does not directly act to physically stop traffic by lowering a gate or some such thing. The conversion from logical to physical is achieved by drivers following driving rules. Traffic lights are therefore logical implementations from a systems point of view.

In software, the purpose of the logical model is to show how the data is captured and used by the application to satisfy business requirements. It shows how this data is related (identifiers, attributes, types, and relationships), and explores any integration requirements with business areas outside the scope of the development project. It is created without any specific computer environment in mind. The purpose of the physical model, on the other hand, is to show how this data capture and usage will be implemented and stored (tables, indices, foreign keys, columns).

Physical models may introduce elements and notions such as throughput and response time, ensure that the application falls within the physical constraints imposed by the computing environment (CPU, disk space, RAM), etc.

One cannot do away with either model — business users will want a logical representation, while coders will want the physical details from the DBA (database administrator). The point is to realize the importance of each and be aware that we maintain the connectivity between the logical and the physical, and use it to our advantage in requirement gathering, estimations, and delivery.

Products, Projects, and Processes

It is essential to keep *projects* and *products* separate in planning. In developing a software product, the *product* is the application being built and the *project* is the development project. The parties involved decide what falls within a project and what does not. For example, in a development project, preparing the online documentation may be in scope but preparing the user training material may not be within the scope of the project. At the same time, the product has its own scope, which is identified in its specifications. Keeping the two scopes — project and product — separate, while dealing with both of them, is key to proper management.

Both projects and products have their own life cycles. Project management processes would include activities such as initiation, execution, or closing the project. Such processes tend to be applicable to many different kinds of projects. For a software product, the processes could be analysis, design, development, test, etc. In a project, the life cycles and processes for both the product and the project are playing out simultaneously. (Note that the term "product" includes service products such as accounting or medical services.)

How do these two life cycles interact? The product life cycle could consist of a number of projects. Prototyping could be a project; beta testing could be a separate project. The development project that we are talking about could be one of the many projects in the product life cycle. Or the entire product development could be handled as a large project with many phases or sub-projects, each phase or sub-project requiring some or all of the project management processes. For the prototyping phase, one needs to initiate the design, execute it, and close it. When one moves on to the next phase, say, detailed design, it would again require initiation, execution, closure, etc. The two life cycles and processes are like two separate threads woven together.

Separately track these two life cycles — project and product — and two scopes — project and product — at all times. A lot of frustration is caused by not recognizing that there are two threads in action, not one. Sometimes, project managers will start "interfering" in product issues that are not project issues, thereby angering the engineering teams. Product leads may not recognize the project management processes that repeat with each phase and get frustrated with the project management "over-head" that keeps cropping up every time they start a new phase. It helps to lay out the separate life cycles and scopes — the multiple process architecture, so to speak — to the leads and the team at the start of the project.

Critical versus Important

Something is considered *critical* if its absence (or presence) causes the system to cease functioning. *Important* things are significant — things whose absence (or presence) will impede the system but not prevent it from functioning. Air and water are critical for human survival — vitamins are important. We all recognize the importance of identifying the critical components. It is the mistake of treating merely important items as critical that causes problems.

Customers treat most of their requirements as critical; vendors may not. One will have to use one's expertise, and analysis skills, to distinguish the critical from the important. Sometimes the difference in opinion is due to differing viewpoints and granularities. The customer is perhaps taking the (understandable) stand that everything has to be delivered according to the contract, and thus is critical. The project manager, on the other hand, is looking at the classification of critical versus important to help better allocate some of the scarce resources, to help identify the requirements that need careful monitoring. While all requirements are important, the planning is guided and driven primarily by the critical ones.

Whenever the term "critical" is used, one must ask what critical stands for. "Critical path" is a frequently misused term. It stands for a specific meaning. The term "critical activity" is used in PERT (Program Evaluation and Review Technique) to mean that the activity is on the critical path. These are activities that have no "slack" — that is, if they slip, the entire project will run late. Some of these activities may be "trivial" compared to the more "important" tasks within the project. Deciding on a name for a new server is obviously less important than creating the test plan, for example. The naming could be a critical activity because it has no slack — any delay will affect the entire project, whereas a few days' delay in the creation of the test plan may not because it has what is called a "float."

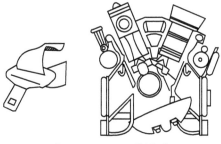

Important versus Critical

Figure A.2   Seat belt versus engine.

PERT deals with schedules. Many think that by calling something a *critical activity* on the schedule that they have raised its priority. They have not. Critical paths change during a project. As such, an activity may be critical today, but not (critical) next week due to something else happening in another activity.

A set of related terms often used is *essential* versus *nice to have*. Features are often classified according to these categories (Figure A.2). A confusion arises because, in the customer's mind, "nice to have" is also part of the delivery, only less important than the other ones. The customer expects the entire list — essential *and* nice to have — to be delivered. However, the delivery team may treat "nice to have" as optional items and ignore them.

Horizontal versus Vertical

This has been a topic of constant discussion in computer science circles and a perennial source of confusion among management and marketing people. An ERP (Enterprise Resource Plan) offering is considered horizontal by its product design teams. Its version for a particular industry, such as oil and gas, is considered a vertical. On the other hand, the oil and gas company may consider its ERP as a horizontal application, while its software to manage the *offshore exploration platform* is considered vertical. For developers, it is the struggle between using a BFS (breadth first search) tree traversal algorithm or the generic branch-and-bound (vertical traversal) technique. Is the definition of horizontal and vertical arbitrary?

In marketing and general usage, something that is more foundational is called horizontal. It meshes with the visual imagery of horizontal. A platform — ERP, CRM, etc. — is horizontal. Such systems provide the grounding for specialized services (e.g., a reporting engine for reports). Extending that visual, verticals are built to balance themselves upon these horizontals. One needs to keep in mind that some recursion is involved in such models. The verticals may themselves be structured as horizontal and vertical within its space.

Problem Solving

Although it appears that the vertical approach may lead to optimal results and help focus on a problem, it is quite likely that horizontal deviations are required along the way. This is because, in real life, most systems we deal with do not work in isolated silos and the information required for solving a problem crosses boundaries. So while one is going deep (vertical) in one area, one may have to make a lateral shift to deal with another system or sub-system. For example, to buy a car, while the deepest interaction might be with the auto dealer, one will need to work with financial institutions (loans), government agencies (registration), or one may wish to look up consumer research reports before closing the deal. If each of these — dealerships, financial institutions, government agencies, and consumer research organizations — is considered verticals in their own right, the solution jumps between them horizontally.

This choice or necessity between horizontal and vertical (going deep) movements is built into effective prototyping (Figure A.3). Many auto manufacturers, for example, start by building many prototypes of their next-generation automobiles (horizontal). They then select one or a few, based on some criteria, and then go deeper (vertical) into it, perhaps all the way to a production version of it.

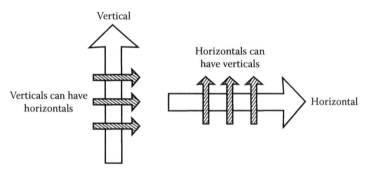

Definitions of horizontal and verticals are arbitrary. One person's horizontal could be another person's vertical, or vice versa.

Figure A.3 Horizontal versus vertical.

Upstream versus Downstream

Upstream and downstream definitions are sometimes very clear, yet sometimes they are arbitrary. If the system consists of a number of processes transferring data across each other, as often happens in batch processing, upstream is more easily identified as the process that happens earlier. When a number of applications are updating the same database (for example, a purchase order database), it is not clear whether one can be considered upstream and the other downstream, even if there is some logical business-related ordering in time. There are situations where this clarification is necessary. If one is trying to plug a problem, one should try to attack it at the most feasible upstream location. This makes sense because it would have the most impact. If a new data validation must be applied, it should be put in at the data entry screen, which is the most upstream for that data.

Because the upstream and downstream metaphor links us to rivers, there is an expectation that there is some source for even the mightiest rivers, some glacier or spring in a cave that is most upstream. The river image also implies that only upstream can affect downstream. Pollution occurring downstream cannot affect upstream water. A downstream application that has messed up some data cannot affect an upstream application, but only itself and others further downstream. How valid is this in our systems?

If we were to take our familiar SDLC (software development life cycle) and cast it in upstream and downstream terms, this would suggest that requirements are upstream and design is downstream. However, we know that software development does not maintain such pristine unidirectional flows. Design can end up affecting requirements. It is better to view such models as merely sequential, rather than upstream and downstream.

When two systems are interacting and there is flow of data in both directions, then it is still beneficial to identify the upstream and downstream points in each direction. In such situations, the point to note is that an application or process is not always upstream or downstream, but can change its position.

Import versus Export

Import is *taking in,* while export is *sending out.* These differing directions have different implications. The repercussions of import are more damaging than those of export. With import, one is bringing something *into* the system. If it is data that is imported, then without proper validations this data can be harmful to one's system. The import and export of data should not be treated with the same degree of seriousness. Such an error of judgment is frequent in off-the-shelf implementation projects as well as platform migration projects.

Data enters a system in many ways. It often comes in through applications that do adequate validation, hopefully. However, when data import utilities are used to import data directly into the system, the security and validation logic is bypassed. This happens because sometimes the need for import utilities is not recognized until it is too late and one does not have time to build the appropriate import utilities. Sometimes the validation must be skipped because the data volumes are high. This approach ignores the security and validation logic, which would otherwise have been invoked had the data been entered using the data entry screens, or system APIs (application programming interfaces).

Even if data fields in the two systems match, there may be problems with duplicate entries (acceptable in the source system but not the destination due to a different indexing scheme) or mandatory fields. The latter is a frequent cause of problems. When data is imported at the database level, optional fields in the source system can be mapped to fields that are considered mandatory for some business logic in the destination. Because the data is supposed to have entered through the screens or APIs (where NULLs would not have been permitted), the business logic assumes it will always get a non-NULL value. This results in bad data getting in and a possible system failure.

Sometimes utilities provided with the database are used to handle bulk loads. Many of these utilities are data movers designed for speed or throughput. They rarely allow the expression of any validation or security-related logic. With some tools, clean-up can be a big issue if the import job terminates abnormally.

By the same logic that imports are important, exports from a system can be critical for the proper functioning of other systems (Figure A.4).

Files are often used for communicating data across processes. This method is common in legacy and mainframe systems where one job outputs a file for another job. Such outputs need not be called exports because the job is expected to transform an input file to an output file. The term "export" carries a connotation of being an extra facility, beyond the main features of the application. The work required to create a simple comma separated (csv) output should not be underestimated.

Do not assume that off-the-shelf software that has an export facility will meet one's data integration requirements. While planning to move data from one process to another, one needs to verify that the destination process has import facilities and that it can import data in the format exported by the source process.

Going across boundaries is not easy. Both the format and the content must match. One system's purchase order number may not directly map

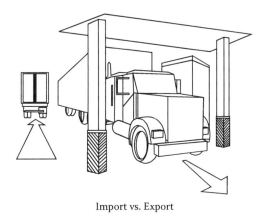

Import vs. Export

Figure A.4   Imports require checks — exports are easier.

to another's customer order number. The destination system may require fixed-length files. Generating fixed-length files from relational databases is nontrivial. Small programs may have to be written to support exported data, which requires some codes to be expanded.

People use export tools as a means of generating reports. They feed the data to an analytics engine or a spreadsheet. A symbiotic relationship has developed between applications and spreadsheets, one exporting data to the other for further processing. It raises the issue of whether the designer considers this post-processing outside the scope of the system.

Both for import and for export, determine a normalized data format that is well understood and agreed upon by both source and destination systems (Figure A.5). XML (Extensible Markup Language) is often used very effectively in most systems nowadays. It reduces errors that result from improper interpretations of data semantics. Using such a normalized format will allow one to plan better and estimate one's resources correctly. As with any technology, there are trade-offs.

Push versus Pull

Push and pull present themselves as options in many design and processing situations. Telnet users have encountered this choice through *get* and *put*, deciding whether to push a file from machine A to machine B, or pull a file from machine B to machine A (Figure A.6). Just as in import and export, or upstream and downstream, there is an asymmetry to push–pull. It is not always feasible to change positions and replace one with the other.

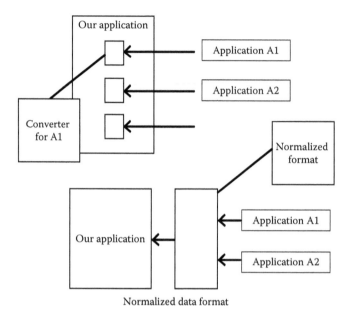

Figure A.5   Normalization helps in data transfer.

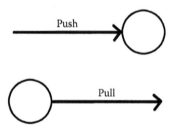

Figure A.6   Push versus pull.

Push and pull issues are often architecture issues hidden from the user. Push does not always mean that the system is pushing something to the user, or that in pull, the user is pulling something from the system. Push and pull interact in many different ways, muddling the separation between the two: the push may follow a pull, the pull may be the result of a push ("Your statement is ready."). Many solutions are hybrid solutions.

Push and pull — both do the work. They require some infrastructure or resources to do that work. If one is trying to push to the edges, then the resources should be at the center. If one is trying to pull to the edges, then the edges should have the resources. The edges may not always have the required resources.

Along with the notion of work is the requirement for control. If what is to be pushed is event dependent (e.g., a file is to be created or a Web page to be formed), then using push allows one to wait for that event to occur, or complete, before triggering the push event. Push also allows control over scheduled events.

Push also appears to allow more efficient creation and broadcast. The file or data is made ready once and sent to everybody, perhaps in a broadcast mode. The normal issues with broadcasts and availability come into play — for example, how to handle the situation if the receiver is not ready. The data sent out is as of the time that the pusher scheduled its creation; this may or may not be acceptable to the receiver. Push can appear simple but has a tendency to become complex.

Push does not mean being pushy. Permissions may be required, such as in proper e-mail marketing. One may have to set up subscriptions or memberships. Push can interrupt something, while pull appears more polite. In many situations, taking an interruption approach is more efficient. Phone rings interrupt us and tell us that someone is calling us. If the occurrence of an event is less frequent than its nonoccurrence, interruption is more efficient. One designs the system to handle or store less frequently occurring, or fewer, values or states. This is somewhat similar to the data modeling strategy when faced with choices whether to keep a table of positives or negatives: should the table record employees who are enrolled (for an event) or those who are not enrolled?

The control point for pull is more with the party doing the pulling, which requests data at a time of its choice. This data may be ready to be pulled or may have to be put together at the time of request, possibly because the requests are random or customer specific or parameter-driven values must be supplied before anything can be done. Each creates a different kind of load on the systems. The demand pattern on certain resources may become variable, although not totally unpredictable. There may be patterns to business or human behavior patterns driving such requests — people coming to the office at approximately the same time, month-end statements, and others, making them somewhat predictable even in on-demand situations.

Pull does not imply total freedom of choice. One can pull only from what is offered, such as in a restaurant menu.

Sometimes there is a third party doing the controlling, asking someone to do the push or someone else to do the pull. Sometimes the process is partially push and partially pull. A certain amount of processing is completed and pushed to an intermediate point, ready for subsequent pull. Maybe there is some notification involved in the completion of push or the readiness for pull.

Push may be overwriting stuff on the receiving end. This can happen because the filenames are repeated, or because the latest encapsulates the past and makes the older versions unnecessary or unreliable.

Push–pull terminology is used in marketing, communications, and other similar domains. "Push your message and repeat it" underlies many an advertising or marketing approach. The objective of some of these efforts may be to generate pull — come to our Web site or walk into our store — to get more information or buy something. The mechanics of push and pull are intertwined in many situations.

One must draw attention to Marshall McLuhan's concepts (Chapter 2, Systems) of hot and cold media, and its relation to, or inclusion of, push–pull terminology. McLuhan's statement that "the media is the message" is often repeated but is less well understood. He categorized media as hot or cold. Hot media deliver a lot of information, thus allowing the user to remain passive. Examples are photographs, the radio, and books. Cold media offer less information, thus forcing the user to engage with the media using his or her imagination, either to fill in the blanks or understand what is happening. Examples are the telephone and drawings. Hot corresponds to push, and cold to pull, for the purposes of our analysis. The application one develops may encourage or demand engagement, or it may cater to a passive user — the monthly report that lands on my desk and requires me to do nothing more than look at it.

Which of these are examples of push, pull, both, or neither?

1. Master code table updates
2. Ordering in a restaurant
3. Stock price quotes on Web sites
4. Phone calls and text messages
5. Change in government regulations
6. Electronic billpay
7. Renewal of medical prescriptions by the pharmacy
8. Doctor's referral to another doctor
9. Patient's admission to a hospital
10. Flight status information at an airport display

11. Filling a gas tank
12. Writing a check

Roles versus Responsibilities

The two are often confused. A project is broken down by functions (e.g., architecture, development, and QA [quality assurance]). These functions identify roles (e.g., architect or developer). Each role has a certain distinct responsibility; for example, it is the responsibility of the regional sales manager to manage sales in the region.

Certain things to watch out for are:

- It is important not to mix people's responsibilities across roles. Crossover will cause delays and confusion.
- When there is more than one person performing a role (e.g., multiple sales representatives in a region or a ten-person QA team), responsibilities within the same role become more important. Each person must have a clear set of tasks that they own and for which they are accountable.
- Individual contributors and those who work independently on their operations must also have their roles and responsibilities clearly defined.
- A good set of metrics is needed to determine how each person is suited to, and fits into his or her responsibilities. A simple exercise is to take any process, say the QA process, and ask each team member to speak about his or her role and responsibility. However, before stating their own role and responsibility, they need to state the role and responsibility of the person speaking immediately before them, as understood by them. This provides an opportunity to correct any erroneous perceptions of roles and responsibilities, and ensures that each person realizes how he or she fits into the overall vision.

If a person's responsibility increases while working in a predefined role, it might lead to a process failure. If a person is hired for a specific role but is then utilized to pick up work in other areas, this could signal another person slacking, a missing role, or an inadequately staffed role. Although multitasking is a necessity in all business environments, staff tend to lose their focus and motivation in such environments.

Role (cop) versus Responsibility (crime fighting)

Figure A.7   Clarify roles and responsibilities.

Clarifying roles and responsibilities in matrix organizations is not easy (Figure A.7). Dotted-line relationships can lead to vagueness in understanding one's roles and responsibilities. Job titles are supposed to reflect roles and responsibilities but often they do not. Furthermore, new roles evolve all the time. Examples include Web masters and security architects. New roles are likely to be even less understood, and thus must have well-defined responsibilities.

The question often asked is if you know your role, do you not automatically know your responsibilities? Yes, if both are well defined. The problems arise in assuming that they are.

Scale Up versus Scale Out

Scalability is the ability to increase or decrease computing capacity, while delivering on value. Scalability is delivered through two methods: (1) scale up and (2) scale out. It is important to realize that these are not mutually exclusive choices. The scaling method used, scale up or scale out, depends on the types of applications being used and on the type of functionality needed. Hardware vendors have responded to the need for scalability by creating multiprocessor machines. *Scaling up*, from a hardware perspective, means increasing the number of processors, disk drives, I/O channels, etc., all on a single machine. *Scaling out*, on the other hand, means getting scalability using incremental hardware, not bigger hardware itself. When one scales out, the size and speed of an individual machine do not limit the total capacity of the network. Scale out, however, requires the centralized management of the multiple hardware servers. Applications such as transaction processing applications and CRM or ERP (customer relationship management or enterprise resource planning) are architected to perform best on a single, monolithic server requiring scale-up capabilities. FTP servers, load balanced Web servers, VPN (virtual private network) servers, and proxy servers are examples that benefit from scale-out technologies.

Adding more processing power by scaling up is as simple as buying a larger, faster system. If running an application on a two-way machine feels limited, then moving to a four-way system should give a significant boost to the response times. It does not require redesigning the application, nor does it require any changes to the data management and system management policies. Scaling out, on the other hand, is not as simple as scaling up. One cannot just add a new machine to a network and hope that the application can make use of it. Using scale-out technology requires redesigning the application so that it can be made to run on two or more machines. It also may require partitioning the database. Messaging and caching may be necessary to get the machines to communicate. Finally, one may need to implement a new component health check process to monitor each machine.

It is important to understand that not every application lends itself well to scalability, and not every hardware configuration is capable of providing the desired level of scalability. Sure, moving from a Pentium 133 MHz, 64 MB RAM system to a Pentium IV 1.4 GHz, 512 MB RAM system should most likely achieve an increase in performance. Creating multithreaded applications can also help in scalability, especially when there are high volumes of both data processing and data I/O. However, for graceful scaling under increasing load conditions, the application should be capable of performing its tasks in parallel and one must have hardware that is capable of multiprocessing.

Before treading on the arduous task of trying to make an application perform well by scaling up or scaling out one's hardware, one needs to observe the behavior of the application to determine the bottlenecks. Quite often, the delays may not be in the data processing, but rather in the I/O. Using RAID disks, single-threaded application can also improve I/O performance because the operating system is able to read data from multiple drives simultaneously. Better performance can be achieved by choosing intelligently between investing in hardware, upgrading I/O systems, making use of networked resources, reorganizing the data, and redesigning one's software application.

Validation versus Verification versus Testing

Many of us use the terms "verification" and "validation" interchangeably, as if they were the same. Let us look at the definitions of "validation" and "verification." To validate something is to use a known or documented procedure to establish the correctness of its characteristics. Verification, on the other hand, involves a process to establish that the expected set of results can be obtained with a previously analyzed set of inputs.

Software validation is used to establish that software requirement specifications conform to user needs and intended uses. In practice, software validation activities may occur both during, and at the end of the software development life cycle, to ensure that all requirements have been fulfilled. A conclusion that software is validated also can depend on comprehensive functional testing of various user scenarios.

Software verification provides objective evidence that the outputs of a particular phase of the software life cycle meet all the specified requirements for that phase. Software verification looks for consistency, completeness, and correctness of the software and its supporting documentation. Structural software testing (path, code, and statement coverage) is one of the many verification techniques intended to confirm that software development output meets its input requirements. Other verification techniques include detailed analyses, and code and document walk-throughs.

In terms of computer science theory, one validates a program's correctness by testing it against a set of inputs that one has analyzed as plausible in the real world, for which the program has been written. Program verification for correctness, on the other hand, sometimes uses theoretical proof techniques to establish that the program does exactly what it is supposed to do. As difficult as the latter may be, it can be made more complex (impossible to solve) if one tries to prove that the program has no incorrect behavior in it.

Validation can refer to points outside the software itself. Many a product has failed in the marketplace because its requirements were never validated against market needs. This brings us to an important aspect of validation: what should the validation be against? Market validation can perhaps be obtained through early prototypes before creating production versions. Frequent validation of assumptions, objectives, and progress is essential in any development project. Setting up these validation points correctly is a project management responsibility and should be undertaken with care.

Asynchronous versus Synchronous

If two known events happen at the same predetermined rate, they are called *synchronous*. If they happen at the same "time," they are called *concurrent*. The operative words are "known" and "rate." "Known" implies that it is important that the events be predestined to happen. Automobile accidents in Los Angeles and those in Washington, D.C., may happen at the same rate but cannot be called synchronous. "Rate" introduces the notion of time — the events should occur together or with a predetermined interval separating them. Traffic lights are synchronized at an intersection to prevent cross traffic from moving at the same time. Further, they can be synchronized to give the green corridor effect for rush-hour traffic on important roads. They may not all turn green at the same time but are timed so that they turn green by the time traffic from one intersection reaches the next intersection. This also gives cross traffic an opportunity to flow. The periodicity of each light turning from red to green and back to red is preset — based on the distance between the intersections and the prescribed minimum and maximum speed in the zone.

Conversely, in an asynchronous environment, the two events do not have to happen at the same time or rate. The entities are still known; however, one event occurrence has no impact, or causal effect, on the other in any deterministic way. Phone conversations are typically asynchronous although both parties must be connected for any voice signals to travel. Within that connection we can always switch topics, speak at the same time, or even discontinue talking. An e-mail is also a form of asynchronous computer-mediated communication. One should not confuse asynchronous as something that is not "live" and real-time. Do synchronous events always need to happen in real-time?

Most digital design is based on a synchronous approach. Interacting systems (and their subsystems) defined as finite state automata are governed through a clock. They change states on the edges of a regular clock. In asynchronous design, however, there is no single clock to determine the timing of state changes.

Synchronous transmission may be more efficient but because asynchronous transmission is simple and inexpensive to implement, it is the choice of most architects. A word of caution: debugging an asynchronous design is extremely difficult. Because synchronous events are causal in nature, investigating failure, providing fixes, and, more importantly, testing them, are doable. In an asynchronous system, events can happen at any time. Most problems occur when interacting systems get into an "unknown" state because of the timing of events. Once the problem has occurred, it is extremely difficult to retrace the failing logic path, and the event timing that made the problem occur.

In computer science, quite often *synchronous* is also associated with the concept of waiting. If events are synchronous, it gives an impression that they would need to wait for each other before the execution of the system can proceed. This indicates an element of inefficiency. The converse is most likely the case — when discussing linear execution traces of systems, where asynchronous events may still need to be accounted for at some point in time. The hope is that multi-tasking, multi-programming, and multi-processing can effectively utilize the resources in a system, at various times, instead of forcing a certain predetermined order.

Is the two-phase commit a synchronous event? The parallel is often drawn to the exchange of marriage vows where both must say "I do" for the marriage to be finalized.

Hierarchical versus Structured

When one hears of a structured approach to solving a problem, one immediately thinks of partitioning the problem into smaller tasks and then working on each of them — the "divide and conquer" approach that has served us so well in the past. The structure of something is its framework that shows how its parts relate to each other, how it is "put together." When things are put together, sub-assemblies are created, physically or logically. This raises the question: is all structured problem solving hierarchical?

The answer is important because most people reach for a hierarchy when they need to structure something. Hierarchies seem to be ingrained in human thinking. Such hierarchies can be based on "superiority," as in the military where the upper levels of the hierarchy are considered "superior" to the lower in many ways. They can be based on "containment," where the upper levels comprise the lower ones, in different ways, such as in geometry, where the class of polygons includes triangles and quadrilaterals, which in turn could include isosceles and rectangle, respectively.

Both can be visually represented as tree structures — classical node-link diagrams that connect nodes together with line segments (Figure A.8) — or diagrams that use indentation, sometimes called "bullet points":

- Polygons
  - Triangles
    - Isosceles
  - Quadrilaterals
    - Rhombus
    - Rectangle

Structure is also used to denote "order" in a set of things. Structure is not necessarily limited to a hierarchy. Hierarchy is one of the options. One could also have an enumerative approach to order lists of items, for example, by value, date, weight, or size. The alphabets of the English language are given a structure but do not work in a hierarchy.

Data structures were previously a popular term in systems design: "are the data structures ready?" was a common question. The selection of the appropriate data structure spelled the difference between efficient and

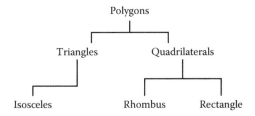

Tree structure for data representation

Figure A.8 Hierarchy is not the only structure.

inefficient processing, a solution that worked and one that did not. It is still formally studied in computer science courses. It appears to not be expressly discussed in development environments. It is as if the relational model has done away with the need for thinking on this.

Task versus Activity

A task is defined by its goal; an activity is defined by its start and end time. A task is typically associated with a target, a goal, or a job that needs to be completed. An activity refers to the various steps needed to achieve the task. The distinction is with respect to the granularity of the work being performed. Preparing the training manual is a task. It would require a number of activities: finding a technical writer, getting access to the system, duration or length of training, etc. Activities should be reviewed only if the task must be analyzed further.

What then is a milestone? Managers review the status of projects through milestones. Each milestone is linked to the completion of a predefined set of tasks that have been specified in the project plan. The milestone metaphor comes from roads. Looking at a milestone, one should be able to know how much of the journey one has completed, and how much is left to do. That is why every task and activity in a project is not a milestone. They are needed to complete the work but do not convey any valuable status information.

Online, Real-Time, Interactive, Batch, Offline

The lines between these concepts are definitely blurred. People use these words interchangeably, depending on the context. An E-banking application can provide an *interactive* browser-based *online* interface to do *real-time* financial transactions. "Online" conjures an image of a "live" connection between the source and destination. At the same time, most people, when asked what *online* is, will probably say that means *interactive*.

Real-time in common usage often refers to the outside real-world time. Real-time means to process data as it is generated. This is the concept used in the real-time virus scan of a computer system — the anti-virus program is constantly scanning all inputs to the system for potential threats, as they come in. This must be done in a way such that users cannot sense a slowdown. The fact is that there is nothing such as "true" real-time. The advantage of real-time in such situations is that the threat is discovered at the earliest.

Real-Time versus Batch

Real-time updates to a database, as compared to batch updates, signify that the inserts, updates, or deletes are taking effect immediately instead of at a later time. Transactional systems are said to operate in real-time. This is an expectation that is related to the online, interactive nature of systems. If one enters a purchase order and hits "Submit," one expects it to have been recorded in the system and be available to others at that same instant. If there is batch processing of such information, then it is not likely available immediately. This may not be obvious to all users.

There are some important considerations when deciding to build real-time systems. Is the data entered all the time or intermittently? Furthermore, who is the consumer of the data and in what frequency? Batch systems have been found to be better in terms of spreading bulk work from high-demand periods to low-demand periods (banks do bookkeeping at night when the number of customer transactions decrease). One advantage with batch systems is that one can do a simple rollback if the data does not appear consistent. However, the downside is that time delays inherent in batch processing mean that one's systems reflect an earlier state of what is happening in one's business. It is as if one is driving by looking at the rear-view mirror.

Note that batch processes can be run at various frequencies. For example, if the Purchase Order database was being updated in a batch mode every 15 minutes, then the real time of this batch system is 15 minutes.

There are many situations where the real time should not be instantaneous. This is a design choice and introduces what is called an "error gap." An example is a self-service account creation program. New account information is saved and reviewed by a person before being allowed to update the Account database. Automation of this error gap could be done through formal workflow systems. By retaining a manual error gap in the processing, one can prevent costly mistakes from propagating through the system.

The real time of a system is a design parameter and must be based on requirements. A designer should not assume that the requirement is always for real "real time," that is, instantaneous.

Internationalization versus Localization versus Multilingual

The word "internationalization" is sometimes abbreviated as *i18n* because there are 18 letters between the "i" and the "n." There are several definitions of internationalization in books and on Web sites. In its most ordinary form, internationalization is the process of making program code generic and flexible so that standards and specifications from markets around the world can be easily accommodated. Part of internationalization is making the product neutral to any locale, that is, enabling the graphical or user interface to be translated with minimal impact on the program code. It is important to note that internationalization is not just about allowing the data processing to handle characters and data formats from across the world. It includes date time formats, currencies, text orientation, search and indexing capabilities — essentially things that also will affect the business and program logic.

Internationalization can be of two kinds:

1. *Monolingual internationalization*: enables the creation of localized versions of a product, where each localized version supports only its target locale. This is like a book that has been translated into French for a certain audience in the world.
2. *Multilingual internationalization*: enables data processing and display in multiple languages and locales simultaneously, for example, mixing Mandarin and Arabic text in a single document, or having one's cell phone text interface capable of supporting many international languages.

Most online or Web services (even Web pages) must be able to simultaneously handle user requests in different languages, and with different cultural conventions (e.g., <Firstname Lastname> or <Lastname, Firstname> or <Salutation Firstname Lastname>; or date formats such as mm/dd/yyyy or dd/mm/yyyy or yyyy/mm/dd). However, creating a multilingual system may not be a trivial task. To overcome this, product ISVs (independent software vendors) these days work toward the concept of multilocalization. This refers to the capability of *generating* a system for supporting a particular locale at runtime.

High Availability versus Fault Tolerance

The availability of a system is defined as its uptime, as a percentage of the total time being considered for measurement. High availability, as the name implies, indicates that the system is available "most" of the time. Actual percentages can vary but the figure is usually in the 90s. Sometimes, we talk of "five nines availability" when referring to a system that is up 99.999%. In a year, this would mean a total downtime (both planned and unplanned) of a little over five minutes.

Interestingly enough, availability is only measured in terms of an application or computer usage. It does not refer to the business impact that downtime or an outage might have. A computer outage of a few seconds might cause an irrecoverable business outage in terms of rework that may have to be undertaken (e.g., in online stock trading). The system may still qualify for the five-nine availability criteria while being down for five seconds at a time, sixty times a year. High availability should be defined from the viewpoint of the customer, not that of the system.

If a system is experiencing repeated failures, although the durations are small, the user is justified in losing trust in the system. In the case of online users who have been assured that they can reach their data at any time, such lack of access can undermine the business proposition.

High availability must be designed into the system through failover, redundancy, or a number of other techniques. If that is not being done, then the expectation of high availability should not be set.

It is also likely that the term "high availability" may be applicable only to a subset of the active systems. For example, there may be a high availability failover solution installed, which fails over machines but does not guarantee that the application comes up on the new server without interruption or manual involvement. From the vendor and the OS (operating system) point of view, this might be a high-availability solution. From the customer point of view, it is not.

A fault-tolerant system is one that will continue to operate, possibly at a reduced level, rather than terminating abnormally when some component (or components) of the system fails. The term is most commonly used to describe computer systems designed to lose no time due to problems either in the hardware or the software. This is achieved in either of the two ways: (1) by using fault-tolerant components, or (2) by instituting redundancy by using additional or duplicate components that can start if the primary one fails. Tandem Computers (now part of HP) was famous for its fault-tolerant systems. Its systems were equipped with two pieces of every component (CPU cards, mirrored disks, etc.), linked in a parallel setup, almost like two identical systems in one box, arranged as primary and backup.

Fault-tolerant systems are difficult to make, and even more difficult to maintain. Their costs can also be high. Their cost versus benefits is also questionable (what if the backup also component fails?). It is easier to implement fault tolerance in software than in hardware, but the problems are similar.

Index

9 780367 403539